I, Fellini

The Ultimate Seduction

Hello, I Must Be Going: Groucho and His Friends

Nobody's Perfect

BILLY WILDER
A Personal Biography

Charlotte Chandler

SIMON & SCHUSTER

New York   London   Toronto   Sydney   Singapore

SIMON & SCHUSTER
Rockefeller Center
1230 Avenue of the Americas
New York, NY 10020
Copyright © 2002 by Charlotte Chandler
All rights reserved, including the right of reproduction
in whole or in part in any form.
SIMON & SCHUSTER and colophon are registered
trademarks of Simon & Schuster, Inc.
Designed by Dana Sloan
Manufactured in the United States of America
10 9 8 7 6 5 4 3 2 1
Library of Congress Cataloging-in-Publication Data
Chandler, Charlotte.
Nobody's perfect : Billy Wilder, a personal biography /
Charlotte Chandler.
p. cm.
Includes index.
1. Wilder, Billy, 1906–2002. 2. Motion picture produc-
ers and directors—United States—Biography. I. Title.
PN1998.3.W56 C49 2002
791.43'0233'092—dc21
[B]   2002021790
ISBN 0-7432-1709-8
For information regarding special discounts for bulk
purchases, please contact Simon & Schuster Special Sales
at 1-800-456-6798 or business@simonandschuster.com

Acknowledgments

WITH SPECIAL APPRECIATION:

Chuck Adams, I. A. L. Diamond, Groucho Marx, Audrey Wilder.

WITH APPRECIATION:

Jan Anderson, Michelangelo and Enrica Antonioni, Linda Ayton, Kevin Brownlow, Horst Buchholz, Henry Bumstead, Charles William Bush, James Cagney, Christopher Challis, Claudette Colbert, George Cukor, Tony Curtis, Danielle Darrieux, Olivia de Havilland, Marlene Dietrich, Kirk Douglas, Mitch Douglas, Lisa Drew, Jean-Louis Dumas, Willy Egger, Douglas Fairbanks, Jr., Rudi Fehr, Federico Fellini, Jean Picker Firstenberg, Joan Fontaine, Joe Franklin, Roy Furman, Greta Garbo, Bob Gazzale, Dick Guttman, Dolly Haas, Robert Haller, Harry Haun, Edith Head, Audrey Hepburn, Arthur Hiller, Alfred Hitchcock, William Holden, Lenore Hornblow, Peter Johnson, Fay Kanin, Bronislau Kaper, Howard G. Kazanjian, Marthe Keller, Theodore Kheel, Klaus Kinski, Alexander Kordonsky, John Landis, Ted Landry, Fritz Lang, Robby Lantz, Christopher Lee, Ernest Lehman, Jack Lemmon, Shirley MacLaine, Fred MacMurray, Dean Martin, Walter Matthau, Ray Milland, Juliet Mills, Kim Novak, Nancy Olson, Robert Osborne, Genevieve Page, Sydney Pollack, Walter Reisch, Paolo and Elizabeth Riani, Ginger Rogers, Sidney Sheldon, Mark Shivas, Curt Siodmak, John Springer, Barbara Stanwyck, James Stewart, Lee Strasberg, Gloria Swanson, Jon Teckman, Pamela Tiffin, Samuel Vaughan, King Vidor, Ray Walston, Mae West, Cheryl Weinstein, Ken Wlaschin, Michael York, and Fred Zinnemann.

Academy of Motion Picture Arts and Sciences, American Film Institute, Anthology Film Archives, British Film Institute, Cinémathèque Française, Film Society of Lincoln Center, Filmmuseum Potsdam, Museum of Modern Art, New York Public Library for the Performing Arts.

To Billy Wilder
Somebody's perfect.

—Contents—

PART II: HOLLYWOOD

PART III: A LEGEND IN HIS OWN TIME

PART IV: A LEGEND

IN SOMEBODY ELSE'S TIME

Nobody's
Perfect

—Prologue—

 "'Nobody's perfect' is the line that most sums up my work," Billy Wilder told me. "There is no comedy, no drama about perfect people."

"Nobody's perfect" may be the most famous line in a Billy Wilder film, as well as being one of the most famous film lines of all time. "And 'Nobody's perfect' wasn't even mine," Wilder said. "It was Iz's."

Iz was I. A. L. Diamond, Wilder's longtime friend and his writing collaborator on the film which ends with the line "Nobody's perfect," *Some Like It Hot,* as well as on *The Apartment, Irma la Douce, The Private Life of Sherlock Holmes, The Front Page,* and others.

"A good writing collaboration is more difficult to achieve than a good marriage," Wilder said. "And it's more intimate. Iz was not only my writing partner, but my alter-id, my alter-Iz."

Wilder considered collaboration to be an art, not a science, and finding a collaborator had the same element of magic as finding romance or ideal sex—"a wife, a mistress, or even the most challenging of all—a perfect dancing partner.

"It's like with married people. It's important to learn how to fight. You have to be able to argue about something so you don't destroy anything basic about the relationship. It's like boxing with rules. No hitting below the belt. No biting. You have to be able to come back for more. Like lovers, it's better not to go to sleep angry."

"'Nobody's perfect' was ad-libbed by Iz," Wilder told me. "We were trying to finish the script for *Hot* so we could send the thing out to the mimeograph outfit. We wrote and wrote away, and finally it got to be one o'clock in the morning. We were tired, we were bored, but still we needed a line, and Iz says, 'Well, "Nobody's perfect."'

"I said, 'Look—let's just put it down on paper for now. Then we can send it out to the mimeograph and we know we've got it. Later, we're gonna come up with something better. There's still another two months while we shoot, and it's the last scene in the picture, anyway.' We were so exhausted at the time, it never occurred to us that we already had the best line.

"We couldn't hear it because it came too easily. We didn't value it because it just popped out. Nobody's perfect!"

Some days later, discussing *Some Like It Hot* and his collaboration with Billy Wilder, I mentioned to I. A. L. Diamond that Billy had been quick to give him credit for the most famous line of the film.

"Oh, no," Diamond said. "That's not true. 'Nobody's perfect' was *his*. It absolutely was *his* line."

Now, *that* was a collaboration.

—Introduction—

Film is the Cinderella Art of the twentieth century, and Billy Wilder is one of its legendary figures.

In the early part of the twentieth century, the motion picture, like Cinderella, was an orphan stepsister of the theater and of literature, relegated to the penny arcade and the nickelodeon. By the turn of the next century, film had become the preeminent new art form, and our collective memory.

Billy Wilder was born at the time that the movies were born, a part of the first generation to take them for granted. Though he began his creative life in Vienna, and his film career in Berlin, Wilder became an American writer-director whose movies speak to the world. Recognized as an artist, and critically acclaimed, he made films to entertain a mass audience.

When I mentioned my concept of the "Cinderella Art" to Billy Wilder, he began by puncturing my balloon.

"Cinderella married Prince Charming, and bought too many shoes. She wasn't satisfied anymore with her glass slipper. Prince Charming dumped her for a younger woman. It's *The Foreskin Saga*.

"Movies used to be made by people who didn't want to do anything else because they loved what they did so much. Even those dear old studio moguls we used to love to hate.

"We miss them because the people out here who control the movies get worse every year. And now, we have next year's people.

"When next year's people go home, their television sets watch *them*.

"They could sell neckties or films or condoms. It's all the same to them. Hollywood isn't about making movies anymore. It's about making a buck, a lot of them. Everything is about selling. We're forced to be salesmen—or beggars. I was never good with a tin cup. I made movies when the picture was still more important than the *marketing* of it, more important than its trailer.

"Individuality isn't valued the way it used to be. Individuality is something that has to be humored, supported, nurtured. Now, there doesn't seem to be time, because time costs too much money. Everyone thinks he is a 'character.' I saw someone wearing an 'I'm a character' T-shirt. It was probably manufactured on a production line in Taiwan.

"I've had a good run. No complaints. But I'd like to make just one more movie.

"If I could have chosen a picture to end my career with, it wouldn't have been *Buddy Buddy*. I didn't know that was going to be my swan song. If I'd known, I would have bet on a different swan. My last picture would have been *Schindler's List*. But maybe mine wouldn't have been as great as Steven's."

———◄◦►———

It was Groucho Marx who introduced me to Billy Wilder.

Groucho and I were walking in downtown Beverly Hills during the mid 1970s when he saw his friend Billy Wilder. "It's good to meet someone I don't have to insult," Groucho said to him. "But people expect it. If I don't insult them, they are disappointed and go away unhappy. I've been insulting people all morning."

"I know what you mean," Wilder said. "To sell and promote my pictures, I've had to become a jokester because it is expected from me."

Groucho told him that I was writing a book about him, called

Hello, I Must Be Going. Many of Groucho's frien
in the book as well, and I was in the process of i

He invited Billy Wilder to come over and l
responded, "I can't sleep for nights if I know I
viewed. I have to go into traction to relax."

"Then let's do it tomorrow," Groucho said,
one night's sleep."

Wilder arrived at Groucho's home exactly on time. He wore an open sports shirt, a cashmere pullover, peccary moccasins, a jaunty hat, and trousers with a perfect crease. Afterward, Groucho said to me, "And he had *two* of them, two creases. They didn't look like the pants my father used to make. His tailor must've used a tape measure."

Groucho asked about Audrey, Wilder's wife.

"I hope she's out buying a Christmas gift for me."

"Where's I. A. L. Diamond?"

"I don't take Izzy *everywhere* with me. I'm glad you liked my last picture."

"*The Front Page* was great! But it got some bad reviews."

"That doesn't paralyze me," Wilder said. "I just get more anxious and determined. In Europe they think you're as good as the best you've ever been. In Hollywood it's 'What have you done lately?' I don't look back. That would be like looking up a girl you slept with thirty years ago. The bad reviews hurt for a week, and then you get over it. If you think about it, and feel they're going to kick you in the stomach again, you can't do the next thing. You have to get right back on the horse."

Groucho's friend, Erin Fleming, carried in cake and coffee. "Aaaah! A *Streusel-kuchen,*" Wilder exclaimed. "Do you have a *Kaffeeklatsch* like this *every* day?"

"No," Groucho answered truthfully, "we're just doing it to impress you."

Wilder looked around at the paintings. "That's *The Peaceable Kingdom.* And what is that?" He indicated a painting on the opposite wall, showing three women.

"Those are my three hookers," Groucho said. "It's my three ex-wives." Actually, it was just something he had found at a street market.

...ould be in the bedroom," Wilder said.

...oucho offered him some chocolates. "Someone sent me these ...m Fortnum & Mason in London."

"When I was making a film in London," Wilder said, "we had the Greek king and queen on the set, the parents of the deposed king, and one of the electricians hollered down, 'Hey, Queenie, where were you when I needed you for my inside straight?' The queen didn't understand at first, but someone translated for her. Then she laughed and applauded."

"I wish we'd worked together," Groucho said. "*The Marx Brothers at the U.N.* was a good idea." This was a film Billy Wilder wanted to do after *One, Two, Three*.

"You guys were great," Wilder said. "You got to try your stuff out on the road with audiences. I should have fought for more rehearsal time, too, before it's costing by the day after you start shooting. You know, after the war has started, after you're over the top, you've got to go all the way."

Groucho said, "Duck Soup time."

——◦——

After completing *Hello, I Must Be Going,* I went to see Billy Wilder to talk with him for my next book, *The Ultimate Seduction,* about creative work and people who were lucky enough to do successfully what they loved to do. Wilder's office was located in the Writers and Artists Building on Brighton Way in Beverly Hills. There was no name on the door. You had to know which office was his.

I told him that I wished to do an interview with him for my next book. He said, "We could do some spitballing, my word for brainstorming—stimulating talk about things, and you see what comes out. I think it's important to walk around an idea."

I placed my tape recorder on his desk. Then I put a second recorder next to it. I said that I liked to use two recorders when an interview was really important to me, in case the tape broke or one of the machines failed.

"That's good," he said. "That's a pessimistic outlook. You're much better off with that, because you'll sleep better. There are people, you

Charlotte Chandler with Mervyn LeRoy, Douglas Fairbanks, Jr., and Billy Wilder during the party for her book The Ultimate Seduction *at the Beverly Hills Hotel in 1984.* (Photo by Charles William Bush)

know, who when they are flying have two parachutes. Those are the suspender and belt people, so as not to lose their pants. If one gives out, there's still that emergency thing. If you were a man, you'd have to wear a pair of suspenders *and* a belt with your trousers."

During his days as a newspaper reporter in Vienna and Berlin, Wilder had interviewed many famous people, including Freud, Schnitzler, Richard Strauss, and Prince Yussupov of Russia, the man reputed to have killed Rasputin. I asked him what he felt had made him a successful interviewer.

"It was a long time ago," Wilder said, "and I was about nineteen, maybe younger. I had plenty of nerve and I was good at being in the right place at the right time. That's not just a matter of luck, but luck helps.

"Sometimes, I was a failed interviewer, like with the good Dr. Freud in Vienna. Well, not exactly failed. I have reconsidered the event, bigger in my life than in his. He threw me out. Not physically. With a few words. From Herr Doktor Freud, it did not take more than that. Verbally, he got me out by the seat of my pants. But I think now it was more of a success to be thrown out by Freud than to be welcomed by someone no one remembers now. He is dead, and most of the people who ever met him are in the past, but his name is with us."

Billy Wilder and I frequently ate breakfast at the Beverly Hills Hotel, in the Polo Lounge, and occasionally at the counter of the basement coffee shop.

Perched on a counter stool of the coffee shop, Wilder had the best vantage point from which to oversee the cooking. He always chose the corner, closest to the waitress who was frying the ham and eggs or pancakes. While our order was being prepared, we were silent, so that he could direct the preparation, if and when direction was needed.

"There is greater privacy here than upstairs because everyone is anonymous," he told me. As he spoke, everyone in the coffee shop was listening, aware of who he was. They heard every word he said, and if what he said called for a response from me, whatever I said.

When I had almost completed my book, which included the conversations with Billy Wilder, I told him that I hoped to write my next book about him.

"Why are you choosing me for your book?" he asked. "You should be talking with someone more interesting."

"Whom would you suggest?"

"Well, Coppola would be interesting. I wouldn't mind having made *The Godfather.*

"What are you calling this book of yours? *The World's Oldest Living Director?*"

"It isn't a title I was considering."

"I think it's a good title. I like it. With a book, like with a film, as soon as you have chosen a subject, you have chosen whether you will succeed or not."

I asked how he would like to have me describe him in the book.

"You can say I am tall, but not too tall, that I am *not* overweight, and that my mind is always in play. And though it may not show, I am shy."

At that time, there was a strike among actors in Hollywood, and production had ground to a halt. Wilder was frustrated. What hurt him was not being able to find a constructive outlet for his creative energy:

"There's nothing more terrible than to want to ride and not to have a horse. This gives a man a terrible sense of impotence, because a man *is* his achievements. To be able to work twenty-five hours a day, eight days a week, doing what you want to do, is a privilege. To have this desire, these hopes and dreams, and the creative energy without anywhere to put it, that is hard. Those are the people who are unlucky."

No Hollywood director enjoyed greater success while knowing what it was to face bleak times than did Billy Wilder.

"Slumps can't be figured. You're the same person, same abilities. It's the secret element that you can't figure—when your timing, your luck goes off. It happens to ballplayers, film directors, even to vineyards. When

"You're not supposed to laugh until you hear the punch line!" Billy Wilder with Charlotte Chandler in his Beverly Hills office. (Photo by I. A. L. Diamond)

you want a home run too badly, you press and strike out. The problem is that the lack of success changes you, and as you act more defensively or more desperately, you hurt your own chance of success. You look too hard for a script and then read into it the qualities you want so badly to find. But I'm still not ready to do the one about the scientist who has a secret formula tattooed on his penis that can only be read when it's erect.

"After a string of failures, you get a different 'hello' in the supermarket, a different reception from the maître d' in the restaurant, from your barber, and from the doorman at the studio gate, who looks at your car instead of at you. You can hear that different tone right away."

Wilder, however, was in good standing at MGM, where I visited him, just before *Buddy Buddy* began shooting. When he, I. A. L. Diamond, and I went to lunch at the studio commissary, we were seated immediately at a choice corner table in the Lion's Den.

The Lion's Den was an area that jutted out from one side of the MGM commissary. There, one would find studio executives and leading directors currently working at the studio. You knew that you were at the MGM commissary because of the ubiquitous box of matzos on every table. Rumor had it that these matzos on the tables were a stipulation in the will of Louis B. Mayer.

In a world of high-powered instability, the stale matzos lent an air of unchanging continuity. The Lion's Den charged more for exactly the same food the extras were eating in the main section of the restaurant.

I asked him if, after a failure, the most disheartening words one could hear might be, "There's no more room in the Lion's Den."

"Worse," he said. "You're not asked to be a pallbearer anymore, and what's really terrible is when you start getting invited to be a judge at the Orinoco Film Festival somewhere in South America because they know you're not working. The last step before they bury you is you're a legend and everyone wants to honor you in your wheelchair.

"The festival circuit comes before you are a legend. It fills that time between working and admitting that you aren't going to work anymore. Now that there are so many festivals, the ranks have opened to those who previously would not have had enough celebrity. Being invited to attend film festivals, especially to serve on the jury, caresses one's ego and gives the illusion of working. Just all that packing. Those who have mastered the technique of being invited to film festivals can easily fill up seven months with the illusion that they are working when, in fact, they are only busy."

———◇———

Several years later, I walked with Billy Wilder to the shop of a picture framer in Beverly Hills. He was taking a sheet of Marilyn Monroe commemorative stamps and a photograph of her to be framed. His attitude toward the actress had mellowed over the years.

"You're a candidate for a lot of honors if you live long enough. I qualify for some just because I am still breathing. The one I don't qualify for is a postage stamp like Miss Monroe's.

"You don't get the fun of putting yourself on your letters. You have to die for that one, so only your relatives get the fun of pasting you on their phone bill.

"I knew Miss Monroe when she was married to Joe DiMaggio, and we were making *The Seven Year Itch*. I knew her when she was married to Arthur Miller, and we were making *Some Like It Hot*.

"Her marriages didn't work out because Joe DiMaggio found out she was Marilyn Monroe, and Arthur Miller found out she wasn't Marilyn Monroe.

"There are more books on her than there are on World War II, and I think that there's a great similarity. Working with her was not easy, but just to give it to you in a condensed *Reader's Digest* form, it was hell, but well worth it once you got it up on the screen. Lots of actresses are pleasant to work with, and you may have a very good ten weeks shooting with them, and then it stinks forever. I have forgotten all the trouble I had with Miss Monroe. Well, almost forgotten. All the times I thought, 'This picture will never be finished.' Then, it's all forgotten once the picture is done.

"One side of Marilyn was wonderful, and the other side was terrible. She was two of a kind.

"I have never had an affair with one of the leading ladies in my films. Not because I would not be able to be unfaithful to my wife, but because I would not be able to be unfaithful to my film. In order to remain faithful to your film, you can have an affair with the stand-in of your leading lady, but never with the leading lady herself.

"Under ordinary circumstances, I would certainly not expect my wife, Audrey, to forgive me if I were unfaithful to her; but she would have forgiven me if I had an affair with Marilyn Monroe—*more* than forgiven me! She would have gone to her beauty salon and proclaimed to all the women there that her husband was having an affair with Marilyn Monroe. It would have enhanced her status. She would have notified the newspapers, like parents announcing the engagement of their daughter. It would have meant she was not married to an ordinary male. Both our images would have been improved. It would have given me mythic proportions, and that would have reflected on her— the man who could sleep with Marilyn Monroe had married *her.*"

"What do you think was the secret of her great appeal?" I asked.

"When I met her, she did not impress me. When I saw what the camera saw, I knew she was special. She was Cinderella, without the happy ending."

———<◦>———

After the tearing down of the Berlin Wall and the city's reunification, Wilder, in his nineties, gave permission for a café to be named after him, located in what was formerly "No Man's Land," that strip in Berlin which had separated East and West Germany.

At the turn of the twentieth century, the Viennese coffeehouse had been a center of social life, and it was a phenomenon that had helped to shape Billy Wilder. At the turn of the twenty-first century, the Billy Wilder Café is a place where writers, journalists, artists, and filmmakers can go and sit for as long as they like. With one cup of coffee, they can read the newspapers, meet people like themselves, write, draw, or study their parts for the theater. Wilder hoped in the twenty-first century it would be the heir to the Romanisches Café, the legendary café he had frequented, "a hangout for the creative people in pre-Hitler Berlin." It was destroyed a few weeks before the end of World War II.

It was *La Ronde.* The circle was complete—from the Romanisches

Café in Berlin where Billy Wilder *felt* he had been born to the Billy Wilder Café. Unable to travel, he said somewhat wistfully, "Now I can only see the Billy Wilder Café in my mind."

———<o>———

While denying that his films were autobiographical, he recognized that the films do have "details" from his life. Wilder clearly drew from the experiences of his own life as well as from his unique perspective on the world of his time. He was born into the Austrian provinces of the early twentieth century; a world marching backward into the future, still living out the nineteenth century. He lived virtually his entire life in the twentieth century, most of it, more than two thirds, in Hollywood. He managed, as he put it, "to tiptoe into the twenty-first century at the age of ninety-four."

———<o>———

At ninety-three, Billy Wilder recalled joking with me, years before, about the title for this book:

"Do you remember when I suggested *The World's Oldest Living Director?*" he asked. "It was a joke then. Not now. I was only a young man of about eighty then.

"You know, you've taken so long with this book, maybe I'll stay alive as long as you're still writing.

"So don't hurry . . ."

PART I

Europe

—Eugenia's—
Dream

 "I do not wish I had made something else out of myself," Billy Wilder told me, "it's been a life I look back on fondly.

"I have had a good career which I have enjoyed. Even the suffering, I have enjoyed.

"I have done some good work and entertained a few people. I've had a very interesting life. I've survived a long time and a lot of people. When I went back to Vienna, I couldn't find anybody who went to school with me who was alive.

"I lost my mother, my family, my friends—Auschwitz, which I could not imagine because it was unimaginable. And here I am.

"To know me, you must think of me in terms of what Austria was like in 1906, when I was born. Austria in those days was a huge monarchy of 56 million people—the Austro-Hungarian Empire. The monarchy seemed indestructible. People in Vienna thought they were really something. It was a world of whipped cream and cream cakes. I have never tasted cream like that since.

"The town where I was born is still there, but the country is gone. I can't remember anything about it, but I guess my mother pushed my baby carriage on a street that is now called Billy Wilder Avenue, or something like that. If I had stayed there, I wouldn't be here to tell the tale, and they wouldn't have been naming a street after me."

Billy Wilder was born into a world of what was believed to be perfect stability. The Austro-Hungarian Empire had existed for centuries, and many thought it would last forever—just before it vanished.

His father, Max, owned railway cafés in towns along the line to Vienna, and he, his wife, and their baby son were passing through Sucha, a small town in the Austro-Hungarian crown province of Galicia, at the moment Billy Wilder was born. It wasn't at all where Eugenia Wilder, Billy's mother, had imagined she would be. She had wanted to be in New York City.

At the turn of the twentieth century, before Max Wilder had come into her life, Eugenia Baldinger had stayed for a time in New York with her uncle and his family. The uncle owned a jewelry store on Madison Avenue.

Genia, as she was called, was born in Nowy Targ, Galicia, in 1885. Nowy Targ had been Eugenia's world, and nothing in it prepared her for what she found in New York City at the turn of the twentieth century. All of her expectations were surpassed. Eugenia especially loved to see the ladies promenading in their finery. Some day, she promised herself, she would be one of those ladies.

She wandered about the city alone, exploring the variety of neighborhoods, walking or riding the new electric trolleys which were rapidly replacing the cable cars and horse-drawn streetcars. Sometimes she would get lost, but only temporarily. She found her way back by locating shop windows she knew, those with dresses she had admired, or by finding a cigar store Indian she recognized, whose familiar wooden feathers indicated that she was going in the right direction. Decades later, Wilder used a Manhattan cigar store Indian to show Don Birnam the right direction in *The Lost Weekend*.

As the end of her visit drew near, Eugenia begged her uncle to permit her to stay in New York and help in the jewelry shop. All that she needed was her mother's consent, but it was not forthcoming.

Eugenia was determined to return to New York just as soon as she was of age. This made going back to Galicia bearable. The image of the cigar store Indian was one of the last to fade of those wonderful memories she took back with her.

Not long after Eugenia returned, she met Max Wilder, an ambitious headwaiter who dreamed of a better life.

This time Eugenia had her way. The two dreamers had met and fallen in love. Now they could dream together. It was only much later that each was to find that their dreams were not compatible.

———◦———

In 1872, Hersch Mendel Wilder was born into a German-speaking Jewish family in Stanislawczyk, a Galician town close to the Russian border. "The farther east you got in the Austro-Hungarian Empire," Billy Wilder said, "the less social status you enjoyed." The Wilders considered themselves Austrians.

German was the official language of the vast empire, causing even more resentment among the minorities whose languages as well as national aspirations were suppressed by edicts from far-off Vienna. The constitution of the Austro-Hungarian Empire was liberal, but its system of government was clerical.

Young Hersch found the world outside his home unwelcoming toward a small Jewish boy whose language was German. As soon as he could, Hersch Wilder changed his name to Maximilian. He wanted to be an Austrian without the burden of being Jewish in the violently anti-Semitic world he inhabited. "Maximilian was the name of some Holy Roman emperors," Billy Wilder said. "My father became known as Max."

Being a waiter seemed an obvious and attainable choice for Max. He could start low in a restaurant in the eastern province and move on through a series of jobs to his goal—Vienna.

At the very first Kraków restaurant where he applied, Max was hired. "As my father was leaving, he heard the wife of the owner say to her husband, 'He's such a nice-looking boy, isn't he? All the ladies will love him.' I'm sure my father was thinking, 'It's a good thing I don't look Jewish!'"

Eugenia was taken by some friends to the restaurant where Max worked. It wasn't long before she and Max were seeing each other outside the restaurant. Max proposed, and against the wishes of Eugenia's mother, they married in 1904.

Max wanted to own his own restaurant, maybe even several restaurants. "It wasn't a matter of money. He probably could have made just as much money working for someone else, but he wanted to have control over what he did. Maybe I got some of that, wanting to be in control, from him.

"My father became the owner of a chain of railway restaurants at the stations where the trains from Vienna stopped. These were not ordinary snack bars. This was the Austro-Hungarian monarchy. Everyone couldn't eat like the Emperor Francis Joseph, but they tried. They said the old emperor, as they called him, ate chicken consommé which took twenty-four chickens to make.

"At important stops, a guy would ring a bell and announce, 'We'll be here for one hour.' It was a hungry captive audience. They would rush for the printed menu. They expected the service to be fast, but good. My father, who had been a successful headwaiter, understood exactly how to please them. Service was important, but the food had to be good, too. And it was."

To Max, the Austro-Hungarian Empire of the new century was a place of unlimited opportunity. He believed this before 1914 and never lost faith even after 1918 when the country shrank from 56 million to 7 million people.

"Timing in life is everything," Wilder told me, "and my father had perfect timing. But not for success. Wrong time, wrong place."

—Billie, the Kid—

 In 1905, Max and Eugenia's first son, Wilhelm, known as Willie, was born. Their second son, Samuel, known as Billie, was born a year later, on June 22, 1906. Billy Wilder never used the name Samuel, and he was known as Billie until he came to America.

"I became Billie when my mother used to play games with us about Buffalo Bill and Wild Bill Hickok. I was 'Wild Billie.'"

Young Billie began hearing his mother's stories of America even before he could understand all the words. She told him about the wonderful Wild West show she had seen and stories about Buffalo Bill. She spoke vividly about Coney Island, New York's elevated trains, and the wooden cigar store Indians who had become like friends. Wilder remembered his mother as "a wonderful storyteller, like Scheherazade. I think I have always seen America partly through her eyes."

Sucha, Billy Wilder's birthplace, was in the southwest portion of what is now Poland, then Galicia. Throughout the vast Austro-Hungarian Empire, no province was more scorned and ridiculed by the Viennese elite than Galicia, with more than a soupçon of anti-Semitism thrown in.

"The Viennese especially didn't like Galicia. It was full of Poles, Gypsies, Jews, Bohemians, and a lot of other untouchables the people in Vienna looked down on. They told Galician jokes in Vienna. I remember one:

"It is winter, and a young Austrian army officer is stuck in a snowed-in Galician garrison. He has fallen in love with the daughter of the town's mayor, Annemarie. One night, when his love for her won't let him sleep, he gets out of bed and goes to the mayor's house and stands outside his beloved's window. Feeling the need to somehow make his feelings clear to Annemarie, and feeling another need even more urgent as well, he pisses a message in the snow: 'I love you, Anne . . . ,' only he cannot complete her name.

"So he runs back to the barracks and awakens a young Bohemian soldier, and orders him to come back to the mayor's house with him. Fortunately, it hasn't snowed anymore. When they get there, he points to the unfinished message and says, 'Here! Piss "Marie" in the snow.' But the soldier stands there, not able. 'What's the matter, Prohaska? Aren't you even able to piss?'

"'I piss well, Herr Lieutenant,' he says, 'but I don't know how to write.'

"This is not a true story, but it gives the idea of how people felt about Galicia."

——◁◦▷——

The Wilder family was constantly on the move, visiting one railway station café after another until Max Wilder had saved enough to buy a hotel with a restaurant in Kraków, which he named Hotel City. "My father wanted my mother's family to see that, after all, she hadn't made a mistake.

"My father was an entrepreneur. Maybe not a very successful one, but our family had plenty to eat. I had a wonderful childhood going around on the trains with my parents to visit my father's train station restaurants.

"He was disposed to be a happy person with high spirits. He tried to look at the upside of things, but life did not cooperate. He was always trying for his little family, but it was all too hard for him.

"My father was a dreamer, a kind of adventurer, though not the kind who climbed mountains. He was always searching for something without knowing exactly what, only that he knew he wanted to change his fortunes overnight and become rich. He was like Don Quixote, except that Don Quixote fought windmills and my father bought them. And then, as soon as he bought them, there was no more wind.

"It is easy to go on when you're successful. But to go forward in the face of failure—that is valiant. My father had pride, and I would say he had a certain nobility.

"He specialized in things he knew nothing about. One day at lunch, he announced, 'By the way, Monday, I'm going into a new business. I'm importing Swiss clock works.' Two rooms of our apartment in Vienna became the offices for 'Fränkel, Pytlak und Wilder.' I have no idea what this firm actually did.

"As soon as my father went into that business, I think clocks went out of fashion. My father was a backwards alchemist. He could turn gold into sawdust.

"Then, he invested in a trout farm. We didn't find out until we had to move. 'What in God's name do you know about trout?' my mother asked him.

"'What's to know?' he said. 'It's just another fish.'

"It turned out there was a lot to know about trout, and my father lost the trout farm. My mother was very unhappy. We had to move from our comfortable home at Fleischmarkt 7, in the First District of Vienna to a tiny flat on the Billrothstrasse in the Nineteenth District. I never order trout in a restaurant.

"When I was a little boy, my mother took me with her when she went for the cure in Marienbad. My brother stayed behind with my father. The water had a dirty color and was lukewarm. I did not see why I should have to drink it, but my mother said it would make me live a long time. It looks like she was right."

Wilder remembered his mother as strict. "She had strong ideas about right and wrong, and she let us know about it. She hit us when she thought we needed it. I don't know if she was right or wrong. I know I didn't like it. She could hit pretty hard. Then, she would cook a delicious meal and want me to eat everything on my plate.

"I guess it's the way she thought mothers were supposed to act. I got hit a lot more than my brother because I deserved it more. But as I grew bigger, I never got hit anymore. I think she thought hitting me would make me a better man, and then she decided she could not change me anymore. My father never hit us. Never.

"But my mother was a good mom. She was always there for us, and she was a good cook.

"She and my father did not argue much—not in front of us, if they did—but they did not talk very much to each other. They did not seem to have much to say to each other. They were mismatched."

Whenever Billie visited his grandmother in Nowy Targ, he stayed in her hotel, the Zent'al. The hotel had originally been the Zentral, but when the "r" dropped off at the turn of the twentieth century, it became the Zent'al. Many years later, the East Berlin Grand Hot'l in *One, Two, Three* had an "e" that didn't light up except when the sign was turned off.

The Zent'al, a very good hotel for its time and place, had nine rooms and one bath. Since his grandmother was religious, the Zent'al's restaurant offered kosher meals for Orthodox travelers as well as standard Austrian fare. Billy Wilder recalled childhood summers:

"I slept in my grandmother's bedroom, and every evening she would look under the bed and say, 'Lately, I've been *so* afraid of a robber!' I don't know if she was speaking to me or if she did that when I wasn't there.

"Anything I know about being Jewish came from my grandmother and from an uncle who lived in Lodz." David Baldinger, his mother's younger brother, was an engineer who fought in World War I, and was interested in music, literature, and Judaism.

"My uncle encouraged me to read the Greek classics and avoid the Nibelungen saga. When he saw I was more interested in other things, he gave up on me. Later, he went to Israel, and we wrote many letters, until he died.

---◦▸---

After the war began in 1914, Billie spent August with his grandmother. It was hot, and he stayed indoors much of the time, sitting in a Thonet rocking chair, reading and thinking. "I had never stopped my active life before just to think. At the age of eight, I discovered thinking. I liked it quite well."

Then, suddenly, they had to flee Nowy Targ because the war was getting too close. Billie insisted on taking his "thinking" rocking chair with him. A horse and carriage was waiting to transport them. There was no time and no room. His grandmother told him that he had to make a choice: the rocking chair or her. He chose the rocking chair.

"For that, I got a slap, a light one. I was only joking, but she did not have my kind of sense of humor. I looked for a rocking chair like that for many years after I was a grown man. I found Thonet furniture, but I never found a rocking chair like that one."

It was the beginning of Billy Wilder's life as a refugee, though for a small child, it seemed an adventure. They went to Hotel City in Kraków.

Hotel City was at the foot of a medieval castle in the neighborhood of the university. It had a large outdoor terrace, on which, in the summer, guests sat drinking coffee, *mit Schlag,* with a peak of whipped cream on top, and eating rich butter *Kugelhuft,* dusted with powdered sugar, while a salon orchestra played Johann Strauss or von Suppé.

The Wilders ate well, but there was little food for thought. "In our house, there were no readers, no art collectors, no going to the theater, no dedicated opera- or concertgoers, no intellectuals, real or pretend. My mother did not collect Meissen. She had a hotel mentality, because she had always lived in hotels, and she had to leave places.

"My father read the newspaper. It gave him something to talk about with customers. Except for the very nice music that was played on the terrace, my parents were not very cultural people."

Hotel City was successful enough to enable the Wilder family to find a place in a Viennese neighborhood, generally thought the best, the First District. Then, the seemingly unchanging world of the Austro-Hungarian Empire changed.

"I was in my father's hotel in Kraków in June of 1914, and people were sitting on the terrace eating and drinking while the orchestra played von Suppé's Poet and Peasant Overture. My father walked to the music podium, and he signaled to the orchestra to stop. He said, 'Ladies and gentlemen: There will be no more music today. Our Archduke Ferdinand has been murdered in Sarajevo.'"

World War I began about a month afterward. In what turned out to be a disastrous decision, the monarchy's reserve forces were sent to the Serbian front in late July, exposing the Galician front to a Russian advance.

Fearing an invasion from the east by the Russians, those who could, left, filling the trains. The Wilder family, unable to get space, had to travel back to Vienna in a rented horse and carriage. Unlike many, however, they had a home to go to in Vienna.

"My father's time was against him. A bullet in Sarajevo killed the son of Francis Joseph, but it got our family, too. The world still has not gotten over it. It wiped out the world I was born into, the Austro-Hungarian monarchy.

"We did not know what was coming. No crystal ball."

—The—
Dream Prince

On November 21, 1916, after a reign of sixty-eight years, Emperor Francis Joseph I died at the age of eighty-seven. He had been born in 1830 and had reigned since 1848, eleven years longer than Queen Victoria.

Max Wilder, aware of the magnitude of the moment, chose an ideal place for him and for his ten-year-old son to view the funeral cortège. He took Billie to the Café Edison from which vantage point they could observe the entire procession.

Max purchased a souvenir program for his son from a vendor, and told him to save it. "It was just like the kind you got in the theater. It was lost a long time ago—like my life in Vienna. A memory.

"Someone told my father that before the coffin was closed, Katharina Schratt, the emperor's actress-mistress, placed two white roses on his chest. I did not know at that time what a mistress was. I hardly knew what an actress was, but I was very struck by those two white roses. I remembered those roses years later for the funeral in *Fedora*.

"My father said, 'You will remember this day all your life.' He lifted me onto a marble table by a window on the second floor where I could look out and watch the people in long, silent lines all along the street. I'll never forget that silence.

"After a long wait, the funeral procession came by, slowly, all of the people dressed in black. I had never seen so much black.

"I was impressed by the black horses wearing jewels. The men wore black suits, and the officers, black uniforms. The ladies in the crowd wore black, too, black dresses, black hats, some with black veils, black gloves. Some had umbrellas with them, black. People wore black mourning bands as though a member of their own family had died.

"Then, right in the middle of all that black pomp, there appeared bright white, a shining apparition. It was the Crown Prince Otto, a child like me, maybe a few years younger, dressed completely in white, in the uniform of the Hussars, wearing a sort of a white helmet with a white plume on top.

"I envied him. I have never been an envious person, but I can remember how I felt then. He would be the emperor, the ruler of the world. He was the prince of everyone's dreams, and I was nothing, standing on the marble table of that café as he passed by.

"I thought, if I disappeared, would anyone care? I guessed my parents would have missed me. Then, for a moment, I lost myself in the procession, as if in a dream.

"I imagined myself the white prince in the white uniform. I became, during that vision, one with him, I took his place. It felt wonderful. Suddenly, I knew how it felt to be born into greatness. Not everyone had to struggle as my father did—and worse. But it did not last long, and I was back on that table—and I was only me.

"My father pointed to the hearse and said, 'There is the last of your old emperor.' Then, he pointed to the little boy riding the white horse and said, 'There is your future emperor, Otto von Hapsburg. Someday you will come here with *your* son and that boy will be your emperor.' Well, my father wasn't *always* right."

Twenty-five years later, after Billy Wilder had become a leading screenwriter in Hollywood, he received a visitor at Paramount who reminded him of that moment.

"I was sitting in the Paramount commissary eating lunch," Wilder recalled, "playing Scrabble with some colleagues. I have always liked words, and I was hoping to make my English better. A guy from the front office came to our table and told me he had a fellow countryman of mine. He said, 'I don't know what to do with the guy.'

"I agreed to help him out. I got deep into the Scrabble game when he came back with a man, about my own age.

"'I'd like to introduce a fellow countryman,' he said to the man, and he introduced me. Then, he turned to me and said, 'Mr. Wilder, Otto von Hapsburg.'

"There before me stood the youth in the white uniform, the one who glowed, only now he was just a man in a gray suit, not made by a tailor. He had thinning hair. My hair had thinned, too, but *I* was only mortal.

"It turned out that the majestic being I had envied that day was on a lecture tour of universities. We talked about life in Vienna. I told him about the *Hungerwinter* during the war—how my brother and I had to stand in a line for hours in bitter winter weather waiting for a handful of potatoes. That was not part of *his* memories.

"What he really wanted to talk about was movies. He told *me* all about movies. He wanted to know about stars like Nelson Eddy and Jeanette MacDonald. I think they must have reminded him of operettas he saw, in what were for him the good old days.

"Then he got to the point. He wanted to know whether the time was right for an extravaganza film about the Danube monarchy. If so, he wanted me to keep him in mind, because he could be available as an expert on the Austro-Hungarian Empire. But how could he? He never had the chance to be an expert.

"I learned a lot about life that day in Hollywood. Maybe too much.

"My father had told me, 'You will remember the funeral procession of Francis Joseph all your life.' He was right, and that was a lot longer than he expected. It was a lot longer than *I* expected."

—Vienna,—
City of
Broken Dreams

 "In Vienna during World War I," Wilder told me, "everyone was hungry. I swept the streets to pick up a little extra money to buy a little food. My brother and I stood in line all day for a few potatoes.

"Sometimes it was very cold, but I was always jumping around so much, because I never could stand still, so I wasn't as cold as my brother, who kept our place. He would say, 'You'll lose our place.' And I would say, 'No, I won't, because you are standing there.' That made him angry.

"My brother and I never talked much. We were never close in anything except age. We lived in the same apartment until my brother left home when he was about fourteen without finishing high school. He went to some relatives we had in London. We were only one year apart, but we never had the same friends; he had his, I had mine. We never had much to say to each other.

"My brother was more like my mother. I was like my father.

"From London, my brother went to America. He had a good business in New York. He was in leather, but he sold his company to make movies. They weren't anything that interested me, so I didn't see them. I saw one. I didn't expect much of it, and it didn't let me down. It wasn't even bad, which is worse. He should have stuck with leather purses.

"We didn't share memories. We shared experiences. Then, we each remembered the experiences differently. My memories of my brother are like old, faded photographs from a long time ago when we were children in the Austro-Hungarian Empire, which was in the Dark Ages.

"I remember him in his place on Long Island when he met me at the ship—when America was new for me and when the snow was white and fresh.

"My father never blamed anybody else for his failures. He claimed them just like he claimed his successes.

"During the war, my father was a guard for the army reserve. It was the only time I knew him to have a regular job. In the war, people did what they had to do. It was a time to survive a day at a time."

When Hotel City became a failing enterprise in a foreign country, Poland, Max Wilder was forced to sell his dream for what he could get. "The Austro-Hungarian Empire was all broken. So many had died for nothing."

The armistice in November 1918 sparked anarchy in Vienna. "The soldiers came back, and there were many who did not come back, as in all wars. And there were those who left a valuable piece of themselves on fields they never should have known—a leg, an arm, an eye. None of these grows back.

"They believed they would be received as heroes. Wrong. People didn't want to be reminded. Soldiers were quick to change to civilian clothes. You could tell they were soldiers because they hadn't eaten well at the front, and their clothes hung loose on them. The rest of us were thin, too, but our clothes got used to it.

"People used to say, 'I remember when I had a big slice of Sacher torte at the Sacher Hotel, or a nice warm *Milchrahmstrudel* at Demel.' I always say, 'Why torture yourself?' It's better to think about something that can come your way. I preferred to think about two potatoes.

"When I arrived in America and had to live on canned soup till I got a start, I was never hungry like in Vienna. Sometimes I hear someone say, 'I'm starving,' and I think all these years later, 'You don't know what starving is.'

"Then, one day it was all over. The American trucks came with their aid. I can remember the American flags waving. They brought food and got us out of hunger. It was the relief program organized by Herbert Hoover, who was the head of the American Relief Committee. Suddenly, there was milk and butter and eggs and meat.

"My mother had told us about America, New York, how wonderful it was. I decided I was going to see that wonderful place, but in school when we were given the choice of studying French or English, I chose French because it seemed easier. I was no student.

"I was bored in school. I could have done better, but I didn't care. I started to get interested in English when I heard the American dance bands on records, especially Paul Whiteman's. I could sing the songs before I knew what the words meant."

As a student, Billie was better on the playing field than in the classroom. "The soccer field where I played was a few miles from where we lived. My mother gave me very exact streetcar fare. There was never extra money in our family. There was a woman near the field who sold sausages so tempting they should have been illegalized.

"Many were the times I had to walk home because I couldn't resist the temptation of a wurst with mustard and pickle. My mother would worry because it took me so long to get home, and because I didn't have any appetite for dinner.

"I had a soccer accident when I was a boy, but it wasn't on the playing field. I was kicking a stone like a soccer ball. Accidentally, I kicked the stone through a store window. The store owner knew me, so I told him I would bring the money if he wouldn't tell my father.

"When I got home, I told my father I wanted to take some classes in typing and stenography. He agreed to give me the money for the classes. It was enough to pay for the broken store window.

"One day, my father was in a hurry to send off a letter, and he asked me to use my new skills. I wrote a lot of gibberish, and went to the typewriter and typed furiously. When my father saw it, I told him what really happened. He didn't do anything. We had an unspoken understanding, my father and I.

"I knew something he didn't want my mother to know. I had a half-brother, and no one knew about it except me and my father.

"One day, I went to get the mail, and I saw a card for my father, an invitation from a boarding school to a party at the school his son was attending. It was not about me or my brother. This was a son our family had no idea existed. His name was Hubert, but I never looked for him.

"My mother was waiting for the mail. I hid the card under my shirt. When my father came home, I gave him the card. He didn't say a word. We exchanged a look.

"It was our secret, for life, a bond. We never spoke of it. It made me feel like that day I was a man. He knew I could be trusted to keep a man's secret. We were men together."

—Viennese Tarts—

Wilder remembered himself as a poor student who did only enough to get by. He was not a "problem" student until he was caught with an Egon Schiele nude in his notebook.

"I saw a wonderful picture of a nude by Schiele. I was about fourteen, and the naked woman was more interesting to me than the artist. It was before his name called out to me, but his drawing did. That picture I clipped from the magazine, you could say, was the start of my art accumulating. I always was an accumulator. As a child, I collected buttons.

"I took this picture to school with me, and began passing it around secretly. Not secretly enough. The professor said, 'What do you have there, Wilder? Is that something you want to show me?' I no longer had the drawing, or I would have tried to eat it.

"The teacher looked at it like he had never seen a naked woman before. I never saw the picture again.

"When my parents heard, they were not surprised. I was a constant disappointment to my mother. My father understood better. My mother had a lot to say. My father did not say anything."

Billie was sent to the Realgymnasium Juranek in the Ninth District, a school for "problem boys." From the window of his new school, he was offered an interesting view which served to distract him.

Across the street was a small hotel which did an exceptionally good business. People went in and out all the time, but no one carried a suitcase. The guests seemed to be mostly men. A few women entered separately. Sometimes the men looked around furtively before they entered.

"I never thought of asking my parents. It was another time, back when you did not ask your parents anything that possibly involved sex, and they did not volunteer much. Sometimes somebody's father told him something like, 'Don't get a girl into trouble,' without explaining what that 'trouble' might be. Mostly us boys just exchanged our misinformation for the purpose of showing off our experience of which we didn't have any.

"I had a friend named Anton, and one day his father caught him masturbating. He said, 'If you don't stop doing this terrible, terrible, terrible thing, you will die the fiftieth time you do it.'

"My friend got so scared, he didn't masturbate anymore unless he absolutely could not help himself. He kept track of how often he slipped.

"All too soon, he reached number forty-nine. He wrote a farewell note to his parents, signing it, 'Your Son.' Then, he did it for the last time . . .

"He survived, and from then on, he didn't believe a word his father said.

"The next morning, the story spread through the school. We all met in the boys' room and chanted, 'Parents lie! Long live masturbation!' In a bold act of defiance, we pulled out the cigarettes we hid in our shoes and smoked them."

———◦———

It was in Vienna that Wilder discovered movies. "I don't remember the first movie I ever saw, but my mother said I watched it without crying." Living in the First District put Wilder close to the exciting new medium. His desire to see films then was as strong as it later was to make them.

"I was always on the lookout for ways to earn *kreuzers* for cakes, sausages, and especially movies. Around the corner from where we lived on Fleischmarkt, there was a woman with a dachshund. She was a professional whore and the dog was only part-dachshund. The other part of him was some very unfriendly dog, probably a big one, and the dachshund didn't know how little he was. He barked so much that he distracted and terrorized her customers, so he was bad for business, but she was crazy about him. So, when she found a customer, she would pay me to watch the dog.

"One time, she got picked up by the police, and I was left with the dog. The dachshund didn't like me, but when I was all he had, he stopped barking and got small and scared.

"I couldn't take him home with me, but I couldn't leave him. I just sat on a step holding the dog. Lucky for me and the dog she came back to claim her 'dackel,' a German pet name for a dachshund. I guess she had made some deal with the policemen. She gave me an extra couple of kreuzers.

"I thought the next day when I went to take the dog, he would remember me. He did. He bit me. He was a long-haired dachshund with a short memory."

Billie liked westerns with William S. Hart and Bronco Billy Anderson. His favorite cinema was the Kreuz-Kino, which was nicknamed the "Revolver Kino" because it specialized in American westerns. He liked American comedies, too; his favorites, Buster Keaton and Charlie Chaplin, both of whom he believed influenced him.

"I liked Keaton best because he was unsentimental. I learned from him that you should never laugh at your own jokes if you want other people to laugh at them."

In spite of so many hours spent at the movies instead of studying, Wilder graduated from what he called "the misfit high school of Vienna." On his last visit to Vienna, he tried to locate some of "my fellow misfits."

"I let it be known that I wanted to see anybody who went to school with me. No one. The guys were all gone.

"Then, just before I was leaving, the hotel concierge called and said there was a gentleman there to see me, named Martini. I remembered him. I said please send him right up.

"I'm standing there with the door open. I'm so glad to see him. He looks pretty old. I hope I don't look that old. I say, 'Do you remember that professor we—'

"He stops me. 'That was my father. He died. I am the son of Martini.'"

—Raincoats—
and Freud

 "The hope that I would do something with my life still beat in the hearts of my parents, though I had done little to inspire that hope. Doctor. Lawyer. The dream of a Jewish family for their son. My brother, Willie, left school and went to London. One down, one to go. There were always the fallback hopes, dentist or accountant.

"I never went to the university. I passed the test. In Vienna, you did not have to attend classes, just take the exams and be a lawyer. [Otto] Preminger told me he went to about two classes. If we had done what we were supposed to do, Preminger and I, we could have become lawyers and stayed in Vienna, waiting for Mr. Hitler. We would have died without finding our lives in films.

"I was eighteen when I decided not to go to college. I could have gone, but I did not want to be dependent on my father's pockets. I told him I wanted to be a newspaperman.

"In the American movies, I saw all these bright-eyed young guys in Burberry raincoats with press cards stuck in their hatbands. I pretty much made up my mind. I wanted to wear one of those raincoats.

"Reporters interviewed movie stars and the luxury-liner rich. I was looking for an interesting life, not doing every day the same thing.

The work looked glamorous and not too hard, and I was full of confidence.

"I was brash, insolent, full of bravado. I was persuasive. I knew how to exaggerate. I never liked to lie. A little exaggeration, I was never above.

"You have to get the opportunity to develop yourself. I had the energy, which is important. I was good at thinking on my feet. And in every other position, too.

"There were two problems. I did not have a Burberry raincoat, and I did not have a press card to put in my hatband. Also, there was a heavy unemployment problem in Austria, especially in newspaper work. There were no jobs even for experienced reporters. There's always a depression in those jobs. It was the old chicken-egg problem. Which came first, the raincoat or the job?

"I tried the best papers, but I could not get to see anyone. I tried the scandal sheets, but no welcoming mat there either. I had few qualifications, but I was not afraid to use shoe leather. I got ignored like I was the Invisible Man.

"Then, my hour came at *Die Stunde,* which means *The Hour.*

"*Die Stunde* came out at noon. I figured they were busy in the morning and the best time to catch them would be after the bigwigs had lunched with some beer and wine.

"I was met by the cleaning women. One of them pointed up to the second floor. I walked up the stairs.

"The place looked empty. From behind one closed door, I heard heavy breathing, moans, what sounded like enjoyable agony.

"I knocked, kind of tentatively. I knocked again. The sounds like asthma went on. I opened the door.

"There was an overweight man and a woman on a sofa. He was on top of her. The man's face was red. He stood up and pulled up his pants and the woman stuffed a breast back into her blouse and pulled down her dress. She grabbed a steno pad and ran into another room.

"The man said, 'What are you doing here?'

"'I'm looking for work.'

"He said, 'You're lucky. I have some work for you.'

"I never knew if I got the job to shut me up or because he had a spot for a nervy kid.

"I became a sort of newspaperman, what they called 'space rate.' You only got paid if they printed your stuff. It was a jungle, the competition, but right away I liked seeing myself in print.

"Editors didn't do too much to what I wrote. I thought it was because it was good, but they were just lazy. I learned not to turn my stuff in too early. They changed less if they didn't have time to put their touch on it, something I learned later for film. I didn't give them too much extra celluloid to work with.

"I was doing sports and the dirty work of crime reporting. Some of this I remembered for *Ace in the Hole,* which critics called cynical. It was kinder than what I saw, sanitized.

"Can you imagine taking the streetcar to see the parents of a murder victim, and then to see the parents of the murderer? Murderers have parents, too. You ask them how they feel. Then, I was supposed to ask them all for old photographs and to arrange for a photographer to come and shoot them, all the while a mother was crying. Sometimes I just made up the answer about how they felt because I couldn't bring myself to ask a lot of questions.

"We reporters sat in a coffeehouse across from a police station where we had a deal going. There was a red light in the café, and the agreement was the light would flash when a criminal was being brought in, a signal for 'breaking news,' like two stolen Lipizzaners were spotted pulling a delivery wagon. Or there was a double suicide in the Imperial Hotel with Mayerling implications, only this was no crown prince with a countess.

"I was having a good run of interviews, and I am a believer that when the cards are coming your way, you don't get up from the table and leave. So I headed for Berggasse 19, one of the best known addresses in Vienna. It was the domicile and office combination of Sigmund Freud. The worst that could happen, I would be out on my ear in the street. Then, I could always turn the other ear. I had enough practice hearing the word no.

"The door of the apartment where he had his office was answered by a housekeeper, who thought I was a patient. I gave her my card. In those days, everyone had a calling card or you didn't exist. She ushered me into the living room and went into the next room. The door was open a little, and I positioned myself so I could look into what was a library-study-office. It was cluttered with stuff I later found out was ancient art. I was surprised how small that famous couch was. The back of the woman blocked my view of the person behind the desk.

"Then, the woman came back past me without speaking. Dr. Freud rose and entered the living room.

"I was surprised to see how small he was.

"I clicked my heels, as the custom of courtesy was then, and said something like, 'Herr Doktor Freud, this is a great honor . . .'

"The good doctor was wearing a large white linen dinner napkin, tucked into his shirt. It was obvious I had disturbed his lunch.

"Freud was holding my card in one hand. 'You are a reporter from *Die Stunde*?' he said in an authoritative voice. With his other hand, he pointed toward the door.

"I bowed deeply and thanked him for his hospitality, and I left. At the time, I remember I was annoyed. Later, I rethought it. It was an honor to have been personally rejected by Dr. Freud!"

———◁○▷———

In May 1926, Billie Wilder interviewed Paul Whiteman, America's "King of Jazz," who had just arrived at Vienna's Bristol Hotel. Whiteman and his twenty-eight-piece dance orchestra were in Europe for a concert tour. Wilder had been a fan since he was fifteen.

"I wanted to understand every word, and there I was with my lousy English, but nobody in Vienna knew more than I did about Paul Whiteman and American jazz."

In his review of the concert, Wilder stressed Whiteman himself, rather than the music, understanding that his readers would find the man interesting even if they didn't like what he played.

"I had this idea to bring with me some songs by some popular Viennese composers and get Paul Whiteman's opinions. It seemed a good slant for the article. I wanted to hear what he would say, and I also wanted something in case I ran short of material. I wasn't the one who was going to bring the interview to an end.

"We talked about his records, 'Whispering,' 'The Japanese Sandman,' 'The Wang-Wang Blues,' 'Dardanella,' and all the others. I sang the songs in German, which he found funny.

"We hit it off so well, I became his tour guide. He liked to eat and drink, and I knew all the best restaurants and beer halls.

"I brought him one of his biggest hits. In German it was called 'Madonna,' and it was very popular in Austria and Germany, but much more popular when he recorded it as 'When Day Is Done.' It was a best-seller for years.

"The Whiteman band was full of great jazz musicians. Matty Malneck, a great jazz violinist, became my friend. Many years later he arranged songs for *Love in the Afternoon* and *Some Like It Hot.*"

Whiteman liked the young reporter and what he wrote, so he invited him to come along and write about the band in Berlin, their next stop. The German capital was the goal of every ambitious young journalist in Central Europe, but Wilder didn't have the money for a ticket. This was solved when Wrede, the music publisher promoting the Whiteman concert tour, agreed to pay his expenses.

"I got my trip and three days in Berlin. I agreed without negotiating for the round-trip ticket. I had no intention of going back."

Wilder informed *Die Stunde* that he was taking a few days off. He told his parents that he was making an extended trip to Berlin.

"My parents had a pretty good idea that I might stay in Berlin because I told them Berlin was where I wanted to be."

—One-Way Ticket—
to Berlin

"When I saw Berlin, I knew I wanted to stay there forever. How wrong can you be?"

Wilder arrived there in 1926. He was twenty years old. "Vienna was gray, but Berlin was colorful like a kaleidoscope," he remembered, despite the very high rate of unemployment that plagued the city and its citizens.

He had one suitcase and a letter of introduction from the Viennese correspondent of a German publishing house. He filed his review of the Berlin Whiteman concerts and found a job as a reporter, and a furnished flat on Pariser Strasse. Agent Robby Lantz's father, Adolph Lantz, was the managing editor who hired him at *Die Nachtausgabe.* Lantz remembered:

"I was only a boy, but I saw how likable and energetic Billy was. Everything seemed to come easily to him, but looking back, I think he tried very hard."

"When I was a young man, I could write anywhere," Wilder said. "I liked best to write in the coffeehouses on my portable typewriter. I liked a little noise and activity. The smell of good coffee, the sight of the rich layer cakes, the sound of conversation, the dancing of dishes—this stimulated me. I didn't like writing alone in my furnished rooms."

He also liked the newspapers attached to sticks on the wall. He kept up with the news while studying the style of each paper without having to buy them.

While Wilder was a reporter at *Die Nachtausgabe,* he met a chorus girl named Olive Victoria, a tall, beautiful English girl. She became Wilder's first love in Berlin.

Olive Victoria was a dancer in a Berlin revue. "They liked to hire English girls because they had such beautiful long legs. Hers were the most beautiful. She was younger than me, but she must be an old lady now."

Olive worked late into the night, so he had to court her in the early hours of the morning, after she finished work. "I was so tired after staying up every night chasing her after the show, I was falling asleep in the office."

One day, he fell asleep in the editorial office phone booth. He was rudely awakened, and out of work.

"I was stuck on her. I practiced my English with her. I wanted to practice more, but she was sleeping with the American actor Eddie Polo. She is a faded vision from my youth."

While looking for his next job, Wilder wrote a poem about Olive which appeared in the newspaper in July 1927 under the title "Fifth from the Right." There was a photo of Olive Victoria's troupe in which she was identified as "fifth from the right."

Between newspaper jobs, Wilder worked as an *Eintänzer* or tea dancer. "Since I was kind of a very good dancer, I did a stint as what you might call a gigolo. I was a dancer for money in the Hotel Eden in Berlin. But it was not romantic. I got the idea in order to write a series of articles on what it is to be a gigolo in Berlin. And it made a bit of scandal.

"An American journalist, years later, who didn't know any better, wrote that I was a gigolo, so I could use older women to make money from. Others copied what he wrote, so the story has always haunted me. I heard that lies travel on short legs, but it is not true. They travel on stilts.

"The women I danced with, some of them were with their husbands who did not dance well enough to keep them happy. I was light on my feet and light on theirs, and I had the best dialogue.

"The Eden Hotel male dancers were not exploiters. The exploited were *us*. It was an honest way to earn my bread. I was thinking all the time of being in my chair that night with my shoes off.

"I had a girlfriend who came back from a trip to America and brought the Charleston with her. She taught me, and I gave private lessons as a sideline. We did it together. She danced with the men.

"These days I am retired from dancing as I am from many things. The only ball to which I am likely to be invited is the Moth Ball."

<hr />

Wilder recalled interviewing famous Americans who came through Berlin. "We're talking now about before World War II, where America was the moon to the Europeans. I mean, the idea of Chaplin coming to visit Berlin, the crowd was standing on its head. In Berlin, anyone who had ever been in America, you just wanted to touch him, because he had been to the moon."

Wilder prided himself on putting some zest into his interviews with the visiting celebrities. His article on Jackie Coogan hinted that Coogan's parents were exploiting the child star, which turned out to be true. Wilder went to the Cornelius Vanderbilt, Jr., interview armed with the question: "Mr. Vanderbilt, how much money are you carrying?"

Vanderbilt didn't have any money at all, just as Wilder had surmised. A rich man didn't need to carry money. He was born with automatic credit, the name Vanderbilt. Wilder found this out when Vanderbilt let him pay the check at their lunch.

In Berlin, Wilder was an avid theatergoer. As much as he could, he tried to see everything. He liked to keep up, and he was always looking for inspiration, celebrities, and stories.

On the opening night of a play about Rasputin, he learned that Prince Yussupov, who was the leader of the group that killed Rasputin, would be in the audience. Good at cultivating waiters, ticket sellers, theater managers, and "those concierges who knew everything," Wilder

was able, with a few, well-placed marks, to purchase the seat exactly behind the prince.

Between acts, Wilder tapped him on the shoulder and asked what
he thought of the play. Prince Yussupov replied, "We killed the wrong
man. We should have killed Lenin. And Trotsky." Wilder had his story.

———◦———

In 1928, Wilder's parents were thinking about visiting his older brother,
Willie, in New York. After he was successful, Willie Wilder invited his
mother and father to come to America.

Money was short, so it was decided that Max, who hadn't seen
America, would go there for a visit to see if he would like to make the
permanent move. Eugenia stayed in Vienna. On the way back, Max
planned to pass through Berlin to see his younger son. During the
return voyage, Max didn't feel well.

On the rail journey to Berlin, his condition worsened. By the time
he arrived and met his son, the pain had become so severe that an
ambulance was summoned. Max died in the arms of his son on the way
to the hospital.

Wilder used what money he had to bury his father in the Jewish
cemetery in Berlin. Then he had to wait until he could borrow some
money to call his mother in Vienna.

—Ghostwriting—
with a
Shoehorn

 Berlin was the film capital of Europe in the 1920s. Everyone was discussing the films of Fritz Lang, G. W. Pabst, and F. W. Murnau.

"I had always loved movies," Wilder said, "but I never tried writing one until I went to Berlin. Then, I saw Eisenstein's *Potemkin,* and I knew what I wanted to do for a living. *Potemkin* is still number one on my list of favorite movies.

"My movie career began with an illicit love affair—not mine—and I squeezed in with a shoehorn. It is a story I have told before because one of the questions people ask of me, second only to 'What was Marilyn Monroe like?' is, 'How did you get started in pictures?'

"I wanted to break into the movies, but I didn't know how. I was living in a rooming house. The daughter of the landlady was engaged to one guy and also kind of playing around a little on the side.

"One night, someone pounding on the front door woke me up. My door opened, and this guy rushed into my room. I recognized him as the head of Maxim Films. It was the fiancé knocking, and the girl's little affair would probably sink the marriage plans.

"The old man had his shoes in his hand. He asked me, 'Have you got a shoehorn?'

"I said, 'I have a shoehorn, and I have a script I want you to read.'

"He said, 'Yes, of course. Just send it to my office,' and he looked for his card.

I said, 'No. I want you to read it now.' He took the script from me, sat down, and read it. On the spot, he said, 'I'll buy it.' He gave me 500 marks, and I gave him my shoehorn. That's how I became a movie writer.

"I was twenty-one when I first got into the commercial picture swim. I'd write from two to five pictures a month, which gave me this great experience. Now, remember these were silent pictures, and I'd write twenty, twenty-five pages, maybe thirty-five.

"It was that time of monumental unemployment, and one was glad to get any kind of work. As a ghostwriter of screenplays, I came to know a lot of film people, especially since they often frequented the same bars and cafés as we journalists did. I met Joe Pasternak, who was at that time Paul Kohner's assistant at UFA, which was affiliated with American Universal. The year before, this same Pasternak, as a waiter at the Universal commissary in Hollywood, had gotten to know the great director and film pioneer Allan Dwan.

"Dwan came to Berlin in 1927 on his honeymoon. He needed a tour guide. Pasternak, knowing my miserable circumstances, recommended me. I went to the Hotel Adlon where I met Dwan and his bride, a gorgeous young Ziegfeld girl, at the bar. I guess it wasn't his first honeymoon. He was pretty loaded, so in spite of my lousy English, we got along, and he hired me to show him Germany.

"Except for the train ride from Vienna, I had never been outside Berlin. But when I was offered 100 marks a week, I put that small problem out of my mind. I purchased a Baedeker and studied it.

"First stop, Dresden. I schlepped Dwan and his wife through the state art gallery, Rembrandts, Rafaels, Rubenses, Dürers. Pretty soon, Dwan asked if I could cut the lecture short so they could return to the hotel. He was anxious to get to the bar. They had Prohibition in the United States, and he had come to Europe to catch up on his drinking.

Four double martinis went down like water. His young wife tried to keep up. I only drank lemonades. I was on duty.

"That was the pattern from Dresden to Munich to Baden-Baden: fifteen minutes museum, fifteen minutes classic architecture, and four hours of martinis. I put aside Baedeker and started improvising.

"In Heidelberg, an English tour group appeared with a real guide who overheard my rendition of nonsense, and spilled the beans to Dwan.

"Dwan said, 'Okay, kid. You're fired.' Then, he turned to the English tour group and shouted, 'Never trust a son of a bitch who doesn't drink!' He paid me for the whole week, even though it was only Tuesday, so I was able to get back to Berlin without walking."

———◦———

In 1929, Wilder received screen credit on *Der Teufelsreporter: Im Nebel der Grossstadt (The Devil's Reporter: In the Fog of the Big City)*.

The film was a vehicle for Eddie Polo, an American circus performer, film stuntman, and Hollywood actor, whose most popular role on screen was as serial hero Cyclone Smith. British film historian Kevin Brownlow told me that it was one credit Wilder would have preferred not having:

"The one time I talked with Billy Wilder, I mentioned this picture, and he was *furious!* He said, 'You people don't do us any favors by finding this crap. You should bury it!'

"It opens with a wonderful sequence in which an open bus filled with schoolgirls drives around the center of Berlin, and you see the city that's completely disappeared. I think it's in this film, there is the most amazing stunt I've ever seen in films, in which Eddie Polo has to get to the top of a tall building in Berlin, and the girls are acrobats. They stand on each other's shoulders until they are the height of the building. Then, Eddie Polo climbs the chorus girls to get into the building. An amazing stunt!"

—People—
on Sunday

 "It was 1929, and I ran into a group of young guys at the Romanisches Café who were interested in making movies. We turned a meeting in a café into a movie, a good movie." The Romanisches Café was the favorite meeting place of film people in Berlin.

The "young guys" were Moritz Seeler, Eugen Schüfftan, Robert and Curt (then Kurt) Siodmak, and Edgar G. Ulmer, and the "good movie" was *People on Sunday* (*Menschen am Sonntag*). Anxious to see their careers move ahead, they believed a good film could be made for a lower budget than films currently being distributed.

"My friend Robert Siodmak, who at that time was selling advertising for the *Neue Revue,* arrived at the Romanisches Café, very excited. He wanted to make a film, and a relative had given him 5,000 marks. Curt Siodmak, his brother, suggested we shoot on the streets of Berlin with unknown people. That was a brilliant idea, because we could not afford professional actors. I wrote a script, and we shot on Sunday. We had to work at other jobs all week, like the people in the film, and only had Sunday to shoot. So, the people behind the camera were people on Sunday, too."

Seeler, a theatrical producer with his own theater, was thirty-five.

Robert Siodmak had been a stage actor, and he had some film experience. He was related to Heinrich Nebenzahl, a successful film producer who had given Robert a chance to work as a film cutter. Robert was twenty-eight. Curt Siodmak, a published writer, was twenty-seven.

Eugen Schüfftan (later Shuftan) was already a recognized cameraman and the inventor of the Schüfftan process, a method of using mirrors to create special effects, blending live actors with miniatures. It was a process Fritz Lang employed extensively in *Metropolis.* Schüfftan was thirty-six.

The Czech-born Ulmer had worked in Hollywood, where he directed low-budget westerns at Universal. Ulmer was a production assistant for F. W. Murnau on *The Last Laugh* and *Sunrise,* and a production designer for Cecil B. DeMille on *King of Kings.* In Germany, he had designed sets for Robert Wiene on *The Cabinet of Dr. Caligari,* was a production designer for Fritz Lang on *Metropolis, The Nibelungen,* and *The Spies,* and had worked with Max Reinhardt. From his Hollywood earnings, he contributed money toward the film they all wanted to make. He was twenty-five.

They were joined by Fred Zinnemann, who was, at twenty-two, a year younger than Wilder, and the youngest. "I carried the camera brilliantly," Zinnemann told me.

Robert Siodmak became the director because, as Wilder put it, "When kids play baseball, the kid who has the bat and ball is manager. On our team, Robert had the camera.

"Except for Schüfftan and Ulmer, we were amateurs. The only money that mattered was to make the picture and live while we did it. Fred Zinnemann was assistant cameraman. Ulmer was codirector, Curt Siodmak and I were writers. Moritz Seeler knew how to get a picture distributed."

Zinnemann was born in Austria in 1907. To the great disappointment of his family, he chose to study music rather than medicine. Then he discovered cinema and wanted to become a cameraman. "It never occurred to me at that time that I would be a director."

Zinnemann studied at the Institute des Hautes Études Cinémato-

People on Sunday—*Billy Wilder and Fred Zinnemann, both of whom got their start in 1929 with a film in Berlin, visit more than half a century afterward.* (Collection of Fred Zinnemann)

graphiques. He wanted to stay in Paris, but his visa expired, so he went to Berlin.

"I became an assistant to Eugen Schüfftan," Zinnemann told me in London many years later. "He had agreed to make a small film, which had almost no budget, about some young people spending a Sunday at the lake. I checked film, carried the camera around, and never dropped it. That was my total contribution.

"None of us had a car at that time. We all went by bus. We had to work without lights. We had some brilliant talent and strong personalities, and a lot of temperament, though not with the nonprofessional actors. There were several leaders in the group. I was a follower.

"Robert Siodmak would have inspirations on the set as we were making the film. Billy Wilder didn't like that, doing something different from what we had planned. They were two high-strung personalities, with Billy Wilder being the higher-strung of the two. They were not compatible, and both had a lot of energy.

"I remember once when Wilder and Siodmak took the negative to the laboratory to be developed. It seemed a good idea to have the two of them watch over the valuable film. They needed a third person to go with them to referee, as it turned out.

"They got to arguing about something and left the film on the bus. They spent the whole day chasing buses. It represented three days work, and it had to be reshot. That was terrible, since we didn't have any budget. We never knew which was better, the three days of film we lost, or the three days we reshot. Everyone but me forgot the incident. I never did. They were different personalities from me, and they looked at the big picture. I was more detail-oriented. I was happy I wasn't the one who lost the film. I'd *never* have gotten over it."

People on Sunday used real locations, such as the zoo train station and the beach at Nikolassee. The actors worked at jobs like those they had in the film. After shooting, they went back to those jobs.

"We had no unions to deal with," Wilder said. "No studio, no producers to look over our shoulders. We had cheap stock, and we shot silent. We didn't know any better, so we just did it.

"There was a scarcity of paper, so when we first began talking the script, I wrote on the backs of envelopes and pieces of paper I had with me. Sometimes I used menus.

"Sometimes everyone was talking at once. Everyone was an authority on the subject of Sunday. We all had jobs six days a week, and looked forward to how we would spend our Sunday.

"Seventy years later, when every day can be the same, when I can sleep late if I want to and not work, somehow, Sunday still seems different.

"It was a simple story that captured a sense of everyday life in Berlin. The style was that of a rough documentary in contrast to the elaborate kind of films being done at the time. It was more than fifteen years ahead of Italian neorealism. We were doing that in Berlin long before Rossellini did it in Rome."

People on Sunday may have saved the lives of those who made it. The doors that *People* opened permitted all of them, except Moritz Seeler, to leave Nazi Germany, and he might have left, but he chose to stay until it was too late.

"That day in the café, Seeler picked up the check," Wilder said. "He stayed in Germany. He had more life built up there, so he stayed too long, and he died in one of the camps."

People on Sunday begins by announcing, "The five people who appear in this film have never stood in front of a camera before. Today, they all go back to their real jobs."

Erwin, a taxi driver, lives with Annie, a neurasthenic model. He's the first of Billy Wilder's "suspenders and belt" characters, wearing both in case one fails. They plan to spend Sunday at the Nikolassee beach with Wolfgang, "an officer, gentleman, antiquarian, gigolo, at the moment a wine salesman."

After an argument, Annie stays at home while Erwin joins Wolf. Wolf has brought along a new girlfriend, Christl. Brigitte, Christl's best friend, joins the group. Brigitte is the manager of a record shop.

At the beach, Wolf tries to kiss Christl, but she rejects him, and he turns his attentions toward Brigitte, who is more receptive. After swimming, a picnic, and a walk through the Grünewald woods, Wolf and Brigitte go off together, and he seduces her.

Back on the beach, Wolf and Erwin, now tired of their dates, flirt with two other women as Brigitte and Christl look on, appalled. They have small satisfaction when the men have to borrow money from them to pay for the paddleboat they were renting.

As they part at the end of the day, Brigitte hopes Wolf will see her next Sunday, but he and Erwin have other plans. The bond between the two men is the one that counts. They have really spent the Sunday with each other. Erwin returns to his flat to find Annie still in bed.

The next day, he is driving his cab, Wolf is selling wine, and Brigitte is selling records, all waiting for next Sunday.

"*And then on Monday,*" the titles proclaim over many scenes of Berlin as the great metropolis starts a new week, "*again work,—again everyday life—again a week.*

"*4—million—wait—for—the next—Sunday!*

"*End.*"

Each word appears separately on the screen to give the effect of how long all the other days of the week seem compared to the one free day of pleasure which all hopefully await—Sunday.

People on Sunday premiered at a small UFA theater on the Kurfürstendamm in early 1930. Curt Siodmak told me, "The projectionist, who said he was always right in predicting a success or a failure, predicted *more* than failure—a disaster!"

Its critical and popular success was unexpected. Silent films were already out of favor, and *People* was considered a silent "art" film, which also limited its access to theaters abroad. "It was a tiny picture," Wilder said, "but people seemed to love it. *People* was a big surprise for all of us. It wasn't 'cinema.' It was a movie!

"After our success, I knew I could make a living the six other days of the week. We got offers of jobs at UFA, the giant film studio, the largest in the world outside of Hollywood." Pronounced "Ooo-fah," UFA was the German acronym for Universum Film A.-G., Hollywood's chief competitor during the 1920s.

"I was about twenty-four. The time ahead seemed endless. I couldn't imagine how it would feel to be old. Just as well.

"Robert Siodmak got just what he wanted—the offer of a contract to repeat his success from UFA with a big salary and a big budget. I went along and worked on the screenplay for one of his UFA pictures with his brother, Curt. Ulmer returned to Hollywood, and we all soon followed. Everyone except Seeler, poor soul."

People on Sunday can never be seen again in the same way it was seen through the eyes of those pre–World War II audiences. The real end of the movie was about to happen.

—UFA—

Billy Wilder received writing credit on thirteen German pictures before the Nazis came to power in 1933. On all but one, *Emil und die Detektive,* he worked with a collaborator.

"After *People on Sunday,* I decided I wanted to go to Hollywood. I had always wanted to go to America, but it took Mr. Hitler to make me leave UFA.

"UFA was a very different situation than Hollywood. The studio itself was something like ten miles outside Berlin in what became East Berlin after the war. They had some smaller studios around town. The big company was UFA, but there were a dozen other companies, too. You didn't have writers or directors under contract. There was no such thing as a writer being on the set. Everything was too far out of town, and most of us didn't have a car. Mr. [Erich] Pommer, who was the Irving Thalberg of the UFA company, ran everything. There were some outstanding directors at UFA: Murnau, Lang, Wiene, Pabst. It was a director's world at UFA. In Hollywood, it was a producer's world."

———◄◦►———

After the collapse of the American stock market, more than one million Germans lost their jobs. "People looked to the movies for escape and laughs. They didn't want grim and sad because they had enough of that in their lives already.

"Writers are not so much affected by bad economic times, because most writers know bad economic times very well."

Having endured furnished rooms and hard-hearted landladies, Wilder was happy to have a roof over his head. "*People on Sunday* opened just before the crash. One year later, we were all living in a different world. The people on a Sunday in 1929 had only one day for their private pleasures. They worked hard six days a week, but they were working. In 1930, it was different."

Far beyond the grandest expectations of its creators, *People on Sunday* turned out to be the last important silent German film. The arrival of sound ended many successful film careers, but not Billy Wilder's.

"All I *had* was future, and sound was good for me. I liked dialogue. I always had a lot of dialogue in my head for the characters, and with sound, I could get it out."

———◇———

Of his German films, Wilder said, "That was another life." *Emil und die Detektive* (*Emil and the Detectives,* 1931) and *Scampolo, ein Kind der Strasse* (*Scampolo, a Child of the Street,* 1932) are his most memorable German sound films.

In 1928, Erich Kästner's novel *Emil and the Detectives* achieved a popular success, and later became a classic among German children. UFA bought the film rights and chose Emeric Pressburger to write the script in collaboration with Kästner, who had already written screenplays. Pressburger would later become Michael Powell's collaborator in London with their production company, the Archers.

The script Kästner and Pressburger turned in was given to Wilder to "fix." The producers said all three writers would be credited, but only Wilder's name was on the credits when the film was released in 1931.

Young Emil takes the train from the town where he lives, to visit his grandmother in Berlin. During the trip, he falls asleep and is robbed of the 120 marks given him by his hardworking mother for his needy grandmother. He suspects the thief to be a man with a derby.

In Berlin, the distraught Emil meets another boy, who introduces him to one of the street gangs of Berlin, "the Detectives," who help him find the man with the derby. Emil gets his money back, and a reward of 1,000 marks.

Wilder added to the story by having the thief offer Emil a drugged chocolate, which causes Emil to have Caligari-style nightmares.

"I was thrilled with *Emil and the Detectives*," Kevin Brownlow told me. "It's absolutely as perfect as it could be, because it's shot at exactly the right time, with exactly the right character in the lead. Gerhardt Lamprecht, who directed it, became Germany's chief film historian, and it has a marvelous light touch. It's brilliant, and of course, you have the most wonderful locations. It's practically all shot on location. And the kids are incredible."

The film was a big hit in Germany and reached American art cinemas. It has been remade several times since. In the 1934 British version, Wilder got a writing credit.

Scampolo, ein Kind der Strasse was a remake of *Scampolo*, a 1928 German–Italian film. The 1932 film was adapted by Wilder and Max Kolpe from a play by Dario Niccodemi. The original story was from Claude Anet's novel *Ariane*, which later inspired Wilder's 1957 film *Love in the Afternoon*.

> Scampolo is an orphaned teenager who lives on the streets of Berlin. She meets Maximilian, an out-of-work financier, once prosperous, but now homeless like Scampolo. He is ready to commit suicide, but Scampolo cheers him with her indomitable spirit and gives him hope. Even in poverty, they are able to find happiness, but one day Maximilian mysteriously disappears. Feeling abandoned, Scampolo returns to her dreary existence. Maximilian reappears several months later, again prosperous. Scampolo is reunited with him, and they leave Berlin for a new life in London.

Dolly Haas, the pixieish star of *Scampolo*, had seen Billie Wilder around Berlin before his film success. She remembered him as "being everywhere at once." Sixty years later in New York City, where she had lived since before World War II, the wife of artist Al Hirschfeld, she spoke to me about Billy Wilder:

"He belongs to my happiest memories. *Scampolo* means a little left-over. In *Scampolo,* I played a street gamine without parents. I lived in a telephone booth and by my wits. Since I played *Scampolo* on the stage, I made the movie.

"*Scampolo* was written years earlier, so Billy took the character of this girl and put her into the current world. His love for this girl is clear in how he invented wonderful situations for her, so it is something that still can be shown. It was at the Museum of Modern Art a few years ago. The amazing thing is, it still has life. Billy has his own marvelous sense of humor, all based on human frailties.

"This girl showed a wonderful naïveté in her relationship with a successful businessman who finally fell in love with her. He treated her like a little leftover, a scrap, until he realized that there was so much original in this child.

"We shot it in Vienna, and in two versions. It had an absolutely delightful French actress in the French version. I was the German version.

"Every girl liked Billy. He wasn't the most handsome, he certainly wasn't rich, he didn't seem to be looking for marriage, but he had a sense of fun. I didn't know him that way, but I wouldn't have minded. I think his secret was he paid a lot of attention to the girl he was with at the time. Nothing phony. It wasn't that he looked into her eyes, or had a line. It was that he listened. He really listened. Maybe it was his training as a journalist. It's not easy to find a man who really listens to you. And it didn't hurt that Billy was such a wonderful dancer.

"I went to Hollywood when I first came here in 1936, but I was never in touch with him. I hadn't seen him in years and years.

"I was already married to Al, and we were to meet at somebody's house in the Hollywood Hills. I was driving, and the lights of my car illuminated two people sitting in the front seat of another car. I wanted to ask where this address was, so I got out and went up to the car. As the man turned around very slowly, I realized I had interrupted something. He was in a deep embrace, and he had been kissing a girl. He focused on me and said, 'Hello, Dolly.' It was Billy."

During his UFA period Wilder wrote many light comedies, often with music. Two of these, *Ihre Hoheit befiehlt* (*Her Highness Commands,* 1931) and *Ein blonder Traum* (*The Blonde Dream,* 1932), were remade as Hollywood films for which Wilder and his collaborators received writing credits.

Kevin Brownlow was enthusiastic about *Ein blonder Traum*. It concerns the love of two window washers (Willy Fritsch and Willi Forst) for a beautiful out-of-work circus performer (Lilian Harvey) who wants to be a movie star. The window washers, who have solved the Berlin housing problem by taking up residence in an abandoned railway car, take in the homeless girl, fall in love with her, and then help her to find out what stardom is really like.

"It's got a takeoff on Hollywood in it," Brownlow said. "A comic locomotive flies over the Atlantic, and takes Willy Fritsch to Hollywood. And then you see all of the ideas Europeans had about Hollywood."

British-born Lilian Harvey would soon be taking that train herself to the real Hollywood, where her career would be short.

"We got all our ideas about Hollywood from the Hollywood movies," Wilder said. "We believed what we saw. Hollywood represented America for us, unimaginable. I remember a scene in a Hollywood film I saw in Berlin:

"A tramp comes up to a man who just got out of a limousine, and he asks him for the time. The rich man reaches into his pocket and takes out this great gold pocket watch, and he gives it to him. For me, that was America."

—Adieu, Berlin—

Wilder was thinking of Berlin as his home. "It takes a while to find your place, your routine, a group of friends, a place to live with a few possessions that make it feel like home. I had succeeded in doing that when there were ominous signs.

"I was not really worried about Hitler and the Nazis until the end of 1932. We believed that the spook would soon vanish. Then, I read *Mein Kampf.* I listened to Hitler's speeches. The elevator boy at UFA was suddenly wearing a storm trooper's uniform.

"At that time, I had a girlfriend, Hella Hartwig, the daughter of a pharmacist. She was from Frankfurt on the Oder and lived with a nice family on the Kurfürstendamm in two luxuriously furnished rooms. She was a very good dancer, and brunette. I always liked brunettes.

"In January 1933, I invited Hella to come with me to Davos on a skiing holiday. It was the first time I had skied. Hella cut a better figure on the slopes than I did, and in our hotel room, too.

"On January 30, we were in a ski lodge when we heard on the radio that Hitler had become chancellor. Our holiday came to an end. We left on the next train to Berlin.

"On the evening of the Reichstag fire, Hella and I were sitting in the Café Wien on the Kurfürstendamm, about where the Hotel Kempinski is today. We were in love, eating and drinking on the terrace. It was our farewell to the Berlin that I would not see again until it was in ruins.

"I was ready to leave Berlin the day after the Reichstag fire, when they dissolved parliament. I knew it was going to get ugly. Any place Hitler became chancellor, I had to leave quickly. I told Hella, and she talked with her parents.

"I sold all my furniture. I had a few nice things I had been collecting, good things other people didn't understand—Bauhaus, Mies van der Rohe, Gropius. I sold my American Graham-Paige cabriolet, a make of car that no longer exists.

"I did a garage sale without a garage. I got about $2,000 worth of marks. I changed the marks into hundred-dollar bills, stuffed my suitcase with what I needed, and Hella and I took the train to Paris.

"Before I left, I could have shot Hitler. I was close enough once.

"Just before the burning of the Reichstag building, I was in a box at the UFA Palace near the zoo for a premiere. Hitler was in the next box. I don't remember what the movie was. It could have been one of mine, and I wouldn't remember.

"During my last days in Berlin, I had given up my flat. I lived in the Hotel Majestic on Brandenburger Street in a little room, always on edge.

"One morning, around 4:00 A.M., two plainclothesmen came to my room. The evening before, I had fallen asleep reading an anti-Hitler brochure. Fortunately, it had fallen between the bed and the wall, so the officials did not find it.

"I had wonderful times in Berlin. You might say it was a love affair I had, not with one girl or many girls, but with that city. It was the home of my youth. My heart beat faster the first time I saw the Kurfürstendamm. Every journalist, writer, and artist dreamed of going to Berlin, me included, and it was better than the dream. I was robbed of the memory. You cannot think about the good and not remember the bad."

—Émigré Auteur—

When Wilder's last German picture, *Was Frauen träumen (What Women Dream)*, premiered in Berlin on Hitler's forty-fourth birthday, April 20, 1933, the name Billie Wilder was missing from the credits, and the man also was missing from Berlin. He was in Paris, with Hella.

Wilder arrived at Paris's Gare St. Lazare on the morning of March 1, with one suitcase, and more than a thousand U.S. dollars in his hatband. Hella had one suitcase and a purse with some gold coins given to her by her father. Neither had a proper visa, but they weren't too concerned about being sent back to Germany, because Hella wasn't Jewish, and Wilder wasn't German.

They found a place to live at a hotel near the Arch of Triumph. "Paris was beautiful, but we were sad," Wilder remembered.

The Hotel Ansonia, at 8 rue de Saigon, became a haven for German film industry exiles. Peter Lorre, one of the stars of *Was Frauen träumen,* was already there, as were composers Franz Wachsmann and Friedrich Holländer. Wachsmann had left Berlin after being beaten on the street by Nazi bullies. He had arrived with his wife, Alice. Wachsmann and Holländer would emigrate to America, where they would change their names to Franz Waxman and Frederick Hollander, and become leading Hollywood composers. Most of the émigrés were Jewish, but not all. It was the Hotel Ansonia that furnished the setting for

Erich Maria Remarque's novel *Arch of Triumph,* which later became a Hollywood film.

A few exiles fared better. Director Joe May and his wife, a well-known German actress, were living in a villa outside Paris. Ex-UFA boss Erich Pommer became a producer at Fox's Paris studios. Fritz Lang, already famous, found work directing Molnár's *Liliom* with Charles Boyer.

Wilder could not claim Lang's celebrity, and he was uncertain about writing and speaking French. Danielle Darrieux, who was directed by him not long after his arrival, told me that he spoke good French.

"Billy Wilder did our film in French," she told me. "Yes, yes. He was very good. He spoke French, because I did not speak one word of *Allemand.* So, he spoke very well French. Very well. So well, it was so good, I never thought about it."

Wilder had achieved a measure of comfort, success, and celebrity in Berlin, but in Paris, he was just another foreigner looking for work without a work permit, in a city that wanted tourists, not refugees.

"I did not feel the gut-wrenching fear that possessed some of the residents of the Ansonia," he recalled. "Some people talked about suicide." The gold coins Hella's father had given her were sold one at a time, relieving some anxiety and leaving Wilder free to write.

"At the Ansonia, we talked together, which we could do without work permits. Our big hope was to think up something that would make a film and find a producer. But it was easier to think up plots than to find producers.

"I had one idea which I liked, but I had left my notes behind in Berlin. It was about a young man whose wealthy father takes away his car because he's a playboy, so he sort of innocently gets involved with a gang of car thieves. I knew how I felt when I had to sell my car. I loved cars. I wrote up the idea, and a couple of guys at the Ansonia I knew from Germany who had written for UFA, [Jan] Lustig and [Max] Kolpe, liked it, so we worked on it.

"We found a producer who was the solution to our problem, except he had a wife he wanted to make into a star. She was terrible.

"We needed someone with directing credits. We found a guy who had directed before."

Alexander Esway, a Hungarian, had been writing and directing films since the mid-1920s. Esway found a new producer, Edouard Corniglion-Molinier, a French flying hero who had built a personal fortune after World War I and had invested in film studio facilities near Nice. He liked the idea, but he wasn't prepared to gamble much money.

"We did *Mauvaise Graine* [*Bad Seed*] on a shoestring," Wilder said. "We didn't use a soundstage. Most of the interiors were shot in a converted auto shop, even the living room set, and we did the automobile chases without transparencies, live, on the streets. It was exhausting. The camera was mounted on the back of a truck or in a car. We were constantly improvising."

For exteriors, they had all of Paris, a nearby beach, the roads of France, and the docks of Marseilles. For interiors, they had the shop, in which simple sets could be built, such as the apartment where Jean and Jeanette live. "We were doing *nouvelle vague* a quarter of a century before they invented a fancy name for it."

To play the ingenue, they hired sixteen-year-old Danielle Darrieux, already an experienced film actress, having been in films since she was fourteen. Darrieux wore her own dresses as well as some that belonged to her mother, who had been a classical singer and hoped that her daughter would become a cellist.

In Paris, Danielle Darrieux, who was preparing for a new play when we spoke, told me with pride, "Of course, I remember Billy Wilder, I was in the first film he directed, *Mauvaise Graine,* in 1933." She laughed. "I didn't know what I was doing at this time. But I remember well that *he* knew what he was doing. It's an extraordinary life.

"It's funny. Our paths never crossed. I would like to have seen him again. I always remember him. He is the only person I remember from *Mauvaise Graine.*

"I don't remember really how I was given the part. You know, I never had to go around and read for parts, because my first film was a sort of miracle. I was playing the cello. I didn't think at all to be an actress. Someone saw me and asked my mother if I could be in a film. We were short of money. So, it was just like that.

"My mother was very afraid when the producer said, 'This girl is exactly what we want,' for the first film I made, *Le Bal.* I was just four-teen. Well, it was difficult for my mother, because we were three, and my father was dead since I was seven years old. She was alone, so she gave singing lessons, and she was a little bit afraid to let me go into the movie business. But after, she was very happy, so happy, and me, too."

Le Bal, directed by Wilhelm Thiele, was a French remake of his German film, *Der Ball,* and was more successful than the original. After one film, Darrieux found herself a star of French cinema.

"I thought it was normal to be young and to work. I worked from when I was fourteen. You know, I was not especially struck over movies. It was just like that. I was laughing all the time. I did not know what was ahead.

"Oh, my God! It's very difficult because it's so *long* ago. I wish I could remember more of being Jeanette. I do remember we did some—how do you say that when you work outside? Locations. In Marseilles, in the mountain near Marseilles. I was very afraid because I was very young, but Billy Wilder made me feel good. I remember it like that.

"It wasn't anything special he said to me. He was totally in com-mand. I felt I could trust him. Perhaps our being so close in age made me feel closer to him."

Darrieux remembered that it was Wilder, not Esway, who directed the picture. She said that Esway was one of the writers, but never the director. "I remember well Alexander Esway. He was a scenarist. I heard he helped for raising the money. He had his name with Billy Wilder as director, but I never saw him around the set when we were shooting. Billy Wilder was the person you noticed because of his personality. He was the only director working with us actors, with the script, with the sets, with the technical, everything. He was young, but he knew just what he wanted, and he was totally in control, like the other best direc-tors I worked with."

She recalled working again with Esway. "He was a scenarist on a film I made with Robert Siodmak. It was a musical comedy. I think it was *La Crise est finie. The Crisis Is Over,* and everybody is singing!

"I do not know what happened to the other actors. My partner was a very young man, called Pierre [Mingand], I don't remember the rest of his name. I had a very young man as my brother, and I don't remember his name [Raymond Galle], either. No one went on to have any great career afterwards that I know."

Darrieux's character, Jeanette, is introduced by her compact mirror, which fills the screen as her brother is describing her; then it's lowered to reveal her face as she finishes applying her lipstick. The mirror and lipstick are also used to allow her to write down the license plate numbers of a car the gang can steal.

Wealthy Dr. Pasquier (Paul Escoffier) informs his son, Henri (Pierre Mingand), that his playboy days are over and he will have to go to work. The crushing news for Henri is that his 1933 Buick roadster has been sold because of his irresponsible behavior.

As Henri disconsolately walks the streets of Paris, he sees the new owners of his car drive up and leave it parked with the keys in the ignition. Henri can't resist reclaiming it to keep a date with a girl he has just met.

Three men in another car follow him. When they catch up, Henri assumes he will be taken to a police station. Instead, he is taken to a garage which is a front for a stolen car gang. Thinking he is a car thief, too, he is warned not to compete with their operation.

In the garage, he meets a likable young man called "Jean-la-Cravate" (Raymond Galle) because of his fondness for neckties, especially those of other people. Jean invites Henri to stay at his flat that night, where he lives with his sister, Jeanette (Danielle Darrieux), and his extensive necktie collection, each with its own name. Jeanette's role in the gang is to lure men away from their expensive cars so the gang can steal them.

Jean persuades Henri to join the gang. When he picks up Henri's belongings for him, Dr. Pasquier finds Jean sympathetic, though he's still worried about his son.

Henri participates in some ingenious auto thefts, often with Jeanette. After a job involving three expensive Hispano-Suizas, Henri demands higher wages for everyone. The chief (Michel Duran) grudgingly gives in.

Jeanette tells Henri that when she lost her job as a secretary-typist, she couldn't find work and joined the gang. She feels responsible for Jean, who, though grown, is "just like a child."

Vowing to get rid of the troublemakers, the chief sends Henri and Jeanette to Marseilles in a racing car with a bad front axle, expecting it to crack. During a high-speed police chase, the car does crash, but without injuring the pair. The gravel crunching under their feet as they walk along the highway emphasizes their discouraged mood.

Henri and Jeanette decide to board a ship in Marseilles and start a new life together. He returns to Paris for Jean.

Henri arrives at the garage just as it's being raided. One of the less intelligent gang members has stolen a Paris bus and led the police to their hideout. Jean is badly wounded, and Henri takes him to his father.

Dr. Pasquier informs his son that it's too late for Jean, who dies, but not for Henri.

Henri returns to Marseilles with money from his father to begin a new life. Jeanette's grief is shown as she puts her head on Henri's shoulder, seen in a long shot with no dialogue.

"I don't like excessive sentiment," Wilder said. "I have never liked it. I especially don't like to show it on-screen in close-up.

"I remember the picture was shot during late summer and fall, and there were some chilly days early that year. But the actors had to continue dressing as if it were summer, so the shots would match." Henri exhales visible vapor as he does his imitation of Maurice Chevalier to impress a new girlfriend.

"I got that idea from a Marx Brothers picture. The Marx Brothers are trying to get into the United States without passports by pretending they are Maurice Chevalier."

———◦———

Mauvaise Graine is, at this early date, recognizably a Billy Wilder picture, even though he was directing his first film in a country he scarcely knew, and in a foreign language. Not a shot is wasted. Each scene is there for a purpose, to develop a character or advance the plot while entertaining the audience. A great deal of the film is silent, with only a musical background. All of those silent film scripts he wrote with no credit proved perfect training for developing his visual imagination.

Apart from the moving vehicle shots, camera movement is usually restricted to pans and tilts, with the camera mounted on an immobile tripod. Emphasis is achieved sometimes through a change of focus. Action is often telescoped, leaving something to the audience's imagination. Simple visuals such as the spinning wheel of a car or the superimposed hands of a clock serve as transitions. Travel is shown on a map.

Two of Wilder's friends from UFA, Allan Gray and Franz Wachsmann, co-wrote the jazz-influenced score. Wachsmann had already changed his name to Waxmann, dropping the last "n" when he got to Hollywood. Allan Gray, who had changed his name from Josef Zmigrod, would go to England to write music for the Emeric Pressburger and Michael Powell films.

The story is difficult to classify, a characteristic of many later Wilder films. It seems to be a comedy, but there is melodrama, and then tragedy.

Glimpses of the future Billy Wilder can be observed in this film. The opening statistic about automobile ownership in Paris has its counterpart in William Holden's ironic voice-over statistics about Los Angeles. Joe Gillis in *Sunset Boulevard* is about to lose his car just as Henri Pasquier lost his fifteen years earlier.

"I was very happy when I saw Billy Wilder became one of the big directors in Hollywood," Danielle Darrieux told me, "but I was not surprised. I have watched his career. It's marvelous. I was not too surprised, because I think he's a man who has very great talent. I could understand that, even at my young age.

"I loved very much to work with Max Ophüls, too, and Billy Wilder had the same attitude, sensibility, much in common. They have the same background and life. Details are very important to both of them. But I think Billy Wilder is crueler in his view of life than Ophüls, no? Harder. Not his personality, but the way he sees things. I remember a film with Gloria Swanson [*Sunset Boulevard*] that was extraordinary. Oh, my God! It was marvelous! Beautiful, but rather cruel, and I mean that in a positive way. I think it's my favorite of the Wilder films. I have not seen *Mauvaise Graine* since 1934.

"Give my best souvenir to Billy Wilder," she said just before his ninety-fifth birthday. "Tell him I remember him well." At eighty-four, she was about to go on tour with her play.

Wilder said, "Mlle. Darrieux was charming and perfect in her part, but of course I didn't know at the time that I was directing the future Madame de." He was referring to Max Ophüls's *The Earrings of Madame de . . .* "I would like to have made that film. One of the greats, Ophüls. But how could he go back to live in Germany after the war? He did that, you know."

———◁○▷———

When I asked Wilder if he would like to see my tape of *Mauvaise Graine,* he declined. "It was shot a long time ago, about sixty years ago. I can't watch even my best movies without wanting to change them.

"I directed out of pure necessity and without any experience. I cannot say that I had any fun making *Mauvaise Graine.* We were always having to change the script to fit what we had, or didn't have. There was pressure. People depend on you, and you aren't really in control, but you can't show that, or everyone gets nervous. I like to have a script and more or less stick to it. Being inventive is fine, but you want to do as much of that as you can *before* everybody is standing around waiting.

"I, alone, was responsible for everything—*everything!* I had to be everybody from the producer to script girl. I was an extra, not because I was trying to pull a Hitchcock, but because we couldn't afford another body.

"I had heard stories about how everything was taken care of for directors in Hollywood. They said you could sit down without looking to see if there was a chair waiting for you. This was the opposite. I've never been a stool director. I don't direct sitting down, but in Paris if I'd sat down without looking, I would have broken something, and if anyone did put a stool there, somebody would have grabbed it to use in the picture."

———◦———

"When *Mauvaise Graine* premiered in the summer of 1934," Wilder said, "I wasn't there anymore. I'd begun my life in Hollywood. Our little picture was well liked and got good reviews. It looked easy and natural, and the struggles and worries didn't show in the movie theater. The worries can show on your brow, but not on the screen. After how hard it was to make, I was surprised how lively and spontaneous people found it. I still didn't think of myself as a director, not exactly. I wasn't certain I *liked* being a director; but I did know I could do it. That was satisfying.

"It is not an easy thing for a writer to become a director, and it doesn't happen very often—Preston Sturges, George Seaton, John Huston. Writing is a very lonely profession, while directing is very social. My being a writer who liked to collaborate helped me to make the jump.

"I remember *People on Sunday* like I remember the first girl I kissed. Better. *Mauvaise Graine* was more like the first girl I ever went to bed with."

PART II

Hollywood

—"Write Some—
Good Ones"

All of Billy Wilder's memories before the age of twenty-six were in German. After that, except for the year in Paris, he lived his life in English.

As Henri and Jeanette sailed away at the end of *Mauvaise Graine,* Billy Wilder was also looking for a new life. He found it with the help of Joe May, the flamboyant director he had known at UFA, who had left Paris and become a producer at Columbia in Hollywood.

May liked Wilder's treatment of a story, *Pam-Pam,* and he was able to sell the idea to the studio. Wilder was offered $150 a week in Hollywood to write the screenplay, and was sent a one-way ticket to Los Angeles.

"As soon as I read the telegram from May, I ran to the U.S. embassy to get a visa." The telegram requested that Wilder bring with him from Paris, among other things, three bidets.

"Hella was homesick and, not being Jewish, she eventually went back. They put her in a concentration camp, but she survived the war.

"After I married Audrey, she came here for a visit. Then I saw her in Paris. I don't know what happened after that."

They said good-bye on January 22, 1934, when Wilder boarded the HMS *Aquitania* for New York, with some American novels and a few

U.S. dollars in his pockets. His brother, Willie, whom he hadn't seen in twelve years, would be meeting him.

Five days later, his ship arrived at night in New York harbor, delayed several hours by a snowstorm. The outline of skyscrapers through the falling snow seemed magical to him.

"My first impression of America," Wilder told me, "was the daily newspaper being delivered by Cadillac.

"It was a very snowy morning at my brother's house on Long Island. I looked out the window. There was this very long American car. It stopped, and a boy leaned out and tossed the newspaper. So, America was a place where the newspaper boys delivered their papers from Cadillacs! Right away, I knew America was a place I was going to like."

———◦———

Billie Wilder's first impression of Southern California was "the smell of orange blossoms and future in the air." He stepped off the train with $11 in his pockets. "Before I left New York, my brother asked me if I needed some money. I said I had enough."

Wilder's $150-a-week salary at Columbia was for six months, the length of his visa. He stayed with Joe and Mia May in their hacienda-style home in the Hollywood Hills. May charged him $75 a month. This included the kind of German cooking to which he was accustomed and the use of their swimming pool. One of Wilder's first purchases was a 1928 DeSoto coupé.

May had neglected to mention to the studio heads that their new writer didn't know much English. "An actor could speak with a foreign accent, but a writer could not write with a foreign accent," Wilder said.

"Suddenly, I had no instrument that I was playing. I wrote in German, and it was translated, and my forte had always been dialogue.

"It's very difficult to be a writer, to feel it is the only thing in life you want to be, and suddenly you are deprived of the language in which you think, speak, and write. You're more or less dead, so I had to learn a new language or get buried.

"A person is shaped by his language. I wanted to reshape myself and be an American. I wanted to make up for the baseball I never played. I've watched so much baseball, sometimes I remember playing it as a child.

"I knew if I hung around with all of the refugees, I would never learn English, so I searched for the company of young ladies who spoke only English. I read books in English. I went to night school. I listened to soap operas and children's programs on the radio. I read the comics. Meanwhile, I sold a couple of stories I wrote in German which were translated."

Wilder started work on *Pam-Pam,* which like *Mauvaise Graine* was the story of an honest person caught up in a world of crime. With help from a writer fluent in both German and English, he was able to produce a treatment, although it was rejected by Columbia.

The six-month visa seemed like six weeks. To renew it, Wilder had to drive to the border town of Mexicali and apply at the U.S. consulate. While there, he stayed in a small hotel where he met other Europeans who were trying to get into the United States.

"I went to the office of the U.S. consul. I was sweating, and it wasn't the heat. Everything I had, I'd left behind in Germany and Austria. I had my passport, my birth certificate, and a few letters from friends vouching for my not being a criminal.

"The consul looked at what I had. 'Is this all?'

"I explained that I'd left Berlin in a hurry. I had written to Nazi Germany to ask for my papers, but nobody answered. I told him I *could* go back to get my papers, but then I wouldn't need them. This was before Auschwitz, but he understood what I meant.

"He said, 'What do you do?'

"I said, 'I'm a writer.'

"'What do you write?'

"'I write movies.'

"He stamped my passport and said, 'Write some good ones.'

"Later, I found out he wasn't the regular consul, but a vice consul filling in while the consul was on vacation.

"I've lived my life trying my best not to disappoint that dear man."

Wilder drove back to Los Angeles and found a small room at the Chateau Marmont for $35 a month, which he shared with actor Peter

Lorre. "We were both out of work," Wilder told me. "Campbell's soup buddies. And we didn't have enough of it, sometimes only one can between us.

"Lorre was Goebbels's favorite actor in Berlin. Goebbels told him that. They were in an elevator together, and Goebbels said in a very friendly way that maybe it would be good for his career if he toured abroad for a while. Lorre's real name was Löwenstein and he was Jewish. He was an intelligent guy, and he got the message. He was lucky Goebbels liked him. Not many people got that kind of personal warning from Herr Goebbels."

Joe May, directing for Erich Pommer at Fox, arranged for Wilder to collaborate on the screenplay adaptation of *Music in the Air,* an operetta by Jerome Kern and Oscar Hammerstein II, starring Gloria Swanson in her first sound picture. "Billie Wilder" appeared for the last time on the screen in this picture. From then on, he was "Billy Wilder."

In 1934, Wilder collaborated on the screenplay of *The Lottery Lover* for Fox. Afterward, he worked without credit on Raoul Walsh's *Under Pressure.*

The next year, Wilder met Judith, a sophisticated brunette, who was from a prominent California family. Her father was George Coppicus, head of Columbia Artists. After her mother, Maybelle, had divorced Coppicus, she had married Paul Iribe, a former Hollywood art director, and went with him and her children to Paris. When she discovered that he was having an affair with Coco Chanel, she divorced Iribe and returned with her children to California. Judith's uncle was the lieutenant governor of California.

American, intelligent, educated, with a cosmopolitan background, Judith appealed strongly to Wilder. "She was tall, brunette, and attractive. I thought I was ready to fall in love and marry."

With $5,000 Wilder earned from the sale of two screenplays, he made a trip back to Europe. After seeing Hella in Paris, he returned to Vienna for the first time since 1926.

"I saw my mom in Vienna in 1935," Wilder recalled. "I tried to persuade her to come to America, but she had remarried and was set in her ways."

On December 22, 1936, Wilder married Judith Iribe in Yuma, Arizona. The couple moved into a modest apartment on South Camden Drive in Beverly Hills.

Wilder received a $1,000 advance for collaborating on *Champagne Waltz*. When the project was postponed, he was offered $250 a week as a Paramount contract writer.

In July of 1936, Wilder was assigned to work on the next Ernst Lubitsch film at Paramount. "It was incredible being at Paramount at that time. I would see von Sternberg and Dietrich and Gary Cooper, and most exciting for me, Lubitsch. It was creative air you breathed. It gave you a feeling of being very, very alive. I had dozens of ideas jumping around in my mind. They came so fast, so many of them, I could hardly get them down on paper."

The writer assigned to work with Wilder on the Lubitsch picture was Charles Brackett.

—The—
Brackett Touch

"If two guys get together who think the same way," Wilder said, "the same politics, come from the same place and have the same background, well, it's a terrible thing. It's like pulling on one end of a rope. If you are going to collaborate with yourself, you don't have a collaborator. You might as well write alone. You need an opponent to bounce things off of. You need to have that rope stretched as tautly as you can get it. Out of the friction comes the spark and the sparkle, and it's especially good for the dialogue."

Charles Brackett, a Harvard Law School graduate, was the son of a New York state senator. Before coming to Hollywood, he was a published novelist and a *New Yorker* drama critic. In Hollywood, he was a successful screenplay writer, though not as well known as he would later become with Wilder, and he was elected the first president of the newly formed Screen Writers Guild. Fourteen years older than Wilder, he had a different temperament, and proved to be just the kind of "opponent" Wilder needed.

"Brackett was a sort of country gentleman, with political beliefs to the right of Herbert Hoover. I was for Roosevelt and the New Deal. Brackett and I didn't think the same way at all, but it's this difference of opinions that makes for good collaboration.

"Brackett, he would be on the couch with his shoes off and a yellow tablet, and I would be pacing up and down. We would discuss a scene, each of us making notes and suggestions. Sometimes we would argue violently, but that was good. That was how we got along. Brackett forced me to *think* in English, especially when I argued with him, which was a lot.

"Brackett didn't love doing movies like I did. I think he would rather have been Faulkner or Steinbeck or Hemingway.

"Brackett really knew English. He wasn't just an American, but he was educated and articulate. He was patient, and he never laughed when I made mistakes in English, which was most of the time. He understood what I meant, and he showed me the right way."

The Lubitsch picture they were assigned was *Bluebeard's Eighth Wife,* based on a play by Alfred Savoir. Gloria Swanson had appeared in a silent film version. "When they told me Lubitsch was going to do it and asked me if I was familiar with the play, I suddenly became a world authority on French farces. I was excited at the idea of working with Lubitsch. One thing Brackett and I completely agreed on was Ernst Lubitsch.

"We had this secretary to type our script conferences. Lubitsch, Brackett, Walter Reisch, a friend of mine from Germany, and I would dictate the scene, and Lubitsch would be sitting in the back, studying the face of the secretary. We would dictate, like twenty jokes in a row, and she would be typing.

"No sign of laughter. Not even a smile. She was our whole audience, and we're getting back nothing.

"The third day we were dictating the script, again which we thought enormously funny, and Lubitsch said to us, 'Look, this is not gonna work. That secretary, she has not smiled.'

"So I went to the secretary, and I said, 'Don't you think that stuff is funny that you've been typing?'

"'Oh, yes.'

"'Then why don't you laugh?'

"'It's my braces.'

"She could not laugh without showing the braces on her teeth.

Her braces could have stopped Lubitsch from making the picture, and my whole life might have been different.

"People ask me, what was the 'Lubitsch Touch'? If I could explain the Lubitsch Touch, if I knew the formula, I would patent it, but nobody ever knew how to arrive at it, except Lubitsch. You can't steal Lubitsch. It was him. Let me give you an example:

"I am in a classroom with a lot of very bright young people, full of ideas and imagination. I say, 'I'm going to give you a problem and you'll come back with a solution.

"'There is a king and a queen, and a lieutenant. The king is played by George Barbier, a very corpulent actor in his sixties, the queen is Miriam Hopkins, who is very pretty, and the lieutenant, Maurice Chevalier, who was at that time very young and handsome. I would like you to dramatize this situation:

"'The queen has an affair with the lieutenant, and the king finds out. Do it any way you want to.'

"The students come back with good solutions, amusing, a little long, but nobody in the world could come up with a better solution than Mr. Lubitsch did for the opening of *The Smiling Lieutenant*.

"We open in the bedroom of the king and the queen. He's getting dressed. There is a little nose rubbing, and tickling, and it's all very sweet. Now, he leaves the bedroom, and we see at the door with a sword and clicking his heels is Maurice Chevalier. He is now watching the king, and the king is going down a long staircase, boom, boom, boom.

"Now, cut back to Mr. Chevalier. He enters the bedroom of the queen and closes the door behind him. We don't cut into the bedroom. That is very important.

"Now, back to the king. He suddenly realizes that he forgot his belt and sword. He turns and goes back up the steps to the bedroom.

"The king opens the door to the bedroom, goes in, and the door closes behind him. We are still outside in the hallway, never inside.

The king comes out, and he has his belt and sword. And he's smiling. He's going down the steps again, boom, boom, boom, and the belt is not his. It's much too small.

"Back he goes, and of course he finds Chevalier under the bed, right? But it's all done with a kind of throwing it away. That is the Lubitsch Touch.

"He had a skit for another picture which they wouldn't allow him to do on account of censorship. It was with Charles Laughton.

"You are in the exterior of a harem, and you see that the sultan is leaving, his luggage piled up ready to go. Standing at the gate is Charles Laughton, who is a eunuch. The sultan says, 'Abraham.'

"'Yes sir,' Laughton answers in a very high-pitched voice.

"'I'm leaving now. Be very, very careful and watch out for the beautiful girls in there. No girl is allowed out and no man is allowed in. You understand, Abraham?'

"'Yes sir,' again in that very high-pitched voice.

"The sultan leaves. A window opens, and a very beautiful girl leans out, smiles, and calls, 'Abraham?'

"In a very deep male voice, he says, 'Coming.'

"Everybody wants to *do* Lubitsch, and sometimes it is *like* Lubitsch, but it is not the real thing. There have been some wonderful comedy directors who had their own style, but all of them owe a debt to Lubitsch, as do I.

"He wasn't just a gagman, he was the best creator of toppers. You would come up with a funny bit to end a scene and he would create a better one. He would look at our stuff and go, 'Ho-ho, very good,' and scratch out the next line. He'd read a bit more, go 'Ho-ho,' and scratch out another line.

"The Lubitsch Touch is the superjoke. You have a joke, and then you don't expect the joke on top of the joke that tops the first one. The joke you didn't expect is funnier than the one you expected.

"The Lubitsch Touch is a *light* touch. But there are serious over-tones in Lubitsch. He understood life.

"'How would Lubitsch do it?' That has been my motto. I had Saul Bass make a sign of it for me, and it's in my office."

I suggested to Wilder that, one day, young directors would have signs posted in *their* offices saying, "How would Billy Wilder do it?"

"If I'm still alive when that happens, I hope they don't have my phone number."

— "Next Year's — Crowd"

"In *Bluebeard*," Wilder said, "I had the chance to do an idea I'd been thinking about for a long time. You know the old cliché, the boy and the girl in the bedroom, both wearing the same pair of pajamas, him with the bottom and her with the top. Well, it happens that *I* prefer to sleep in the top, and I thought of a funny scene in a picture, in which the man is wearing the top and the girl the bottom. Of course, you couldn't show it then. Now, you could show them without any pajamas at all.

"Lubitsch had this problem of needing a funny way for Gary Cooper and Claudette Colbert to meet at the opening of the picture. This was the 'meet-cute,' and I used to write down every 'meet-cute' I thought of in a notebook. I suggested that Cooper is in a department store trying to buy half a pair of pajamas, the top half, because that's all he ever uses. The clerk can't do that, and they have an argument.

"Enter Colbert, who has come to buy only half a pair of pajamas herself, the bottom half. So, the problem is solved. They both get that part of the pajamas they want, and they meet in a funny way. I, myself, never tried to buy half a pair of pajamas."

Lubitsch elaborates on the idea by having them insist on going all the way to the top of the department store for permission to buy only half of a pair of pajamas. The president of the company has to get out of bed to answer the phone, and the audience sees that *he* is only wearing the top of his pajamas.

American millionaire Michael Brandon (Gary Cooper) cannot forget the beautiful French woman who shared a pair of pajamas with him at the Nice department store. When he learns that it was her father for whom she bought the bottoms, Brandon gives the poor but extravagant aristocrat, the Marquis de Loiselle (Edward Everett Horton), enough money to maintain his high lifestyle because he intends to marry his daughter. The daughter, Nicole de Loiselle (Claudette Colbert), is not so easily bought.

Brandon wins Nicole; but before the wedding, she learns that he has been married seven times before. She marries him only after he agrees to make a generous settlement in the event of their divorce.

Brandon has to accept a marriage in name only, but he's confident he will conquer Nicole. When it seems he won't, he wrongly assumes that she must have a lover.

Though by nature tenacious, he finally agrees to give Nicole a divorce. She loves him but doesn't want to be "Bluebeard's Eighth Wife," a wife he would leave when he tired of her.

Traumatized by the idea that he could lose in any business transaction, even marriage, Brandon commits himself to a luxurious sanitarium. When Nicole isn't allowed to visit him, her father purchases the sanitarium with some of her settlement money.

Becoming violent, Brandon has to be restrained, but when Nicole starts teasing him, he breaks out of his straitjacket and kisses her passionately. She admits that she has loved him ever since their pajama counter encounter.

"I've been asked," Wilder told me, "if Colbert's character really was there to buy the pajama bottoms for her father, or if she had her eye on the handsome American millionaire and saw this as an opportunity to meet him. Of course she was out to meet him. That's part of the

Lubitsch Touch, to allow you to wonder and to figure it out. No hammer on the head. Cooper is pretty visible there in Nice, being six feet four, and having a tall wallet.

"I don't know everything that's in my characters' heads. They have secrets they keep, even from me. Cooper's character is a notches-on-his-belt guy who keeps a scorecard.

"I don't like to get too much into backstory. I believe only what you need should be forced out. It's a good sign if the audience wonders what happens to the characters afterwards."

Costume designer Edith Head spoke with me about Claudette Colbert. "She had a wonderful sense of French fashion, and she encouraged Banton to exaggerate haute couture." Head began her legendary Hollywood career as an assistant to, and then protégée of, Travis Banton. She remembered him talking about Colbert with great admiration, describing her as a perfect lady with a great fashion sense, high-style imagination, who gave a designer a chance to shine, someone who understood how to make her small stature dramatic. She recognized how much a dress could enhance her character, and also help her to get into character when she got into the dress. In *Bluebeard,* Colbert's puffed sleeves are memorable. The actress did her own makeup.

When Claudette Colbert was being honored by the Film Society of Lincoln Center in 1984, I mentioned to her that I had never heard a French accent in her English.

"I've been here a long time," she confided, "but I still dream in French."

Billy Wilder contrasted Claudette Colbert with Marilyn Monroe:

"I guess I would say Colbert as an actress was the opposite of Marilyn Monroe, professionally. Personally, too, the opposite.

"Colbert was never, never late. You could set your watch by her. With Miss Monroe, you didn't *need* to set it; you didn't even need to wind it.

"Colbert was always prepared. She knew her lines perfectly. She'd get completely into her part so you thought that she was just playing herself, and then, the scene ended, and she would be unzipped from her part.

"Miss Colbert did not surprise you. You got exactly what you were expecting.

"Miss Monroe was full of surprises, good ones, bad ones, mostly bad ones, but the good ones were very good."

◄○►

During one of my early conversations with Billy Wilder, he spoke with me about the changed world of Hollywood. He bemoaned the change in the people, saying that "each year the people get worse, and now, we have next year's people."

At that time, I hadn't seen *Bluebeard's Eighth Wife,* but I remembered what he said. Several years later, when I viewed the films, I heard Claudette Colbert on the screen talking about Nice with Gary Cooper, saying, "It's a lovely place, beautiful; but the class of people who come here gets worse every year. And this year, we seem to have next year's crowd."

After *Bluebeard's Eighth Wife,* Brackett and Wilder were loaned out to Universal to work on Joe Pasternak's next Deanna Durbin musical, *That Certain Age,* co-starring Melvyn Douglas. "I don't know if we helped the picture or not, but I think the experience of having already written lines for Melvyn Douglas helped later in *Ninotchka.* It's much easier to write lines when you have an actor in mind than to try and find an actor who fits your lines."

◄○►

In 1938, Wilder left the agency that had been representing him, and engaged Paul Kohner, his old friend from Berlin. As soon as he was able, Wilder became an early contributor to the European Film Fund, which Kohner had helped found in 1937. This organization supported out-of-work European film people until they could find jobs, after which they, in turn, contributed to the fund.

—Every—
Cinderella Has
Her Midnight

Midnight, shot in early 1939, was the first of three films Brackett and Wilder made with Mitchell Leisen, one of Paramount's most successful directors. Wilder did not get along with Leisen. He resented that Leisen did not watch over writers' lines, allowing actors to make changes as they pleased. The other writers submitted, but the obstreperous young Wilder would sneak onto the set and make his displeasure known with grimaces of pain and, on occasion, more vociferous protests.

"I never watch movies on television," Wilder told me. "On the TV screen, I would watch only the picture of a director I hated. And there is no director I hate *that* much. Not even Mitchell Leisen.

"Brackett and I sweated a long time on our scripts so they would work. Then Leisen would drop a line or a whole page, or he would let some actress say whatever she wanted. Here we were setting up for the big payoff in our story, and he was sabotaging us. Charlie hated it, too, but he couldn't complain like I did. I challenged Leisen, and he went straight to producer Arthur Hornblow and demanded I be banned from the set. That made me more determined."

Midnight is a variation of the Cinderella story. Posing as a baroness in Parisian society, a penniless ex–chorus girl (Claudette Colbert) finds herself trapped in a rich man's scheme (John Barrymore) to break up an affair between his wife (Mary Astor) and a playboy (Francis Lederer). She is saved from being exposed as an impostor by an aristocratic taxi driver (Don Ameche) who falls in love with her and finally wins her.

Despite the animosity between Wilder and Leisen, *Midnight* was critically and financially successful. In 1946, it was remade as a musical, *Masquerade in Mexico,* also directed by Leisen.

The next Wilder and Brackett film, *What a Life,* was based on a successful Broadway comedy. "The picture doesn't seem like much now," Wilder said, "but at the time it was a very, very big challenge for me. It was so American. I had never worked on that kind of subject before, and this one was twice as tough, because it was about American teenagers in an American high school. The Europeans in Hollywood usually got European subjects, but with Charlie Brackett, they trusted me. The lines I contributed didn't speak with an accent.

"Paramount's first choice for the lead was a young guy nobody had ever heard of, William Holden. But just then, they lent him out to Columbia for *Golden Boy,* and the part went to Jackie Cooper. Can you imagine Bill Holden as Henry Aldrich, the most unpopular guy at Central High? We would have had quite some trouble writing that one!"

What a Life is the story of a teenage nonachiever who, with the help of an understanding teacher, finds his course in life, art, while clearing his name in a high school scandal and winning back his girl-friend. The film was successful and inspired a series of Henry Aldrich films and a popular weekly radio program.

"I speak at schools a lot now, and they ask questions about my best pictures and some I wish they could forget about. They also ask about the early German ones, but they never ask about *What a Life.* It isn't worth asking about. Even so, it was the first time I felt comfortable in a marvelous new language. I wasn't bluffing anymore. I really understood

the dialogue I was writing. It reminds me of a gag Lubitsch added to
Bluebeard's Eighth Wife.

"There's a sign in a shop window in France. It says, 'English spoken,
si parla Italiano, man spricht Deutsch, American understood.' I remember when Lubitsch added 'American understood' to the script.

"That was how I felt after *What a Life:* American understood."

—"A Ghostwriter—
in the Toilet"

"Whenever our work went slowly," Wilder recalled, "Lubitsch would go to the toilet. If he stayed there more than five minutes, we were certain that he would come back with an inspired idea. We made a joke about this, that he kept a ghostwriter in the toilet.

"On *Ninotchka,* we had a problem that took us a long time to lick. We worked on it for days. How do you show on film how these completely indoctrinated communists are corrupted by the luxuries of capitalism? And how can you show convincingly the moment this change takes place, how the ice of their ideology suddenly melts away? We were stuck. Then, Lubitsch went to the toilet.

"He was there a long time. We figured he was solving it. He came rushing out, and said to us, 'I think I've got it!'

"His idea was that if the three commissars who have never known capitalistic luxury are living in a hotel like the Ritz, they have to pass shop display windows, like you see in the lobbies of luxury hotels. In these windows are the luxury goods—clothing, perfume, jewelry, watches, and hats. The hats are haute couture creations. When Garbo passes the display windows, she would stop to look at an especially crazy hat, and she says to her comrades, 'How can such a civilization survive that permits their women to put things like that on their heads?'

"After she has become acquainted with Melvyn Douglas, and has been up to his apartment 'to inspect the electrical system,' she passes through the hotel lobby, and stops again for a moment in front of the crazy hat. She shakes her head disapprovingly, but with a little less disapproval than she had before.

"A few days later, after she has fallen in love, she opens the curtains of her hotel suite, and a spring day shines through the window, a spring day as one can only imagine in Paris! Even when you are poor in Paris, you get that spring. When I was poor in Paris, I determined I would come back to spring in Paris, but with some money.

"Ninotchka is another woman, completely changed by Paris air and love and material comforts. She sends her three comrades with some francs to have fun in Paris, but not enough money to have too much fun. She hasn't forgotten everything. When she is all alone, a Lubitsch scene takes place.

"Our Ninotchka goes into the bedroom and, very carefully, she locks all the doors. When she knows she is all alone and no one can come in, she goes to the bureau and again, making certain no one is there, she unlocks a drawer, and she takes out the hat. She's gone out and bought it! She walks to a full-length mirror, and puts it on and looks at it in different poses. At that point, everyone knows that communism has lost this woman.

"What makes the magic of this scene is that the audience becomes aware of Garbo being led along the path of capitalism by her locking of the doors and looking around. Lubitsch has prepared the audience for some secret longing on her part. And then, the audience understands: For Ninotchka, the hat is like eating a forbidden fruit.

"I don't remember who wrote what on *Ninotchka*. It was a completely collaborative effort. What I do remember is that whatever Reisch, Brackett, or I contributed, it was always Lubitsch who made the final decision. He would laugh, 'Ho! Ho! Ho!' at our jokes, then make changes or additions. And he was always right. Lubitsch didn't take a writing credit, but he should have had one."

The original idea for *Ninotchka* came from Melchior Lengyel, a

Hungarian writer, who knew Greta Garbo. She liked the idea, and Gottfried Reinhardt presented it to MGM as a possible vehicle for her. George Cukor was Garbo's first choice as director. When Cukor left to direct *Gone With the Wind,* she agreed to do the picture either with Edmund Goulding or Ernst Lubitsch, who had always wanted to direct her. Only Lubitsch was available, so he won out over the objections of Louis B. Mayer, who didn't consider him "commercial" enough for a Garbo picture.

Three Soviet trade representatives (Felix Bressart, Sig Ruman, and Alexander Granach) are sent to Paris to sell some royal jewels, but they are legally blocked by the real owner, the Grand Duchess Swana (Ina Claire), and ideologically by her lover, Leon d'Algout (Melvyn Douglas), who introduces them to the forbidden pleasures of capitalism. Another trade representative, the unsmiling Nina "Ninotchka" Ivanovna Yakushova (Greta Garbo), is dispatched from Moscow to investigate. She falls under the spell of Paris in the spring, and the charm of suave, urbane Leon, who makes her laugh.

The jewels are taken from Ninotchka's hotel room safe and returned to the jealous grand duchess, but Swana offers a deal. If Ninotchka will immediately return to Russia, the jewels will be given back to the Russian government and their sale not blocked, but she must not see Leon again.

In Moscow, Ninotchka can no longer be happy marching in parades and sharing her flat with two other women, nor can the three trade commissars readjust. Leon can't get a visa to visit her, and his letters are so censored, nothing remains to be read.

Ninotchka is assigned another foreign mission by her superior (Bela Lugosi). The three trade commissars, sent to Turkey to sell furs, have defected and opened a Russian restaurant. In Constantinople, she finds that Leon has backed their restaurant so that he and Ninotchka can be together again.

After Leon has offered to introduce the three envoys to the pleasures of Paris, waiters and cigarette girls are seen entering and leaving their suite. Each entrance elicits exclamations of pleasure, but the viewpoint remains from outside in the hallway, just as it was in Wilder's example of the Lubitsch Touch from *The Smiling Lieutenant*. Marx is losing out to popping champagne corks and pretty cigarette girls, but it is only heard, never shown. Later, Russian caps on a hat rack dissolve to formal hats, indicating a change in the Soviet envoys' ideological tastes, and paralleling Ninotchka's interest in the decadent capitalistic hat.

Among the lovely things Ninotchka remembered owning in Paris was a pair of forbidden silk stockings. "You know how it is today," says her roommate, Anna (Tamara Shayne). "All you have to do is wear a pair of silk stockings, and they suspect you of counterrevolution." These lines provided the title for the 1956 Broadway musical, *Silk Stockings,* an adaptation of Lengyel's original story. Rouben Mamoulian directed the 1957 screen version for MGM. Tamara Shayne is not listed in the credits of *Ninotchka,* though she deserves to be.

In the final scene, the illuminated sign of the restaurant shows one of the three names turned off, looking back to the Hotel Zent'al of Wilder's youth and anticipating the faulty East Berlin hotel sign in *One, Two, Three.* Having thoroughly absorbed the ways of capitalism, Kopalski, one of the three commissars, has gone on strike and is picketing his own restaurant with a sign that says, "Buljanoff and Iranoff are unfair to Kopalski."

Ina Claire was Cukor's contribution to the cast. When Cukor was to be the director of *Ninotchka,* he had insisted on Ina Claire as Swana. When Lubitsch was appointed director, Claire remained.

Gossip circulated that there would be "fireworks" on the set between Claire and Garbo, who had shared silent screen *homme fatal* John Gilbert, though not at the same time. "They were professionals," Wilder said, "and maybe both of them were tired of Gilbert." Gilbert had died in 1936.

"The only person who caused any trouble was me. I was always trying to get on the set and hang around, to listen to the lines, and I was anxious to watch Garbo. But Garbo spotted me. I saw she didn't like me watching, so I disappeared quickly. It turned out she had said I was not to be allowed back to watch when she was acting—and I wasn't!

"Years later, I met Garbo. She was running in Beverly Hills. I was driving. I invited her over for some martinis.

"I told Audrey, 'Guess who I brought home. Garbo.' She thought I was joking, but then she saw Garbo.

"We had martinis, and Garbo could drink pretty good. Audrey made a perfect martini, and Garbo got way ahead of us."

At the time Garbo made *Ninotchka* she didn't drink, and she was apprehensive about her drunk scene. She asked Lubitsch if he could take it out, but the scene was an integral part of the plot, and the story had been built tightly around it.

"Garbo was rather obedient as an actress. She liked to be told. We thought Lubitsch might ask us boys to rewrite. But Lubitsch said to her, 'It's perfect for you. You will be great.' And she was.

"Garbo did not attend Lubitsch's funeral. I believe it was because she was too shy. She was so shy, she probably wouldn't even attend her own funeral, if she could skip it. I liked her."

Near the end of Garbo's life, I met her with Douglas Fairbanks, Jr. He asked her what was her favorite part. "*Ni*-notchka," she answered, with the accent on the first syllable. Fairbanks asked her why she liked that part.

"Comedy. I found my laugh. I found a funny voice inside you that makes fun. It was nice to make people laugh after so many tears. I could be sad inside, but I learned how to put on *Ni*-notchka's funny face. When I smile on the outside, I make a pretend smile, but I feel better inside."

—Lovers—
of Fortune

Just after *Ninotchka* was released, Judith and Billy Wilder became the parents of a twin boy and girl. The infant boy, Vincent, died. The girl, Victoria, would be Wilder's only child. The Wilders had moved to Hidden Valley, then an isolated community just off Coldwater Canyon, and a long drive to the studio. The differences in the couple's temperaments were becoming more evident.

After *Ninotchka*, Brackett and Wilder returned to Paramount and worked briefly on a Bing Crosby musical, *Rhythm on the River.* The script was quickly passed on to other writers, and only Wilder received credit, along with Jacques Théry, for the original story, *Ghost Music.* As Wilder remembered it, "We wrote a story about a very popular composer who couldn't write his own songs, so he hired a couple of ghost-writers to do it for him, and they were *too* good."

Their next project at Paramount was a picture with producer Arthur Hornblow, Jr., tentatively called *La Polonaise,* starring William Holden. "We were contract writers working on a story about an American athlete who goes to Warsaw to see his grandmother, and gets caught up in the war. Bill Holden had to do something at Columbia, so Brackett and I were called in to work on a different story, about an

American pilot who is in jail in Spain. They didn't know who'd play the pilot, but the girl was Claudette Colbert." Ray Milland became the pilot, and Mitchell Leisen the director.

> At the end of the Spanish Civil War, fashion reporter Augusta "Gusto" Nash (Claudette Colbert) rescues American flier of fortune Tom Martin (Ray Milland) from a firing squad by pretending to be his wife. Her story on the rescue wins her a promotion to foreign correspondent. When her editor asks for a follow-up, she is slow to comply because Tom has become romantically involved with her, and she is determined to remain a career woman.
>
> Just as Gusto is starting to fall for Tom, she is sent to Berlin as a foreign correspondent. Tom takes the same train to join the Polish air force. The train makes an unscheduled stop at the forest of Compiègne, where they decide to spend a few idyllic days together. Their romantic interlude is interrupted by the beginning of World War II. They book passage on a ship to New York.
>
> The ship is torpedoed, and Gusto and Tom are saved, but separately. Realizing they can't escape their fates, Gusto goes back to reporting and Tom joins the Royal Air Force.
>
> Months later, Tom returns to Paris on his way back to the United States, after having been wounded and discharged from the RAF. He joins Gusto, again in the forest of Compiègne, where she is covering the French surrender. She accepts his proposal of marriage, and they vow to urge America "to arise."

The title comes from Song of Solomon: "Arise, my love, my fair one, and come away." It is Tom's takeoff prayer. According to Martin's passport, Wilder gave Tom his own birthday, June 22, 1906.

"The scene we had the most trouble with," Wilder said, "was when Milland is in the bathroom with those two other guys. The Breen Office sent us a note suggesting all kinds of things we never thought of. They didn't like the idea that Milland was taking a bath without any clothes on. Milland wasn't really naked."

This was the second time cinematographer Charles B. Lang, Jr., worked on a Billy Wilder script. The first was *Midnight* and the last would be *Some Like It Hot*.

"The picture about Poland with Bill Holden never got done, and even with Mitchell Leisen, *Arise, My Love* was successful," Wilder said. When the film was released in November 1940, Leisen told the press that the film was "Charlie Brackett at his best," omitting Wilder's name.

—The Cockroach—
on the Cutting
Room Floor

"Hold Back the Dawn," Wilder said, "was loosely based on my experience in Mexico in 1934. In one scene, the [Charles] Boyer hero is stuck in a shabby Mexican hotel on the border, hoping for his visa. While he's lying on his bed, he spots a cockroach. This roach is trying to reach a mirror, and our so-called hero pushes the spunky cockroach back with his cane. He toys with him as if he were an immigration official preventing the roach from crossing a border. 'Where do you think you're going?' he asks the roach. 'Where is your visa? Where are your papers?' And he keeps pushing the roach back because he doesn't have a visa and the right papers.

"While Leisen was directing this picture, he was able to keep us off the set simply because we were too busy writing the script. He started directing before we finished writing, so Brackett and I wrote as he shot.

"But one day Brackett and I went to the restaurant across from Paramount, and Boyer was sitting there eating, very refined, with napkin and red wine, French from head to toes. I asked him how things were going, and he told me that this afternoon they were shooting the shabby hotel room scene.

"'I like that scene,' I said, 'when you speak to the cockroach.'

"In his French accent, he said, 'We have changed that a little. I do not speak anymore with the cockroach. It is not logical to speak with an insect, so we have cut it.'

"I was furious. I said, 'You are wrong!'

"He argued, 'A normal human being would not speak with an insect.'

"I was ready to explode. But we knew the producer was in too deep at this point and at the mercy of the star. So we decided if Monsieur Boyer couldn't speak to a cockroach, then in the third act, which we were about to write, we would give Miss de Havilland the best lines. We left Boyer virtually speechless while we gave Miss de Havilland all the lines. She was promptly nominated for an Oscar. The cockroach wasn't. If Boyer had said the lines we worked so hard on, the cockroach might have been nominated for best supporting insect.

"For our next picture, I tried to make a list of directors we could work with. I only came up with one name: me. I was inspired to become a director by a cockroach."

Hold Back the Dawn came from an idea by Katherine Hartley (Ketti) Frings, who had worked on *Arise, My Love.* Her treatment, *Memo to a Movie Producer,* was about European immigrants stranded in Tijuana and the American wife of one of them. Her own husband, Kurt Frings, was waiting in Tijuana for a visa. She wrote her story as a novel, *Hold Back the Dawn,* the basis for the film.

"What she had in mind was something like Vicki Baum's *Grand Hotel;* but in Tijuana instead of Berlin, the hotel would not be grand.

"I'd done the research myself in Mexicali, because I was in that situation myself, trying to get a visa. I was lucky. I found someone very kind. Sometimes it seems like he existed only just that day, for me.

"I remembered the most hopeless case I'd seen there, a Romanian with suspicious papers. The quota from Romania was something like one a year, or maybe less. This guy was becoming very fluent in Spanish.

"So, we have a Romanian with a shady background, but not too shady. He says he's a dancer, but he's really a gigolo. The only way this guy can get into America is by marrying into it. We were influenced by

Goethe's Faust, redemption by a good woman. Our Romanian's got to find this good woman he's using so he can become a U.S. citizen. Her goodness saves him, and he's a redeemed cad.

"Paramount had already told us we had Charles Boyer, and we wanted Olivia de Havilland for the schoolteacher. She had a couple of years before been nominated for an Oscar in *Gone With the Wind,* and that's the character we wanted for Emmy Brown—dear, sweet, naive, gullible Melanie. The trouble was, Melanie was under contract to Warners. Brackett knew her, and said he could show her our script."

In Paris, where she was living, Olivia de Havilland talked with me about *Hold Back the Dawn.* "I had just had my appendix removed, and I was staying with my friend Geraldine Fitzgerald while I recuperated. Charlie Brackett invited her to a Sunday brunch, and when he found out I was there, too, he invited me. I didn't feel like it, but I was pretty bored just lying around, so I went.

"Charlie told me about the script he and Billy Wilder were working on and that they wanted me to do the lead. I read it, and I think it helped me to recover more quickly. I phoned Charlie and told him I would love to do the picture if they could get Warners to agree." Jack Warner agreed to loan out Olivia de Havilland in exchange for getting Fred MacMurray.

"The Oscar nomination for that part," de Havilland continued, "helped me to be thought of for many of the fine parts I was offered later." She received an Oscar for *To Each His Own* in 1946, a nomination in 1948 for *The Snake Pit,* and another Oscar for *The Heiress* in 1949.

The film opens with Georges Iscovescu (Charles Boyer) offering the story of his life to Paramount for $500. In a flashback, he describes dancing his way across Europe as a refugee gigolo. When war breaks out, he makes his way to Mexico, but is unable to get a U.S. visa. Anita (Paulette Goddard), an old girlfriend, tells him that the easiest way to enter is by marrying a U.S. citizen.

He meets an innocent schoolteacher, Emmy Brown (Olivia de Havilland), who accepts his proposal only hours after they meet. They marry, and she returns to the United States until he can obtain his visa and join her. Meanwhile, Georges resumes his affair with Anita.

Emmy returns in a week with her life savings, $500, which she gives to Georges. He gives it to Anita, planning to leave Emmy and join Anita in New York. The officer in charge of immigration, however, decides to refuse visas to immigrants he feels have married only to become U.S. citizens.

To prove his good faith, Georges takes Emmy on a honeymoon. In a romantic setting reminiscent of one of Wilder's favorite films, Murnau's *Sunrise,* he falls in love with his bride. When they return, a jealous Anita informs Emmy of Georges's original motive for marrying her. But Emmy loves Georges and tells him she will give him a divorce after he has entered the United States.

Driving back, she is gravely injured in an auto accident. When Georges finds out, he crosses the border illegally, knowing that if he is caught, he will never be granted a visa. He finds Emmy near death, and gives her courage to live.

As he is telling his story, immigration officers come to arrest Georges and take him back to Tijuana. Later, a recovered Emmy appears in Tijuana to plead for him, and Georges is permitted to enter the United States.

Veronica Lake and Brian Donlevy make cameo appearances as themselves, and director Mitchell Leisen plays the director at Paramount to whom Georges tells his story. Wilder's personal animosity toward Leisen clouded his view of that director's substantial Hollywood achievements.

Between *Hold Back the Dawn* and his next film, *Ball of Fire,* Billy Wilder made an uncredited contribution to Julien Duvivier's 1942 film, *Tales of Manhattan.* Wilder described it as "about a dress suit that passes from owner to owner, until its owner is a scarecrow in a field."

—The Slang Gang—

 "He was a good director," Wilder said of Howard Hawks. "His touch was light, and the audience was not aware of the picture being directed by anyone. Everything seemed natural and easy, but it wasn't natural and easy for him.

"Hawks was a fumbler, a hair-splitter, but that wasn't the character he played on the set. With *Ball of Fire,* he seemed patient, charming. He worked long and painstakingly until he found the best solution for a scene, but at the end of the day, all the pressures his easygoing nature had been forced to endure caught up with him.

"Every evening at six after the day of directing was over, on the way home from the Goldwyn Studios to Bel Air, he stopped his car at the corner of La Cienega and Santa Monica Boulevard, got out, and threw up.

"Directing never affected me so that I had to throw up. Just stomach pains.

"*Ball of Fire* was an idea that I brought with me from Germany. It was written in German, in Berlin, before Hitler. It was better in German. The idea of the respected professors who lived life only in their books was more of a German idea. You know, 'Herr Doktor Professor.'"

Wilder and Brackett offered the idea to Samuel Goldwyn. "Goldwyn was a great producer, but he couldn't read. He gave everything to his wife, Frances. He called me and said, 'Frances likes it.' It kept you in your place as a writer but as Goldwyn might have said, I should thank my lucky starlets.

"The picture probably never would have gotten made if Hawks hadn't said he would do it. It certainly wouldn't have had Gary Cooper and Barbara Stanwyck just because of a Brackett-Wilder script.

"For research, Brackett and I sat for hours at a Westwood soda fountain, ordering chocolate sodas while we listened to the students talking 'jive.' We 'dug' it. There were many things outside of our writing Brackett and I didn't agree on, but chocolate sodas weren't one of them. We had to limit our own personal research at the soda fountain, though. We were putting on weight."

The first title was *The Professor and the Burlesque Queen.* Then, *From A to Z,* and finally *Ball of Fire,* which was the description of Stanwyck's character in the tabloid headlines.

While doing research on slang for a new encyclopedia, Professor Bertram Potts (Gary Cooper) becomes involved with nightclub singer Sugarpuss O'Shea (Barbara Stanwyck), whose gangster boyfriend, Joe Lilac (Dana Andrews), is a murder suspect. Sugarpuss uses Potts to help Lilac, endangering the foundation funding of the encyclopedia, until she realizes it's the professor she really loves. Then, Potts and his fellow professors save Sugarpuss from being kidnapped by the Lilac gang through use of their high intelligence, and the professor gets the girl.

"Hawks didn't mind my hanging around, like a fly on the wall. I didn't set out to be like him, but something might have rubbed off.

"I got to know Gary Cooper better than I had before, and I got to know Barbara Stanwyck. Cooper became a friend of mine, and he was in *Love in the Afternoon* many years later. He was a very sophisticated man and articulate. The women really went for him. Off-screen, he wasn't that silent character he played on-screen. He was a good talker, and he was no ideal husband.

"In his last years, when he was dying of cancer, he was as brave as any of the heroes he played on the screen.

"I never got to know Stanwyck well, but this picture helped me to persuade her to do *Double Indemnity*. It's not a great picture, but who knows? If you subtract any part of your life, maybe it changes everything."

The song "Drum Boogie" was chosen not just to furnish Barbara Stanwyck with a chance to sing, but also to give Gene Krupa a chance to play the drums. The Krupa band was an important attraction for teenage audiences of the early 1940s, during the big band era.

Ball of Fire was released just before Pearl Harbor in 1941, and became one of the top-grossing films of the year.

—The Major—
and the Minor

"I loved *The Major and the Minor,*" Ginger Rogers told me, "because it was *my* story, as if they knew my life. Mother and I often didn't have enough money when we traveled, so I carried my stuffed doll named Freakus, which made me look younger, especially when I hugged it and talked with it, and then, at night, I could use it as a pillow. Just like Sue-Sue, I often pretended I was younger than I was, so I could travel half-fare. I *was* Sue-Sue!

"When Charlie Brackett was trying to sell me on doing the movie, he was really enthusiastic. Then he got around to the hard part: 'We have someone in mind who would be a great director for you. He has a wonderful sense of humor. You'll love him. But there's one thing: He's never directed a movie in this country.'

"I was a star. I had just won an Oscar. I could have had any director I wanted. But I said I would meet him anyway. I always wanted to decide for myself."

———◇———

"I remember the exact moment I wanted to become a director," Wilder told me. "I wrote some pictures in Berlin. In one of them there was a kind of discotheque of the '20s. There was a sign at the entrance that said, 'You must wear a tie and shoes to get in.'

"I wrote that a guy with a beard down to the floor comes along. The man at the door looks under the beard. Yes, he's got shoes. Then he lifts his beard some more to see if he's got a tie. Yes, he's got a tie.

"I go to see the picture, and the director has given the guy a little Van Dyke beard. It was obvious he had no tie. What did the director think was funny now? It was not a good joke anyway, but this shows what happens when directors make changes in the script without thinking.

"Arthur Hornblow, who Brackett and I had written a few pictures for, thought I ought to get the chance to direct my own scripts. He gave me my first chance with *The Major and the Minor*.

"Everybody was sure I was going to do some German Expressionist thing sure to fail, and that crazy Wilder would go back to his typewriter and stop bothering everybody. But I was very careful. I set out to make a commercial picture I wouldn't be ashamed of, so my first picture as a director wouldn't be my last.

"Paramount had an option on a property I kind of liked, and I wished I could get Ginger Rogers to play the lead. My agent, Leland Hayward, talked to Ginger Rogers, who had just won the Academy Award as best actress for *Kitty Foyle*. He was her agent, too.

"I wrote the part of the major for Cary Grant. I always wanted him in one of my pictures, but it never worked out.

"I was driving home on a Friday, and I happened to pull up at the same stop light with Ray Milland. In southern California, a friend is someone you wave to when your cars stop at the same traffic light.

"I called out to him, 'I'm doing a picture. Would you like to be in it?' And he said, 'Sure.' We smiled at each other and drove on when the light changed. That was it.

"It wasn't too difficult for Ginger to imitate a girl of twelve, especially in those days. Now it seems a little foolish. To think a thirty-year-old could play a twelve-year-old girl and be believable! Well, she couldn't, but it didn't matter. The audiences were very generous in those days. They had come to have a good time and they went along with you. When Norman Taurog remade the picture in 1955 [*You're*

The Major and the Minor—*thirty-year-old Ginger Rogers emerges from the ladies room a twelve-year-old while thirty-six-year-old Billy Wilder looks on. This was his debut as a Hollywood director.* (Museum of Modern Art)

Never Too Young], it was a different audience, and Jerry Lewis played Ginger's part for broad comedy."

> Susan Applegate (Ginger Rogers), desperate to leave New York City and go home to Iowa, doesn't have enough money for the train ticket, so she rides for half-fare disguised as a child. A kindly army officer, Major Philip Kirby (Ray Milland), believing she is a frightened twelve-year-old, becomes her protector. In doing so, he risks losing his post at a military academy and alienating his fiancée, Pamela Hill (Rita Johnson). "Sue-Sue," however, is able to help him get the military assignment he really wants, and she believes she has saved his upcoming marriage to the shrewish Pamela until "Uncle Philip" drops by Stevenson, Iowa, on his way to active duty in the Pacific, still single and available for the grown-up Susan.

While *The Major and the Minor* was still being shot, Lenore Hornblow, wife of the producer, told me, "Arthur came to New York, and we met. I wore a black and white checked dress, like gingham, but it was taffeta. It was a very pretty dress. He was taken with the dress and I'm glad to say, with me.

"When he went back, he said to Edith Head, 'For that scene on the porch, what would you think, Edie, of having her in a black and white checked dress with a white collar?' And she said, 'Oh, that would be marvelous.' She loved to use black. So, I can't watch that movie, because when I see the black and white dress, I'm overcome."

———◁◦▷———

Wilder turned to experienced film editor Doane Harrison for guidance. From Harrison, he learned to "cut in the camera," not to shoot a lot of footage so that someone other than the director could later determine how the finished film would look.

"It's the scissors that make the picture," Wilder explained. "Cutting is very, very important. It is the juxtaposition of the various shots that makes the picture, so what I do is try not to give *them* any extra film to monkey around with. I didn't always have first cut, but even when you have it, they still have the power not to release your picture. So I shoot the minimum. When I finish a film, there is nothing on the cutting room floor but chewing gum wrappers and tears."

———◇———

Ginger Rogers was the object of considerable, if discreet, attention at New York's Le Cirque restaurant in the 1980s. Some of the dinner patrons recognized her, but even those who didn't couldn't help noticing that she was wearing dark sunglasses with white frames at night, all through dinner. She never took them off, even to eat the soufflé.

When the owner, Sirio Maccione, came by to make certain the soufflé was perfect, she explained to him that while people might assume she wore the dark glasses in order to not be recognized, she really wore them so she wouldn't see the other diners, to put distance between herself and them. The glasses prevented her from seeing anyone except those with whom she was actually having dinner. There were times when she was in the mood to be a celebrity. There were other times she wasn't in the mood, and at those times, she wore the sunglasses.

"Did you know Billy Wilder owes his career to me?" she asked me. "If I hadn't said yes to doing his first directing assignment, who knows? Maybe he wouldn't have gotten to direct, or maybe his first try would have been a failure, and they'd never have given him a chance again. Remember, I was pretty hot at the time.

"My agent, Leland Hayward, told me to expect a call, but I was surprised when the call came while I was on the set. The front gate called during my lunch break to say Arthur Hornblow, Jr., and Charles Brackett were out there to see me.

"I was doing *Roxie Hart,* and I liked to be alone at lunch, to rest, to look at my lines. It didn't seem very considerate of them, or professional. I was working. I was a star. I spoke to Charlie Brackett on the phone, and I said, 'We'll have to make an appointment for another time. All I have is my lunch break, and that's not really enough time.' The real reason was I wasn't in the mood. I said, very politely, but firmly, that it just wasn't the right moment for me, and I would probably say no to anything they presented.

"But he just wouldn't take no for an answer. He said, 'Please, we only need five minutes.' I said I'd have to be on the set the moment the director wanted me, that I wouldn't be late. Charlie said, 'We understand. Just five minutes.'

"Well, it took them ten minutes just to *find* me!

"I had a reason I said yes. I had a great dressing room. It was the best one. Fox had it built just for Shirley Temple, and she had it until she got too old for her parts, which was kind of an omen for the part they were offering me. It was sort of a doll's house. I loved it. I thought these two men were going to be pretty impressed, but feel uncomfortable and out of place. It was very feminine and sweet.

"They rushed in sort of out of breath, and they didn't seem to notice anything. They began talking as they came through the door. They didn't even take time to say hello.

"Charlie did most of the talking, and they went on nonstop, telling the story of *The Major and the Minor.* Then I got my call to be on the set.

"I met Billy Wilder at an Italian restaurant. He was charming, a European gentleman. I didn't find him as funny as they said he was. Maybe it was because he had such a heavy accent, and I couldn't understand everything he said. I've always been a good judge of character. I decided then and there that we would get along and that he had the qualities to become a good director. He knew just how to order in the restaurant, but remembered to ask me what I liked. I felt he would be strong, but that he would listen. He certainly understood how to pay attention to a woman.

"I was told that the reason they had to have my agreement so fast was because they wanted to write the part specially for me, to tailor it for me, just the way Adrian or Jean Louis or Edith Head did a costume. It was true. They created the part, so it was perfect for me.

"We had a lot of fun making the picture. It was that kind of story. And even though it was his first film, from day one, I saw that Billy knew what to do. He was very sure of himself. He had perfect confidence."

Wilder and Rogers each remembered differently how Ginger's mother came to play the part of Susan's mother in the film. Wilder remembered Rogers asking him to consider her mother for the part.

She remembered the director "considerately" asking her who would be a good mother for her.

"We needed someone to play my mother, a small part, but it was key that she resemble me. Billy and Brackett asked me who I thought would make a good mother for me.

"I said, 'How about *my* mother?'

"She was around all the time anyway, watching over me. We were very close. She wanted me very much because she lost a baby just before me. The baby was murdered by a doctor who used forceps. I remember my mother told me I was dancing even before I was born. She could feel me tap dancing in her stomach.

"My mother asked, 'What are you paying?'

"Charlie Brackett, Billy, and Hornblow really laughed. They thought it was a joke. That was until they had to make their deal with her. It took a while, but they worked it out. Lelee never needed a retake, and she knew her lines perfectly. Billy loved that. He really cared about his lines. He didn't want you to change his lines, even as a first-time director. Of course, he was the writer, too. So was Charlie, but I had the feeling that Billy was more devoted to the words. He seemed to know every word, every day, without ever needing to look at the script.

"My mother approved of Billy. He directed her small part as if it were one of the most important. He told jokes and made it a lot of fun on the set, and everybody talked about how funny he was, but I think under it all he was a very serious person. I had the feeling that it might be something that happened in his life. Maybe in Germany. He was German, you know.

"I remember a funny thing he'd do. He never did many takes. When we finished a scene, and he liked it, he'd yell out, 'Champagne for everybody!' After a while, the crew would join in. Finally we would, too, even Ray Milland. Everyone loved to come by our set. I understand that later Billy would have a closed set sometimes, but this was only the beginning, and maybe he didn't know about closing the set. I think my chapter talking about Billy Wilder should be called 'Champagne for Everybody!'

"The dresses I wore were very good for the character. I've always

The Major and the Minor—*Cowriter Charles Brackett goes over a line in the film with Billy Wilder and editor Doane Harrison. Both men were extremely important to Wilder's career.* (British Film Institute)

liked clothes. When we finished shooting, I was pleased with the work I'd done, and I thought our film was going to bring a lot of pleasure, so I went on a fabrics binge.

"When I finished a film, I liked to binge. I didn't drink or smoke, and I couldn't eat much dessert and lose my figure, so I binged on my great love, fabric. I loved buying wonderful material for dresses. When your hand hangs down and brushes a wonderful piece of material you are wearing, it's sensual.

"I would like to have worked with Billy Wilder again, but he never asked. Socially, I didn't seem to be someone he wanted to know. He wasn't like Astaire, who made it clear to people that if they invited him, he didn't want them to invite me. If we met at a party, Billy would nod, say hello, and then he'd hurry over to the other side of the room and talk with a little group. If I walked in their direction, he would be so deep in conversation, he'd fail to see me—and people usually see me.

"Billy was kind of a snob about European culture and food, and I guess he didn't think I knew about those things, because I didn't play that part, but I knew a lot. I've lived very well.

"The thing I didn't think was right was the way he never talked about me when he was interviewed or gave me enough credit for what I did. They told me that they needed my yes so they could write the script for me. Well, that part was true, but I understood later that's how they got the film made, getting a big star like me to say yes. Some people might think Billy Wilder became a director because I agreed to be in his movie.

"I've never been sorry I made the film. *The Major and the Minor* really holds up. It's as good now as it was then.

"Champagne for everybody!

"Then, when the Film Society of Lincoln Center honored him in 1983, out of all the people he could have had, he wanted *me* to be there with him sharing that great evening. So, I guess he liked me and our picture better than I knew."

—Five Graves—
to Cairo

"I was always an admirer of Stroheim," Wilder said. "When I went to high school in Vienna, I first saw his pictures. Then, after I came here and became a director, we made a picture called *Five Graves to Cairo.* I had the idea to get Stroheim to play General Rommel."

Wilder greatly admired Jean Renoir's *La Grande Illusion,* in which von Stroheim plays a German commander who fraternizes with his captured French officers, a part similar to General Rommel in *Five Graves to Cairo.*

"We were in the desert somewhere near Yuma, shooting the tank stuff. I came back to town, and they told me that Mr. Stroheim was at Western Costume and they were fitting him into his uniform. I was pretty excited, but I didn't want to show it.

"I rushed right up, clicked my heels, and I said, 'Herr Von Stroheim, my name is Billy Wilder. The idea now that I should be directing you—little me directing the great Erich von Stroheim! You were always ten years ahead of your time.'

"He looked at me and said, 'Twenty!'

"That was Stroheim. He had special obsessions. He discussed with his makeup man about how Rommel, 'the Desert Fox,' was sunburnt, but from his brow up, absolutely white. When I saw him, I said, 'Aren't they going to finish your makeup?'

"He said, 'It *is* finished. This is a man who always has his cap on! This is a general!'

"You could have gotten von Stroheim for nothing to play a king. He loathed playing enlisted men, but a general, that was absolutely right.

"He came to me and said, 'I will need three different pairs of field glasses, and I will need two Leica cameras with film inside.'

"'With film inside? Who would know it?'

"'The audience, they will feel it. And *I* would know it.'

"*Five Graves* was based on *Hotel Imperial,* a play by a Hungarian author, Lajos Biró. It was about a hotel in Przemysl, a town close to where my grandmother had a hotel in Galicia. In the play, during World War I, when the Russians were coming, the porter would put up a large portrait of Czar Nicholas in the lobby instead of Emperor Francis Joseph. Then, when the Austrians were returning, he would change it back to the emperor, and so on. In *Five Graves,* we substituted Queen Victoria, and then have her covered over by Field Marshal Rommel when the Germans come."

In June 1942, British corporal John Bramble (Franchot Tone), takes the place of a dead waiter in a Sahara hotel to avoid capture by the advancing Germans. When General Rommel (Erich von Stroheim) arrives at the hotel, Bramble learns that the man whose identity he has taken was a German spy. Bramble seizes the opportunity to spy on the Germans.

Mouche (Anne Baxter), a French chambermaid, offers herself to General Rommel in exchange for her brother's release from a prisoner-of-war camp. When Rommel rejects her, his adjutant, Lieutenant Schwegler (Peter Van Eyck), accepts the offer.

Schwegler is killed by Bramble after the German lieutenant discovers his real identity, and Mouche becomes the prime suspect. She does not implicate Bramble, who is leaving for Cairo, because she knows he has secret information for the Allies, forgiving him and the British for leaving her brother behind on the Dunkerque beach.

When Bramble returns with the advancing British forces, he places the pearl-handled parasol she had always wanted on her grave.

"Melodrama isn't easy to do," Wilder said. "If you miss something along the way, or you put something in that doesn't work . . . *Five Graves,* it worked. It's nothing to be ashamed of.

"I was happy to get Stroheim, not to play Rommel, but to *be* Rommel. I wanted him. He did not resemble Rommel at all, but it did not matter. Von—what I called him—could create the illusion of a great general. He was very odd and had invented himself, and people believed every bit of his fiction. He had a heavy accent from the rougher part of Vienna, but he had style.

"He always had suggestions, and I listened to what he had to say. He and Lubitsch were my idols.

"I wanted my old chum from Berlin and Paris, Franz Waxman, to do the music, but he was too busy. I told Miklós Rózsa he wasn't my first choice, and he said I wasn't his first choice, either. I changed my mind. He did four more scores for me."

Five Graves to Cairo was filmed at Paramount and on location, January through February 1943, and released in May of the same year. Locations included the desert near the Salton Sea, Indio, California, and Yuma, Arizona. While *Five Graves* was being filmed, early box office receipts indicated that *The Major and the Minor* was going to be a big success.

Wilder was singled out by the trade papers as a brilliant new directorial talent. While the consensus of newspaper and magazine reviews was favorable to *The Major and the Minor,* far greater attention was paid to star Ginger Rogers than to director Billy Wilder. At that time, directors were generally not recognized, and film critics had less influence than they were later to enjoy.

"I didn't want to be singled out too much," Wilder said. "I wanted only that audiences enjoy the picture, and I wanted to be a working director."

—Double—
Indemnity

Billy Wilder lived by his wits, and his characters often lived by theirs. Sometimes they died by their wits.

"The main characters in *Double Indemnity* have a problem," Wilder explained. "They aren't living the American dream, and they hope to correct that. The game is as important as the gain."

Film noir was a term coined by French critics to describe a type of film produced in Hollywood during the 1940s and early 1950s, usually about interesting losers, often with a bad woman who didn't know how bad she was. Cities at night were favorite *film noir* settings, because there was so much to hide and so many ways to hide it.

"I never heard that expression, *film noir,* when I made *Double Indemnity.* We didn't think we were working for forever, whatever 'forever' is. I just made pictures I would have liked to see. When I was lucky, it coincided with the taste of the audience. With *Double Indemnity,* I was lucky."

———◦———

Charles Brackett found *Double Indemnity* a sordid subject, so he left Wilder temporarily and produced *The Uninvited* (1944). Wilder needed to find another collaborator for this film.

"I wanted James Cain, who wrote the short story, but he was busy. My producer, Joe Sistrom, said, 'Look, there is a good writer who knows the climate of Southern California, and you will like him.' So, we found Mr. Chandler. Raymond Chandler wasn't known then the way he is now.

"He was a marvelous book writer, but he was strange, abrasive, and unpredictable. He absolutely hated me because I knew more about the medium.

"I also was a lot younger, I knew many pretty girls, and I could drink without it ever getting in control of me. Chandler had been an alcoholic. He had stopped drinking, but he hadn't gotten over it.

"Chandler had never been inside a studio, and was bewildered. He read the story very quickly and said, 'You can't have the screenplay until Monday.' He thought *we* thought he's going to write the whole damn screenplay between Thursday and next Monday!

"He had never written a screenplay. I said, 'Look, it's going to take sixteen weeks and you're going to be working with me, the director, in one room together.' By the time we were through, I bet he was drinking again!

"One day, he quit over a Venetian blind. He said, 'Wilder,' in his rude way, 'pull that shade down,' without saying please.

"After three weeks, no Chandler. So Sistrom got in touch with Chandler, who says, 'I don't want to work with that son of a bitch,' he meant me, 'anymore.'

"'Wilder pulls up the Venetian blinds without asking. Broads are calling him. He uses three minutes here, six minutes there. He's not serious about writing. He has two drinks before lunch. He's scribbling notes all the time.'

"You know, this kind of pettiness about my scribbling. But I write down my ideas and save them because you don't know when the muse will touch you on the brow. It is good to be prepared for the day she goes out to have her hair done. I have always been a note-taker, everywhere but in the shower, because the ink runs too much.

"Chandler was a man full of talent, but we were not made for each other. With a collaborator, it's like a marriage, you know. Even though

you may not get along, you can produce something. I was very happy
with the end result of *Double Indemnity.*"

> Insurance salesman Walter Neff (Fred MacMurray) plots with
> attractive Phyllis Dietrichson (Barbara Stanwyck), to murder her
> husband (Tom Powers). After the husband has been tricked into
> signing a double indemnity accident policy, they kill him to make it
> look like an accident.
>
> Insurance investigator Barton Keyes (Edward G. Robinson)
> doesn't believe it was an accident and pursues the case, linking
> Phyllis with everyone but his friend, Walter. Neff, meanwhile, is told
> by Dietrichson's daughter from a previous marriage (Jean Heather)
> that she believes Phyllis killed her mother in order to marry her
> father. Neff suspects Phyllis of a double cross, and she believes he
> has abandoned her for the younger woman. In a confrontation,
> Phyllis shoots Neff, wounding him, and he kills her.
>
> As the bleeding Neff dictates his confession, Keyes enters the
> office. Neff tries to escape, but collapses in the hallway as sirens are
> heard in the distance.

"I performed a major surgery on the end of *Double Indemnity,*"
Wilder explained. "I had an ending, about twenty minutes long, where
Mr. MacMurray was executed in the gas chamber. It was all done with
minute precision. I had the priest from San Quentin, I had the warden,
I had the doctor, and everything was absolutely perfect. I had the gas
chamber with the pellets dropping and the bucket and the fumes, and
outside is Eddie Robinson watching. Their characters are two great
friends, and there is something going on between them, an exchange, a
bond that doesn't need words.

"Then, after I built that whole thing, I saw it was unnecessary. I
found a scene where MacMurray tries to go to the elevator and get to
his car to go to Mexico. Eddie Robinson tells him, 'You can't even
make the elevator.' He collapses there, and he can't even light the match
anymore the tricky way he always did. Robinson has to do it for him.
And in the distance you already hear the sirens of the police car or the

Double Indemnity—*Billy Wilder shows Barbara Stanwyck and Fred MacMurray how he wants a scene played.* (Museum of Modern Art)

ambulance, so you know what the outcome is going to be.

"The other scene, in the gas chamber, would have been very anti-climactic. We knew that he was guilty because he confessed. The ending between the two men, almost a love scene, was the best."

The supermarket setting, where the killers meet and plot, was admired by Alfred Hitchcock. Hitchcock's own preference was for creating suspense and shock in an everyday, ordinary place where, as he would say, "fear wasn't supposed to enter." He told me that he thought *Double Indemnity* "was a lovely film, the cream on the bun." He had been quoted as saying, "After *Double Indemnity,* the two most important words in movies are Billy Wilder."

Barbara Stanwyck approached *Double Indemnity* apprehensively. We talked at lunch in the Beverly Hills Hotel.

"I was worried about playing a woman like Phyllis Dietrichson, who described herself as 'rotten to the heart,' and she had it right. The characters I had played up to that time may have been poor and done a lot of what they had to do or thought they had to do to survive, but they had redeeming features, a kind of gutsy sincerity. I believe sincerity was the important element. That was how I judged a part. Every character I played had to be sincere."

The role Stanwyck most wanted to play was that of Eva Perón, because, as she said, "I always believed that, in her skin, she was sincere.

"I was used to being a bad girl, but with redeeming qualities, so the audience could be with me. I was afraid my fans would confuse me with the character of Phyllis and not like me anymore.

"I did the part because of Billy Wilder. He'd only directed a couple of pictures. I knew him a little from *Ball of Fire,* which he and Brackett wrote. You couldn't help but notice how much he cared about his script. He was always talking about it with Howard Hawks, the director.

"Phyllis is a great part and I thought I could play her. You could feel for her when she got hers." Stanwyck considered the role one of the best of her career.

"Fred [MacMurray] was very, very unsure about whether he should be doing *Double Indemnity.* I tried to reassure him, but I didn't have anyone to reassure me. So, I reassured myself. Maybe this real feeling of insecurity we had suited our characters.

"Billy Wilder said to each one of us separately, 'What do you have to lose?' Well, each of us thought, 'Everything!' But I only *thought* it and never said a word. I think Fred mentioned it.

"Everybody calls me 'Missy,' but Billy Wilder always said, 'Miss Stanwyck,' so I called him 'Mr. Wilder.' But one day near the end of filming, I said, 'Billy.' It was a big thing for me to call him by his first name, but he never noticed, or he didn't show he noticed it. I guess it just didn't make any difference to him. That was the worst thing, when you find out you don't matter. Well, I mattered to him professionally, and that was what really counted, but I don't feel I was a person he ever thought about knowing outside of work.

"Personal relationships, even ones of the greatest love and passion, that you think will last forever, those fade. They can't stay the same, but it's looking like *Double Indemnity* is forever. What we put on the screen, in the end, that was what counted.

"Wilder has great taste. I like pretty things, but I don't know *why* I like them; I don't think about it. He had more education than I did. Actually, just about everybody did!

"When I meet fans, more of them want to talk with me about *Double Indemnity* than any other movie I've done. Someday when I'm a very old lady, I'll be able to go on the road talking to film fans and schools about what it was like making it. I kept the anklet Phyllis wore for a long time, but I haven't been able to find it for years. Actually, there were a few identical anklets around, in case we lost one.

"I met Fred many years after, and I asked him if he was ever sorry he did it. He said it was the best thing he ever did. It didn't finish his career the way he had worried. He worked with Mr. Wilder again. I never did. I would have anytime."

Edith Head's work on a film was an important support for Stanwyck. "You knew Edith would really help to give you your character for the audience. What people don't know is that she helped give me my character for *me*. Edith helped me to *feel* cheap."

Edith Head was able to save some of the clothes she designed from many of her films, and she kept them on racks in her roomy Spanish-style home. She recognized every piece of clothing and remembered what role it had played in which film, and who had worn it. One of Barbara Stanwyck's *Double Indemnity* blouses hung next to the tiny dresses of Veronica Lake. "I couldn't always keep the dresses," she told me, "but Paramount was happy enough to let me keep what they considered junk nobody wanted." She had saved many dresses that otherwise would have been thrown away before they could be collected as part of film history.

For *Double Indemnity,* Head believed, "The clothes shouldn't call too much attention to themselves or be too cheap, but Barbara Stanwyck's figure had to show. She had great legs. No one had greater legs, not even Dietrich. Being so short myself, I've always envied long legs. Stanwyck wasn't very tall, but she had long legs in proportion to her body, and they were so beautifully shaped. Because she knew how to show them off, she created the illusion that they were much longer than they were. Her clothes weren't off-the-rack. Cheap clothes can be more important than the most elaborate costumes, and they need the same attention."

———◄◊►———

Fred MacMurray's career was changed by this film, but when first approached to do it, he was not enthusiastic. "You have no idea how difficult it was to find stars for *Double Indemnity*," Wilder recalled, "to find a leading man who would play a murderer. I wound up with MacMurray. Once we thought of him, I knew he would be right.

"He said, 'You're making a mistake. I can't play that. It requires acting.'

"I said, 'Look, you've got to make the big step. You've got to get over being a saxophone player.' That's the part he was playing in a picture I worked on called *Champagne Waltz* [1937]. 'You don't want to just do comedies with Carole Lombard and Ginger Rogers.'

"He said, 'But I do!' I wore him down and finally he said, 'All right. I'll do it.'"

Wilder liked the use of the voice-over narrative in *Double Indemnity*. "Voice-over," he explained, "is useful if there is a *raison d'être* for it, if it is anchored in the story. Now, I think in *Double Indemnity* it was very good because a man is speaking into a Dictaphone in order to help a man who is believed to be a murderer, to whitewash him, to do the decent thing. There was a reason for telling the story.

"Chandler didn't think that way. He took the treatment home and he came back with a voice-over narrator in his script who knew too much and talked too much. Chandler was used to a narrator in his stories who was kind of an all-seeing storyteller. He would write stuff that Neff could not possibly have known just to get the plot moving along, the way he did in his novels, which was okay for that medium. I kept telling him, 'Movies are different. Backstory must be forced out like steam in a boiler.' That was our first argument. I guess he didn't like a young guy with a funny accent telling him how to write an American story. But he had never written a screenplay, and I'd written hundreds. I wouldn't have told him how to write a novel!

"The worst thing is when a character comes along and tells another character everything the writer wants the audience to know, stuff the character wouldn't ordinarily be talking about. It's usually because the writers are lazy."

The viewpoint is that of Neff, who is telling the story. He's thirty-five, with "no visible scars," and has been an insurance salesman for eleven years. Originally, the Neff character was called Ness, but this had to be changed when a real Walter Ness was discovered living in the Los Angeles area, who was an insurance executive.

We learn almost nothing about Neff's background. He drinks beer, bourbon, and rum. He drives a 1935 Dodge coupé, the right car for a traveling salesman. Wilder cast the cars in his films as meticulously as he cast the actors who drove them. The Dietrichsons have a Plymouth and a LaSalle, the right cars for an upwardly mobile, yet conservative Southern California family.

When Keyes figures out exactly how the crime was committed, he likens the murderers to being on "a trolley car they must ride to the end of the line, and the last stop is the cemetery."

Some years later, in Tennessee Williams's *A Streetcar Named Desire,* Blanche DuBois says, "They told me to take a streetcar named Desire, and then transfer to one called Cemeteries." Tennessee Williams told me that he had seen *Double Indemnity* several times when it came out in 1944. He loved it, yet he didn't think it really influenced *Streetcar.* "There *was* a streetcar named Cemeteries in New Orleans. But, then, who knows what detours the mind takes?"

Since the script was based on an actual case, Paramount didn't have exclusive rights to the story. Another studio made its own version of the news story, *Apology for Murder.* Paramount sued, saying the film too closely resembled *Double Indemnity.* They won, and the competing film could not be shown. In 1973, ABC-TV produced a remake which was very close to the original. Wilder was not pleased.

"Can you believe that I was asked to make a remake of my own picture? Not a sequel—a remake. Someone wanted me to do a remake of *Double Indemnity.* What would they call it? *Triple Indemnity?*"

Double Indemnity was filmed on location in Los Angeles and Hollywood, and at Paramount, September through November 1943. It was released in May 1944. The gas chamber ending was shown at its first preview and then cut. Since the footage belonged to Paramount, Wilder had no idea what happened to it, but believed it might exist.

The picture was nominated for seven Oscars: best picture, best actress (Barbara Stanwyck), best director (Billy Wilder), best screenplay (Wilder and Raymond Chandler), best cinematography (John F. Seitz), best dramatic musical score (Miklós Rózsa), and best sound recording (Loren Ryder), although no Oscars were carried home.

—The Lost—
Weekend

 "One day it happens," Wilder said. "Success happens and it catches you by surprise. One day you are a signature, and the next day, you are an autograph."

For Billy Wilder, that day came in March 1946, when *The Lost Weekend* was nominated for eight Oscars and won four. It was voted best picture and Wilder was voted the best director. He and Charles Brackett shared best screenplay.

"Before *Weekend,* alcoholism was treated as something funny. There were character actors who only played drunks, and always for laughs. There's nothing funny about a drunk."

Wilder discovered the Charles Jackson novel during a cross-country train trip in 1944. "I bought it in Chicago and started reading as the train pulled out of Union Station. The next thing I knew, the porter came by to make up my bed. We were somewhere between St. Louis and Kansas City, and I had missed dinner. I figured if a novel can hold your attention like that during a long train trip, what would it be like up there on the screen? In the morning, I called and got Paramount to buy the book."

He and Brackett were eager to start writing, but Paramount was uncertain, as was the Breen Office, which didn't approve of Gloria, the prostitute. Don Birnam's struggle with his sexual identity would not be included in the film.

The Lost Weekend began shooting in October 1944, before the script was finished. Wilder had wanted José Ferrer as the lead actor, but the studio demanded a handsome star.

"We needed somebody who could be weak but sympathetic, so the audience would be with him even as he slipped into degradation. I knew Ray Milland could carry it off, though in the beginning, he wasn't so sure.

"I figured we were giving Milland a good chance at the Oscar. It's the part that gets nominated, you know."

Ray Milland told me that he was "uncomfortable" playing an alcoholic, but that he wanted to work again with "that well-met pair," Wilder and Brackett. "Later, I got to know the novel's author, Charles Jackson, to whom I owe a great deal. He shared more than I wanted to know of the horror he had experienced.

"To research my role, I was anxious to spend a night at Bellevue Hospital with the far-gone alcoholics, but I lasted only a few hours and bolted. A policeman returned me, but I was finally able to talk my way out of hell and back to the Waldorf Towers.

"They used hidden cameras mounted in the trucks that allowed me to walk the streets of New York, unshaven, unkempt, without attracting attention. Then someone recognized me, and word got around in the gossip columns that I was on the skids."

> Unpublished writer Don Birnam (Ray Milland) is an alcoholic who has alienated everyone in his life except his fiancée, Helen St. James (Jane Wyman) and his brother, Wyck (Phillip Terry). After Don meets her at the opera because of a coat mix-up, he gives up drinking, but returns to alcohol when he can't face her parents as a thirty-three-year-old failure. She vows to help him fight his addiction.
>
> Don will do anything—lie, even steal, to get a drink. One weekend, he begins his novel, but cannot write without a drink. He tries unsuccessfully to pawn his typewriter, and then falls down a flight of stairs, awakening in the alcoholic ward. In the other alcoholics there, he sees his own bleak future.
>
> Helen stops him from committing suicide after he experiences

terrifying hallucinations. A bartender (Howard da Silva) returns his typewriter, and Don vows to give up alcohol and write his novel.

"I think the audience took it as a happy ending," Wilder said, "but our story wasn't really the end of it. Life goes on.

"Personally, I didn't identify with someone who gave up writing so easily, or who let the bottle get control. Birnam sees the bottle as his worst enemy, but *he* is his own worst enemy.

"He wanted the novel to just pour out of him. Maybe it does for some genius, but I never met that genius. I just know people who struggle, and whether it comes out easier or harder doesn't affect whether it comes out better or worse.

"I wanted to do the DTs scene with more than a mouse and bat, but the 'studio beings' didn't like the idea of my going overboard. They were afraid I was going to go crazy with German Expressionism. I was sort of thinking about Hieronymus Bosch.

"Brackett and I argued alone. Usually, I won. Then, we went out with a unified front.

"This time, Brackett didn't like my visual ideas for the scene. He thought it would be conspicuous and out of style for this picture, and worse, people might laugh, so I settled for the bat and mouse."

As I spoke with costume designer Edith Head about the leopard coat that played such a prominent part in *Lost Weekend,* she was petting her large cat, Thomas Gainsborough. "Helen's coat had to be very distinctive, a little inappropriate, showing a more flamboyant side of the *raffinée,* reserved heroine, the side that loves the charming alcoholic, would-be writer. Mr. Wilder only told me that the coat had to stand out in black and white, and be something special the girl would prize. My very first thought was leopard."

The coat plays an important role in the climax. The suicidal Don pawns it to redeem his revolver. Don's coat provides one of the most memorable scenes when he imagines a *Brindisi* chorus of swaying overcoats like his own, a bottle in one of the pockets. Later, Don escapes from the alcoholic ward by stealing a doctor's overcoat. At the end,

Helen shows her determination to stay with Don and help him fight his addiction when she refuses her coat.

Joe Franklin remembered an occasion on his television show when Ray Milland read a letter he had received after *The Lost Weekend*:

"It said, 'Dear Mr. Milland, I am a dedicated movie fan and a chronic alcoholic. I have never been so touched by any movie as I was by *The Lost Weekend*. After seeing your masterful portrayal of a drinker in that film, I have decided to give up movies.'

"Milland said that when he showed Billy Wilder the letter, 'Billy really laughed.'"

Miklós Rózsa was dissatisfied with his jazz–flavored music for *Lost Weekend* and replaced it with a symphonic score. To the orchestration, he added the theremin, which he had just used so effectively in Alfred Hitchcock's *Spellbound*. The theremin was an electronic instrument that sounded like an unearthly soprano. Rózsa was nominated for an Oscar for his *Lost Weekend* score, but he lost to himself, winning for *Spellbound*. Also nominated for Oscars were John F. Seitz for cinematography, and Doane Harrison for editing.

Wilder met his future wife, Audrey Young, during the filming of *The Lost Weekend*. He had been dating Doris Dowling. "Audrey came by for a nothing part, a hat check girl. No words, but I noticed her anyway. She was very young and very pretty. I would have had to be blind not to notice, and I wasn't blind.

"Ray Milland is in this club, all boozed up, and he can't pay his check, so he takes a lady's purse and gets caught, and is being thrown out. The bare arm of a hat check girl barely comes into frame, holding Milland's hat.

"I saw only the arm, and that's all it took. I fell in love with that arm. We started dating." Wilder and Judith had separated and would soon divorce.

"Audrey was a singer with Tommy Dorsey's band, and she did some traveling, but we were pretty much together from that time on.

"If you love a woman after you marry her as much as you loved her before, this is very good. Falling in love is so easy. Being in love is much harder. I love Aud more now than when I married her, and we've been married for fifty years. But I make a point of not saying it to her."

—Colonel Wilder,—
U.S. Army

 After *The Lost Weekend,* Wilder was asked by the Office of War Information to serve in the army's Psychological Warfare Division in Germany for a special mission. Reporting for duty in New York, he was commissioned a colonel in the U.S. Army. His German background and film experience made him an ideal advisor on the rebuilding of the German film industry.

The person giving him his papers wanted to know how someone who had never been in the military could be starting out as a colonel at $6,500 a year. The man asked him what he had been earning in civilian life.

Wilder answered calmly, "$2,500."

The man was outraged.

Then, Wilder added, without raising his voice, "a week."

Though officers had an allowance for custom-made uniforms, Wilder accepted the regular GI issue. He flew to London, and then Paris.

At Hermès, Wilder visited the store's Faubourg St.-Honoré museum. An early nineteenth-century shaving mirror caught his attention. He asked about buying it, but was told that nothing was ever sold from the museum collection. Then, Hermès made an exception.

"I think it was because I was in uniform. The man who was selling it said to me, 'Thank you for the liberation of Paris.' I hadn't done anything.

"The mirror had wonderful glass. They don't make mirrors like that anymore. For shaving, you could see every hair.

"They wrapped it in *Figaro.* I still have the *Figaro,* yellow with age, and the news of 1945."

"I still like the mirror, but I do not like to look in it anymore. The glass is *too* good. I do not see the face that looked back at me in 1945. I regard the shaving mirror as a wonderful decorative object, like a small piece of furniture. But I avoid looking into it."

———◦———

In Bad Homburg, near Frankfurt, Wilder and his group began screening actors, directors, and writers to identify those who had been Nazis or Nazi collaborators.

A flight over Berlin while filming an army documentary stunned Wilder. "I had wanted to see Berlin again. It wasn't there. It looked like the world had come to an end. Kaput. I had mixed feelings. I wanted to see the Nazis destroyed, but to see *the city* destroyed . . ."

Endless ruins had replaced the city he had once loved and thought of as home. He applied for a permit to visit Berlin.

"I felt the need to visit my father's grave, perhaps because he was the only one of my little family I could find. My mother and grandmother had disappeared, taken away. Everyone in our neighborhood in Vienna who was Jewish had vanished.

"As soon as I arrived in Berlin, I had my army driver go directly to the Soviet sector. That was where my father had been buried. We drove through a Berlin I could not recognize.

"The summer of '45 was very hot. It was the hottest summer in Berlin anyone could remember. There was an unbearable smell. Thousands of corpses were buried under the rubble. The stench and the heat were intolerable. The dead were floating in the Landwehrkanal. In the vegetable gardens, there were no vegetables growing, just corpses rotting.

"A stalled panzer tank had sunk halfway down into the hot asphalt of the Kurfürstendamm. I supposed there were bodies still inside. Children played in the streets making friends with the GIs, who gave them chewing gum and chocolate, probably the first chocolate they had ever tasted. It wasn't very good chocolate, but they were crazy about it, having nothing to compare it with. When I was a boy, the best chocolate I ever ate was in Vienna. I remembered how delicious the chocolate was in Berlin when I got there, before Mr. Hitler destroyed the chocolate, and the buildings, and the people.

"It was strange the way my father had died visiting me in Berlin, he who had never thought about visiting Berlin, let alone dying there. I did not have the money to send him back to Vienna to be buried. At that time, Berlin was the place I called home.

"The neat Jewish cemetery in the Schönhauser Allee had been a battlefield. Before that, during the Nazi era, it had been vandalized. It was filled with the broken pieces of gravestones, parts of names, dates without the person. Tank tracks crisscrossed the field. There was the smell of smoke and what had burned. I did not want to think about it, but I couldn't shut it out.

"Then, an old rabbi appeared who looked like he was a dead man who had risen, like Conrad Veidt in *Caligari*. He told me it was not possible to find the place where my father was. He and his wife had been trapped in Berlin.

"Somehow, they had survived the nightmare, almost starving to death, hiding underground, coming out only in the dark for some breaths of air. They had their belief that good would triumph. The Red Army had come to 'rescue' them. The rabbi and his wife rushed out of their hole. It was hard for them to straighten up. The soldiers were Mongolian troops. They raped his wife, and then killed her. Yet he had remained a religious man.

"My driver was a redheaded Irish boy from the South, only eighteen who looked sixteen, and who didn't understand a word the man was saying. But he was crying."

Billy's father had not been allowed to rest in peace. Max Wilder's body had disappeared forever. He would live on in his son's memories.

"There was nothing I could do for my father. Maybe I believed there was something he could do for me.

"It is a terrible thing not to be able to show your success to your parents. I could give them anything they wanted. I don't know what my mother wanted, but I would have given my father money to go and lose at the races."

Wilder never knew exactly when his mother and grandmother were taken away from their home in Vienna. Neighbors later told him that there had been a roundup of all of the Jewish people, and his mother had been seen in a square with the others. Then, all of those people had disappeared. It wasn't until after the end of the war that the fate of Wilder's family and that of all the others became known to him.

Wilder learned from Auschwitz survivors that they had seen his mother in their first days at Auschwitz. After that, there was no record of her. "The Germans didn't keep as careful records as they were famous for. My family, they just threw away without making notes."

Wilder tried through the Red Cross to locate her. He waited for a letter from her. Gradually, when the letter never arrived, he knew the truth.

Eugenia had been taken to Auschwitz, probably along the same route that she had traveled as a girl living in Galicia. Not far from Auschwitz were Kraków and Nowy Targ, and the happy days of Eugenia's childhood. On the train of death, she must have passed the same stations she had passed with Max on their way to inspect their small chain of railway station cafés, in the area where her children were born, close to the hotel in Kraków which was the source of their great hopes until history redrew the map of Eastern Europe. Eugenia Wilder couldn't see where she was, but she knew the route well, and by that time, she may have understood that she would not pass that way again.

The thought of what his mother had endured, retracing the steps of her life, locked in a crowded cattle car, these images had to be shut out by Wilder, as did those of what must have been the last days of her life—but they could *not* be shut out.

———◦———

Wilder was asked to make a documentary out of the Nazi footage taken of the extermination camps, to be called *Die Todesmühlen (The Death Mills)*.

"After I had edited *Todesmühlen,* I wanted as many German people as possible to see the picture, but I was told they wouldn't believe it. They would just think it was some Hollywood trick. I suggested another Hollywood trick, a sneak preview.

"So, in autumn of 1945, we did a sneak preview in Würzburg. We had a harmless old Lilian Harvey musical which was what the audience was looking for. Then, we invited them to stay and see another film. We told them that outside in the lobby were preview cards and pencils for them to write their opinions.

"The film started to run, and so did the audience. Some of them got up abruptly and left. Others slipped out during the film. Of the four hundred people at the beginning, there were less than twenty at the end. None of them filled out our preview card, but all of the pencils were taken."

Wilder also began talking with occupation officials about a film that would treat postwar problems, especially those being faced by the U.S. military in Europe. When he was discharged from the army, he returned to Hollywood with such a film in mind. Two weeks after his return, Judith filed for divorce, asking for custody of Victoria. "My daughter went with her mama," Wilder said.

Shortly after the divorce, Judith remarried and moved to Brooklyn Heights, New York, taking seven-year-old Victoria with her. Wilder was awarded custody of his daughter during one month of the year, in the summer.

He would go to New York to meet her and spend some days taking her to the Broadway theater and dining in the great restaurants. The little girl was dazzled by the glittery life and awed by her glamorous father. Then they would take the train to Los Angeles, the trip giving each an opportunity to know the other better.

After Judith's second divorce, she and Victoria moved back to California, for a brief sojourn in Southern California followed by permanent residence in the San Francisco Bay area. During Victoria's visits to see her father, Audrey Wilder advised the young teen on clothes, makeup, and hairstyles. For her sixteenth birthday, Victoria received a sports car from her father. It was exactly the gift he would have wanted when he was a young man, but an unimaginable one at that time.

When Victoria was twenty-one, Wilder gave her a two-and-a-half-month trip to Europe with all of his special tips on where to eat, and not just which museums to visit, but what to see in each. Audrey provided fashion shopping recommendations. Victoria would have needed more than two and a half months.

Wilder's daughter married twice, first a high school teacher and then a former racing car driver. During Victoria's first marriage, Julie was born, and Wilder was able to introduce a very young granddaughter to the Bistro restaurant in Beverly Hills, where she sat on a stack of telephone books so she could reach the table.

Years later, when Julie's daughter was born, Wilder became a great-grandfather. "When your daughter has a grandchild, it's something to think about," he told me.

After her second divorce, Victoria went to live near her mother in San Francisco, and the family remained in that part of California.

Of his first wife, Wilder said, "She was a nice girl, but she liked country living. I didn't want country living, only a painting of it. And Monet was not my favorite artist."

After *The Lost Weekend* opened successfully in November 1945, Wilder began work with Brackett on the idea about the German occupation which he had been discussing with the army. Another project, however, intervened.

—The—
Emperor Waltz

"I had just come back from Germany, and I was looking for a project to get the images of those camps out of my mind. I had this idea I wanted to do a musical. I like drama when I'm happy, comedy when I'm sad. It turned out I wasn't a musical director. I could be an audience for a wonderful picture like *Singin' in the Rain,* but I couldn't make it."

Bing Crosby was Paramount's biggest star. Billy Wilder was the studio's top director. To make a film with the two together was logical. Wilder and Brackett had already contributed to a Crosby film, *Rhythm on the River,* in 1939.

"I'd liked Crosby ever since his Paul Whiteman days. I imagined him singing Viennese operetta songs with English lyrics.

"But this was not an operetta, and it was not a fantasy in some mythical kingdom. It was Vienna at the turn of the twentieth century, and some of the characters were historical figures. It was a comedy with some songs."

Virgil Smith (Bing Crosby) comes to Vienna to sell Emperor Francis Joseph (Richard Haydn) a new American invention, the phonograph. He doesn't succeed, but he and his dog, Buttons, fall in love with

the Countess Johanna (Joan Fontaine) and her dog, Scheherazade.
At first, both are rejected, then true love wins out over Freudian
psychology, and class barriers.

The Emperor Waltz was based partly on a real incident. A Danish
inventor demonstrated an early magnetic recording device for the aged
Emperor Francis Joseph, who was so conservative that he hadn't
adjusted yet to indoor plumbing. Francis Joseph didn't invest in the
machines, but his voice was recorded.

One of Crosby's songs in *The Emperor Waltz* became a big hit. "A
Kiss in Your Eyes" is based on "Im Chambre séparée," a waltz from
Richard Heuberger's operetta *Der Opernball,* popular during Wilder's
youth in Vienna. "In those days, lovers had separate rooms," Wilder said,
"but they got together anyway."

Sig Ruman, a favorite of Wilder's, played the dog psychiatrist. "It's a
part for a mustache and a lot of accent." Siegfried Rumann had come
to America from Germany during the 1920s, and virtually his entire
film career had been in Hollywood.

Joan Fontaine gave credit to Edith Head for the wonderful dresses
that she designed for the Countess Johanna. "Wilder encouraged Edith
to go overboard with my dresses. They were so low-cut that I was able
to get some attention away from the dogs.

"Edith was brilliant, and Billy Wilder didn't seem to care how much
they cost. Mr. Wilder told Edith, 'Be extravagant.' I think he meant 'Do it
as elegantly as you can.' She accepted it as permission to spend the
maximum amount of money. I was the beneficiary of the largesse.

"Crosby wasn't very courteous to me. I remember he didn't stand
up when we were introduced. I thought, 'Poor Dorothy Lamour!' This
man didn't have respect. Maybe he treated her better. There was never the
usual costar rapport. I never enjoyed his songs after working with him.

"I was a star at that time, but he treated me like he'd never heard of
me. I should have brought my sarong. Crosby's personality was what
you might have expected from the Emperor Francis Joseph. He was the
Emperor of Paramount.

"Bing Crosby had the power over Billy Wilder. Paramount would certainly have replaced Mr. Wilder, and Mr. Brackett, too, any day, if Crosby had wanted it. It wasn't that he had anything against Mr. Wilder. He just didn't pay much attention to him. He told me once that he had some trouble understanding his funny accent.

"Looking back on *The Emperor Waltz,* I would describe it as your typical dog-meets-dog, dog-loses-dog, dog-wins-dog story.

"Crosby was directing himself, and he had writers working on what *he* said, and sometimes he didn't pay any attention to the Wilder-Brackett words, or even the words of his own writers. He said it as he felt it at the moment."

(George Seaton, who directed Bing Crosby to an Oscar nomination in *The Country Girl,* told me, "It's not true that Bing Crosby doesn't say the lines in the script. He says quite a few of them.")

The Emperor Waltz filmed June through September of 1946 at Jasper National Park, Alberta, and at Paramount in Hollywood, and there were delays, causing the film to come in late and over budget. This was Wilder's first color film, and he was dissatisfied with the colors of the region as photographed in Technicolor, so some of the flora had to be repainted. The weather was unpredictable, and Fontaine was sick, as was Wilder for a time.

"Bing Crosby operated for himself, not for the group or the film," Wilder said. "He was a big star, the biggest, and he thought he knew what was good for him. He did. He sensed what his audience expected, and he knew how to deliver that. The picture didn't come out what I wanted, but that wasn't Crosby's fault. It was mine. I was looking back to my childhood in Austria—waltzes, Tyrolean hats, cream puffs—shutting out what came later. I would like to have done the picture as a tribute to Lubitsch. A tribute to Lubitsch, it was not."

<hr />

In 1946, Wilder's divorce from Judith became final. His brother, Willie Wilder, had sold his successful business in New York and arrived in Hollywood in 1945 as W. Lee Wilder, where he became a producer and director of low-budget films at Republic.

—A Foreign—
Affair

"This was in the old days," Wilder recalled. "All the big exec-utives, with their enormous salaries, would run the rushes of the pictures that were being shot. Paramount was shooting like six, eight pictures at a time, because they made fifty pictures each year.

"I was shooting a picture called *A Foreign Affair* with Jean Arthur and Marlene Dietrich, and a guy by the name of John Lund. He was the guy you got after you wrote the part for Cary Grant, and Grant wasn't available. Lund played an American captain in the army of occu-pation in Berlin.

"As we are beginning to set up the camera, on walks Ray Milland, who was in another picture on another stage, in which he played a colonel. He was still in uniform, and I said, 'Hey, I'm going to make that shot with you. I'm going to hold back the one with John Lund, and I'm going to send this one down to the executives when they run the rushes.' So, Ray Milland, who was a good friend of mine, stepped into the scene, and we shot him.

"By this time we had been shooting about six weeks. The next day, I walked into the commissary, and all the heads of the studio were

there. I said, 'How were the rushes?' Nobody noticed that there suddenly was a new leading man in the picture. Maybe they thought they
were watching *Lost Weekend II*."

---◦---

While he was serving with the U.S. Army in Germany, Wilder was
promised government cooperation if he made a film about the objec-
tives and the progress of the occupation. That film was *A Foreign Affair*,
and Erich Pommer helped facilitate Wilder's shooting on location in
occupied Berlin. Pommer had returned to Berlin after the war as the
chief of the Information Control Division, and was in charge of
rebuilding the German film industry. Whatever was left of UFA, or had
been rebuilt since Pommer's days there, was put at Paramount's dis-
posal. The shooting of backgrounds took place in August 1947, much
of it in the Russian zone, which was not yet sealed off.

Wilder was fascinated by GI English. "I listened to GIs talking with
each other, and I took notes. You can't make up that kind of thing. I
talked to the people of Berlin, too, the ones who were left. And I
watched the Russians. We were allies then."

On the way back to America, Wilder stopped off in Paris to see
Marlene Dietrich, ostensibly to seek her advice on who should play
Erika. He wanted only Dietrich herself, but he thought she would say
no to playing the part of a Nazi collaborator. Instead, he showed her
some tests he had made with June Havoc, and asked Dietrich what she
thought, not telling her that the part had been written for her. Neither
did he mention that Frederick Hollander had written songs with her
in mind. He planned to tell her that after her initial no.

"She kept making criticisms and suggestions, and finally I said, like
I had thought of it just that moment, 'Marlene, only *you* can play this
part.' And she agreed with me.

"She was so much against the Nazis that at first she didn't like playing someone who slept with one. I said, 'Marlene, you're an actress. I
want you to play a part, not join the Nazi party.'"

He had based the character of Erika on a woman he saw clearing
away rubble on the Berlin streets. "The woman was grateful the Allies

had come to fix the gas. I thought it was so she could have a hot meal, but she said it was so she could commit suicide."

In postwar Berlin, visiting U.S. congresswoman Phoebe Frost (Jean Arthur) investigates a singer in an off-limits cabaret, Erika von Schlütow (Marlene Dietrich), who had Nazi connections and is now being shielded by an unidentified American officer. She doesn't realize that the officer assisting her in her investigation, Captain John Pringle (John Lund), is Erika's lover.

As Phoebe starts to fall for Pringle, she abandons her natural reserve in a wild night at the cabaret, and is arrested in a raid. Erika uses her influence to help Phoebe save her reputation. Phoebe then

A Foreign Affair—In 1947, Wilder returned to Berlin to film exteriors and to revisit lost memories of his youth. (Museum of Modern Art)

finds out about Pringle's affair with Erika, not realizing that he has been ordered to draw her jealous Gestapo ex-lover out of hiding.

As she is about to leave Berlin heartbroken, Phoebe learns the truth and rushes back to the cabaret, where the Gestapo fugitive has been shot, and she and Pringle are reunited.

Jean Arthur came out of retirement to make *A Foreign Affair.* She was taking some college courses when the offer came to play Phoebe. She and Dietrich were opposite types on-screen and on the set, and Arthur believed that Wilder favored Dietrich.

"In the middle of shooting," Wilder remembered, "at midnight, my doorbell rang, and standing there was Jean Arthur, absolutely out of her mind, shaking, and behind her was her husband, Frank Ross.

"'What did you do with my close-up?' she says.

"'What close-up?'

"'You burned it. Marlene told you to burn my close-up. She doesn't want me to look better than she does.'

"This is typical, you know. It's a small Dr. Caligari's Cabinet that's going on there, and they are all inmates. If you don't stay a little apart, it is dangerous because maybe you can catch whatever it is. It is also better if they do not find out that their director is only a human being.

"I'll tell you the denouement: Many years later, my phone rings, and this voice out of ancient history speaks without identifying herself. I know it's Jean Arthur, because she had this very unique voice.

"Miss Arthur says she is calling from Carmel, California, and finally she saw *A Foreign Affair,* and she liked it. I guess she thought I'd sleep better that night."

Wilder told me that of all the actresses with whom he ever worked, there was none he admired more than Marlene Dietrich. "People talked about her legs. They were very good, and so was the rest of her, and her talent, too. But what was most wonderful was her intelligence. She had the courage of her convictions. She recognized the Nazis early and wouldn't accept their awards or invitations, and she got out, even though she wasn't Jewish.

"The crews adored her. She liked to find somebody with a cold, so she could make chicken soup for him. She loved to cook. She would put on the most terrible hair net. It would be enough to make anyone else look ugly, but not Marlene. She couldn't look ugly."

Douglas Fairbanks, Jr., who had a long affair with Dietrich, told me that she had a prejudice against women. "She was an angel with men, but she didn't trust women. She would say, 'They want to examine you for wrinkles.'"

On Liberation Day of World War II, Marlene Dietrich arrived in Paris by jeep with the U.S. troops. She was attired in a perfectly tailored U.S. officer's uniform, which she had paid for herself. When she appeared at the Hermès store on Faubourg St.-Honoré, large crowds gathered, and she signed autographs.

Her fountain pen ran dry and was refilled until they ran out of ink, everything still being in short supply. The store supplied her with pencils, which were sharpened for her until the stubs were too small to use. Then, she took a lipstick out of her purse and signed her name. That the recipients of the lipstick signatures were able to preserve their autographs is unlikely, but that they remembered the day is certain.

After the impromptu autographing session, she signed Hermès's guest book. Next to her signature was that of General George Patton.

A Foreign Affair was filmed at Paramount, with some exteriors shot in Berlin, December 1947 through February 1948. It was edited in only one week, and premiered in August, just one month after *The Emperor Waltz* was released. Meanwhile, Billy's private life had changed.

On June 30, he and Audrey Young drove to Linden, Nevada, with designer Charles Eames and his wife, Ray, and there, Audrey and Billy became the Wilders "for two dollars in three minutes," as Audrey remembered. She still wears the $17.95 wedding ring they bought along the way.

"I knew I wasn't the marrying kind," Wilder said. "I saw my parents' marriage, which did not work for either one. Compromise, disappointment. They didn't have anything to say to each other. Maybe they had already said everything they had to say and didn't have anything left by the time I was old enough to notice.

"I didn't want to marry young. Then, I met a German girl in Berlin who went to Paris with me, but didn't come to America. I asked her to marry me, but she wasn't ready to leave everything.

"I don't understand people making a mess of their romantic lives. I always had a lot of fun when I was a young man. I thought I was in love, but that was before I knew what love was.

"When I met my first wife, I thought maybe I found the perfect person. Maybe she was, and *I* wasn't. She was a very nice lady and very attractive. If she had been terrible, that would have been easier to understand. When the marriage didn't work, I was *more* certain that I wasn't meant for marriage.

"Then, Audrey proved me wrong. With everyone else, the beginnings were best. But Aud, she got better."

PART III

A Legend
in His
Own Time

—Sunset—
Boulevard

"The idea for *Sunset Boulevard* came out of our heads. It was an idea that Brackett and I had thought of long before we tackled it. We wanted to make a picture about a star who was passé.

"Originally, *Sunset* was going to be more of a comedy. I thought of using Mae West. It's impossible to believe that now."

George Cukor, who was a friend of Mae's, felt that it would have been a disaster for Wilder, *Sunset Boulevard,* "and Mae, too." Cukor saw too many resemblances between Mae West and Norma Desmond.

"Mae, for example," Cukor said, "lived with a man who, unknown to her, not only answered her fan mail for her, but also wrote the letters. She even had a pet chimpanzee, Boogie, whom she loved like a child. The part was too close to her own life, but she didn't recognize it.

"There's a lot of humor in *Sunset Boulevard*, but it's important that the characters never *feel* that they're being funny. It has to be subtle to be a great film, which it was."

George Cukor had arranged for me to meet Mae West for my book *The Ultimate Seduction.* I talked with her at her Hollywood Ravenswood apartment. When the subject got around to *Sunset Boulevard,* she said, "It was a part for an older woman. And you think I'd ever have let Bill Holden leave *me*? He'd've been too tired to get from my bed to the swimming pool."

Pola Negri, who was living in retirement in San Antonio, Texas, was considered for the part. Mary Pickford was approached. "A disaster," Wilder said. "Then, George Cukor saved us. There isn't a nicer man in Hollywood."

"There *is* only one actress for that part," Cukor told Wilder. "Gloria Swanson."

With mock seriousness, Cukor told me that he should have had a credit on *Sunset Boulevard.* "I would have been proud to have made the film myself, but no one, no one could have done it better than Billy Wilder, and I'm proud of the assist I gave.

"I gave Billy the idea of using Swanson. I knew she wanted to get back to movies, and she was good. People didn't give her credit for being as good as she was because we all knew Joe Kennedy was keeping her. It worked against her like it did against Marion Davies, who had Hearst. But they were both damn good actresses.

"When they asked Gloria to take a screen test, she almost threw it all away. But she called me, and I told her it's worth it. Nobody knows about those little humiliations we all go through."

At first, Wilder wasn't sure about Gloria Swanson. "With a few exceptions, I enjoyed working with my actors. I thought Gloria Swanson would be one of the exceptions, but she was so right for the part, I was ready to put up with anything to have her.

"Now, remember, here was a star who used to ride in a sedan chair from her dressing room to the set. When she married the Marquis de la Somebody and came by train to Hollywood, people were strewing rose petals on the tracks in front of her. She'd been one of the all-time great stars, but when she returned to do *Sunset,* she worked like a horse, a very professional horse, a Lipizzaner. Swanson got $150,000 to do *Sunset,* one of the great bargains in film history.

"You know, it's strange, when Swanson made *Sunset,* she was fifty years old, that's all. But for some reason, there was this abyss between the silent pictures and talkies, and some people thought she was seventy or eighty years old. I don't think she liked that part of it. None of us wants to seem older than we are. I told her it was because she was *too* good."

Cukor was also indirectly responsible for William Holden being in *Sunset Boulevard*. Wilder had wanted Montgomery Clift to play Joe Gillis. "Monty asked me what I thought," Cukor said, "and I told him, 'It's not right for you.' That was all, but I didn't need to say more. He understood and backed out. I wish I could have seen it that clearly for some of my own films."

Suddenly, Wilder needed a leading man, and he bet on a long shot. "There was a young actor who had been very good in *Golden Boy,* and some other things, so I gave him the script. I knew Barbara Stanwyck thought he was the greatest, but she wasn't exactly objective about him. It took Bill Holden two hours to read it, drive to my house, and say yes.

"Bill was very much underestimated as an actor. He was such a natural leading man, people didn't notice how good an actor he was. He was so good, they just thought he was the part.

"Bill was always testing himself in every way, always wanting to do better. He could please everyone but himself. He wasn't a happy person. He got everything in life but happiness. He was insecure, but he brushed off any reassurance. Sometimes he seemed happy, but he was such a good actor, you didn't know if maybe he was just playing a person who was happy. If he'd been really happy, he wouldn't have been a drunk, would he? I don't know why he needed the booze. He had it all.

"He'd never traveled. I suggested he go to Europe. He never stopped traveling after that. He liked Africa. He was always longing for something. I don't think he found it, or he wouldn't have died the way he did.

"He wouldn't let people help him. He had total pride. A man doesn't need help. When he was lying there dying, he was too embarrassed to use the phone to call for help. But he died too young."

William Holden did not like to give interviews. He was an actor only on-screen. "On the screen, he played sides of himself," according to Wilder. "Bill was a complex guy, a totally honorable friend. He was a genuine star. Every woman was in love with him."

Gloria Swanson said, "Bill Holden was a man I could have fallen in love with. He was perfection on- and off-screen."

William Holden told me, "Billy didn't give me a complete script, and he didn't tell me much about my character. I'm not a great actor, so I need all the help I can get, but Billy just said, 'Don't worry.' With another director, if you weren't worried, that would have made you worry, but not with him. He had a way of making you feel good."

For Max, the butler who had once been a famous silent director, there was only one ideal choice for Billy Wilder: Erich von Stroheim. An extraordinary bonus was derived from this casting, about which Wilder only later learned. Stroheim had directed Gloria Swanson, in her unfinished *Queen Kelly.*

"Von had a great visual imagination," Wilder said. "He knew how to get you with both knees. In *Foolish Wives,* there was such a potent, potent scene. A high officer in the French army is in a hotel elevator. He has a sort of cape on. An elegant lady, full of furs and jewelry, steps into the elevator and drops her stole. The officer makes no move to pick it up. The lady gives him a dirty look and picks it up herself. Later on, his cape opens a little bit, and she sees that he has no arms. He lost them in the war. It's not part of the plot or anything, but it's Stroheim."

Von Stroheim offered several suggestions of which a few became part of *Sunset Boulevard.* "Wouldn't it be nice," he told Wilder, "if people find out subsequently that I was Max von Mayerling, the director who directed Swanson? That I was her husband, and now I'm her valet, the butler? That I am the one who is writing the fan letters to make her feel better?"

"That was beautiful, a wonderful idea," Wilder said. "Stroheim didn't mind playing a butler so long as the character had once been somebody important."

A key suggestion by von Stroheim was to use footage from *Queen Kelly.* Wilder was able to get *Queen Kelly* from Paramount for $1,000.

"A few days later, Von came and said, 'I think we should dramatize that he still loves her. I wish to wash and press her panties.'

"I said, 'How big a scene do you see?' He wanted me to have him laundering Gloria Swanson's lingerie and finish with a shot of him ironing her panties, a close-up. The audience would have laughed."

There is a scene in *Queen Kelly* which may have given Stroheim this idea. Swanson, one of a group of convent girls, meets the prince. Her panties fall to the ground, and he laughs. She throws them at him, and he catches the panties, smiles, and pockets them.

Sunset Boulevard—*Charles Brackett, Gloria Swanson, and Billy Wilder backstage. Written on Swanson's dressing room star are the best wishes of cast and crew.* (Museum of Modern Art)

Sunset Boulevard—*William Holden and Wilder enjoying each other's company on stairway to Norma Desmond's bedroom.* (Museum of Modern Art)

"Then he said he would like Max to limp. He limped. Such a limp you've never seen!"

The first preview audience did laugh at the original opening scene of *Sunset Boulevard.* "I shot a prologue, a whole reel. There are two reels of stuff that I've shot in all these years that I didn't use, the prologue to *Sunset Boulevard* and the ending to *Double Indemnity.* The original prologue to *Sunset* was very well shot.

"A corpse is brought into the morgue downtown, and I shot it right there, too. It is the corpse of Mr. Holden. He is in the morgue, and there are about six other corpses under the sheets. Then, we sort of see through the sheets to the faces, and the people are telling each other the events leading to their deaths.

"There was a kid who drowned, and there was a guy who came from the Midwest and bought himself a little avocado ranch in the San Fernando Valley who had a heart attack, all very short. Then Mr. Holden started telling his story.

"We previewed the picture in Evanston, Illinois, right where Northwestern University is, and this is not like going to see *The Odd Couple,* where they know what to expect. It is very hard when an audience does not have any idea what mood to be in.

"Well, the picture starts, and they bring the corpse in on the slab, and they put a name tag on the toe of Holden, and it was the biggest laugh I ever heard in my life. It was the kind of laugh I dreamed of getting, but for a comedy. They just screamed with laughter. It was a disaster.

"I left the theater, and I was sitting on some stairs leading down to the toilet. A woman came out of the theater and was coming down the stairs. She had a big hat with a ribbon and a feather. I'll always remember that hat in my worst dreams. She looked right at me and said, 'Have you ever seen shit like this before in your life?' And that was before you were accustomed to hearing that kind of talk from women.

"So that whole sequence, it went. We just kept the notion of a man telling events which led to his demise."

With collaborators Brackett and journalist D. M. Marshman, Jr., a new opening was written. "I wanted a shot of Holden after he had been killed, with the camera looking up at him from the bottom of the pool."

The shot was made by positioning a mirror at the bottom of the pool and photographing from above the water the reflection of the dead body floating facedown. "We tested it with a rubber duck and it worked. The only trouble we had was Bill having to keep his mouth and eyes open facedown in the water for ten seconds. And the water was cold. But Bill was a great athlete, and he did it better than the rubber duck."

Joe Gillis (William Holden), an unsuccessful screenplay writer, escapes the finance men who are trying to reclaim his car by driving into the garage of an old mansion on Sunset Boulevard. Assumed to be someone else, he is led by Max the butler (Erich von Stroheim) to the mansion's owner, silent film star Norma Desmond (Gloria Swanson). Wishing to make a comeback, she hires him to rewrite her *Salome* script, then falls in love with him. Joe moves into the mansion as a kept man.

Secretly, Joe is collaborating with a pretty young screenplay editor, Betty Schaefer (Nancy Olson), on another idea. Though she is engaged to his best friend, Artie Green (Jack Webb), Betty falls in love with Joe. When Betty finds out about Norma, she asks him to leave Norma for her, but Joe can't unsettle her life, too. He decides, instead, to leave Hollywood. As he is leaving, a crazed Norma shoots him, and he falls into the swimming pool. Max, once a famous director and Norma's ex-husband, tearfully directs the newsreel cameramen in Norma's final scene. Norma believes she is back with Cecil B. DeMille making *Salome.*

Nancy Olson, who was a UCLA student in theater arts when she was cast as Betty Schaefer, talked with me about *Sunset Boulevard:*

"I think that Billy never considered me a great actress, but he needed a particular quality on the screen that was in juxtaposition to Norma Desmond. The picture wouldn't really work without Betty's character. Unless the audience cares, they will say, 'Let him go off with the old movie star!' But with Betty he's got another opportunity, another way out. So, the part is pivotal.

"The character of Betty Schaefer was loosely based on Billy's wife,

Audrey, who grew up in Hollywood. She was born in Los Angeles, and her mother worked in wardrobe at Paramount, the same as the mother of my character. But Audrey was much more sophisticated than Betty. She had a wonderful 'Audrey Style.' Audrey would have caught on to Joe Gillis much sooner, which would have ruined the story.

"I thought that when Joe Gillis invites Betty to the house on Sunset Boulevard and says, 'Take a look at what I really am,' that's when he becomes the hero. That is a valiant thing to do. The audience is saying, 'No! No! Go with her. Get out of there! Start over!' But he thinks about the movie business, about what he has done, about life, and he wants to save her.

"My feeling is that if Betty were at all smart, she would have understood that. I don't think she married Artie Green. After an experience like that and the shock of what has just happened, I think that if she really truly was a writer and loved this man and was willing to forgive him, then she went on. I hope she had a good life. I hope something really nice happened to her.

"You know, Bill Holden's career was in great trouble, his marriage was in trouble, he was drinking too much. He was in a difficult place in his life. He didn't really know where everything was going. There was a kind of desperation. Well, can you think of anybody *better* to play Joe Gillis?

"I was told that the cinematographer was one of the great ones. I remember he came over and turned my head. I guess he saw that I wondered if I had done something wrong. He was very nice and kind, and he explained so I would understand, 'I wanted your profile because you have a very good nose.'" John F. Seitz, a Hollywood cinematographer since 1917, received Oscar nominations for each of his four Billy Wilder pictures, including *Sunset Boulevard*.

"Edith Head designed my wedding gown," Olson said. "But in *Sunset Boulevard,* I wore all my own clothes! Whatever she put on me, she said, 'I liked you better when you walked in.' And it isn't that she liked my clothes that much, don't misunderstand, she liked it for Betty Schaefer. It's because I *was* the character.

"Billy said, 'Every character in *Sunset Boulevard* is an opportunist.' It seems to me what he is saying is that this picture is not only about opportunism, but about opportunism and the consequences of it.

"*Sunset Boulevard* was the talk of the entire studio. You know, in those days, they'd show rushes from everything that was being filmed all at once, in a block. Who would sit there through all that? Then, all of a sudden, click! There would be *Sunset Boulevard*. Take three! And people would be excited. People would be rushing to the rushes who never went before.

"I was on the set a lot even when I wasn't working. I was so *intrigued* with what was going on, that it was hard to stay away, plus there was Gloria Swanson's dedication to *Sunset Boulevard*. Billy and she had a rapport in working. I think, of all of us, she understood what the potential of this picture was. She absolutely believed in it.

"Billy was so excited about what was coming on that screen in the dailies that he couldn't wait to get back to work the next day.

"For me, Bill Holden is the glue. He holds it all together. I was just a fresh-faced, eager college girl. There were many young actresses, but you wouldn't necessarily believe that they were ambitious writers. I conveyed that I was educated, that I had a kind of natural intelligence that was straightforward.

"I was scared to death! The first scene was in the office, where you see me come in, and I'm talking about the script and what was wrong with it. I was well prepared, and Billy seemed so pleased. That helped me and made me relax, and I felt maybe I'll stay in this picture, and maybe I'm going to be part of what's going on here.

"As a director, Billy understood my vulnerability. He never suggested anything from a critical point of view, only, 'Why don't we try it like this?' It was always supportive, and I remember being very grateful about that. He said, 'Nancy, just do it.'

"Billy has the reputation for this laser beam wit, and your feeling is, that if the beam ever hits you, you'll be dead. I've spent a great many years dodging that beam, hoping that I will continue to live. What a waste of time! Because he hasn't ever meant to hurt anyone. He is actually a very kind and caring person.

"I got fan mail for years about *Sunset Boulevard*. A lot of the letters asked, 'Who did your nose?' I guess it was my mother."

In the film, Wilder called the producer Sheldrake, a name that recurred in several of his films, notably *The Apartment.* "I liked the name because it already had character. I got it from a basketball player at UCLA."

Sunset Boulevard was the last Wilder picture on which Hans Dreier worked. He had been the art director on every film Wilder directed since *The Major and the Minor. Front Page* art director Henry Bumstead remembered serving his apprenticeship at Paramount with Dreier:

"One of my first assignments was to decorate a man's room. I got a lot of stuff I thought he would have, including shelves full of books. After I'd finished, Hans Dreier, who was from UFA, came in and looked around. He saw all the books and said, 'Is this man an intellectual?' and walked out. I learned something important that day."

In one of the most memorable scenes in film history, Joe Gillis is forced to accept that he is a kept man and that others know it. Norma, despite Joe's protests, is intent on buying him a new wardrobe at a fashionable men's store. A salesman offers Joe the choice between a camel's hair coat and one of precious vicuña. Looking around to be sure Norma can't hear him, he speaks into Joe's ear, saying, "Well, as long as the lady's paying for it, why not take the vicuña?"

Holden's reaction points up actor Michael Brandon's perfect delivery of the line in the same way that Jack Lemmon's underlines Joe E. Brown's "Well, nobody's perfect" in *Some Like It Hot,* two of the great reactions in film history. The salesman's brilliant small part was expanded in the Andrew Lloyd Webber stage musical adaptation of *Sunset Boulevard.*

After Norma has attempted suicide, she draws Joe close in an embrace, and Joe appears resigned to his fate. The screen goes to black. I asked Wilder if they consummated their affair.

"In 1950, no," he answered. "In 2000, yes. It's not just what you can show that is different, it's what audiences are thinking that is different."

In the scene that follows, Joe, in his swimming trunks, emerges from the swimming pool and sits down beside Norma. She doesn't look at his bare chest, his legs, his nearly naked body. The implication is that she already knows it all.

Gloria Swanson told me that she had hoped she would win an Oscar for her portrayal of Norma Desmond, even "expected" it. "But that was not to be," she said, as we sipped our herb tea and ate sugar-free cookies.

At the time I spoke with her, in the late 1970s, she was interested in the sugar-free diet. Still attractive, slim, and energetic, she attributed her well-being to avoidance of sugar, except from raw fruit. I had brought cookies from my favorite French bakery, but she disapproved, saying, "Cookies like that are poison." I was hoping she would give them back to me, but she threw them away. From then on, whenever I visited her at her ground-floor apartment on New York's upper Fifth Avenue, I brought cookies from the health store.

She showed me stacks of scripts she had stored in her closet, piled under rows of glittering cocktail dresses and evening gowns. These scripts, she said, were only the best of the many she had received following *Sunset Boulevard.*

She was annoyed when fans said, "I loved you in *Sunset Boulevard.*" Her career of which she was so proud seemingly had been overlooked, the films that showed her youth and beauty, forgotten. "It was Wilder's fault. Everyone will remember me old, even though I was only forty-nine when I did *Sunset.*

"I *became* Norma Desmond. Every script I received, every one of them, offered me a chance to play an aging actress, usually one who was crazy. I'd had a very successful career for years but one film dominated. Sometimes I wasn't glad I did the film.

"After the film opened to such success, George Cukor said to me, 'You see, my girl, I was right.' Well, I don't know . . .

"When I die, I want to be remembered as Gloria Swanson, not as Norma Desmond.

"It began when I got a call from Paramount, a casting director. He found me in the hospital, recovering from having my appendix out. They wanted to pay all my expenses for a screen test. I told him I'd already had a screen test, years ago, and that he should take a look at the two dozen pictures I'd made for Paramount. I said, 'Why would they need to test me?' and I was very haughty about it.

"The truth of the matter was I didn't do well in screen tests. If my career had depended on a few minutes of a screen test, I probably would have been selling ribbons somewhere.

"The calls continued from Paramount. Then, the call came from Charles Brackett, the producer and writer, who had a wonderful reputation. He told me he was producing, and writing along with Billy Wilder, who would also be directing.

"I remembered Mr. Wilder from *Music in the Air.* He'd only been a writer, but he was one of those unforgettable characters you meet in your life. My tone changed. I didn't want to sound too anxious, but I couldn't think of Mr. Wilder without smiling. I was certain it was Mr. Wilder who had thought of me, and that changed everything. I said I was open to everything, except no screen test.

"Mr. Brackett tried flattery. Then, money. I was offered a first-class trip, a suite at the Beverly Hills, $50,000 a week if the screen test was satisfactory, and he said the role was 'a major one,' which I immediately interpreted as being a good supporting role. That $50,000 was what interested me. That was music to my ears, not music in the air.

"I took my mother with me, but first I called my dear, dear friend, George Cukor, and I told him that I was being asked to fly out to California to 'try out,' to do a screen test, and that I was insulted, outraged. I asked him if I was right to feel that way.

"George always knew the right thing to say, but you could always depend on him for the truth. He was totally honorable and the person in Hollywood I knew I could *always* trust. I didn't really know anything about the project, except that the producer was Mr. Brackett, the director was Billy Wilder, and they were writing the script. I remember George's words:

"'If they ask you to do ten screen tests, do them, or I'll personally shoot you.'

"George was always very direct, and there was no chance that you could miss his message. He said, 'These are the people who did *Lost Weekend,*' adding, 'and I suggested you to them.'

"I was happy, but nervous, like a very young girl with everything riding on her screen test.

"When I met with Mr. Wilder and Mr. Brackett, Mr. Wilder reminisced politely with me about *Music in the Air.* There wasn't really a lot to say about that film, except that it happened. Mr. Wilder had grown a little older. I suppose I had, too, but I preferred not to think about that. I noticed a great difference. Mr. Wilder had become very confident with success. Your Oscar is a companion wherever you go. He still had that fabulous energy, even more, maybe too much. Mr. Brackett was older, quiet, very refined.

"For my butler/ex-husband, they had Erich von Stroheim. I thought he was a good choice, but I had ill-feeling toward him from when he directed *Queen Kelly.* It was never finished because he was crazy.

"Mr. Brackett told me I had the part as far as they were concerned, that the screen test was only a formality, because the studio was requiring screen tests, and because they wanted a look at the actor they were considering for the part of Joe Gillis, Montgomery Clift. I'd never heard of him. I was pleased as punch when I heard the story seemed to be about my character!

"I was anxious to see a script, but they said there wasn't one—yet. They had not committed their ideas to paper, and weren't certain how the story would 'play out.' They hadn't decided the ultimate fate of my character, Norma.

"Mr. Brackett did explain to me a sort of basic idea of the story about an ex–movie queen who doesn't see herself as ex at all and wants to return to the screen in the same parts she played when she was young, because she doesn't recognize the passage of time. She meets a younger man who is short of money and opportunity, and she tries to own him. There was to be a murder, and I asked, 'Am I murdered or do I do the murdering?'

"Mr. Wilder said, 'We don't know yet.'

"He gave me a few pages to study for the screen test, and I thought it might be all they had.

"Well, we did the screen test, and I wasn't even very nervous. I did the test with a young man who was not Montgomery Clift.

"Mr. Brackett and Mr. Wilder were tremendously enthusiastic about my performance, and they let everyone know it. They made me feel very good.

"I signed my contract and rented a house for myself and my mother.

"I asked about Mr. Clift and was told he'd changed his mind because he didn't think the part was appropriate for his image.

"I did publicity pictures, and for one, I posed with Adolph Zukor, who had become chairman emeritus of Paramount. He embraced me. He was the first person to mention the title of the film, which he said everyone was enthusiastic about—*Sunset Boulevard*.

"I thought about my part, and how close it was to myself. It was a little frightening. I was not one of those actresses who like to dredge up personal experiences. I wanted to act a part, not be myself. That was the fun of acting. I could be other people. I could be myself at home.

"Then, they brought in someone named William Holden.

"I'd been worried about looking young enough, so I was surprised when Mr. Brackett said, 'I hope you don't mind. We have to age you a little.' I thought he was just being kind, but he explained that the story was about an actress who was supposed to be fifty, and 'the young writer you are involved with is to be played by William Holden, who is playing twenty-five and is really thirty-one. He is worried you will look too young.'

"I said, 'Why don't you use "just a little makeup" to make *him* look younger?'

"I was exactly fifty by then and didn't see any reason to look older.

"They had rented a marvelous '20s mansion for my Norma character. It didn't matter that it wasn't on Sunset Boulevard. That is what films are all about: magic and illusion."

The mansion was at Wilshire and Irving Boulevards, had been built in 1924 and was torn down in 1957. For the film, a swimming pool had to be put in.

"The strain between Erich and me had passed, if not completely. Mr. Wilder wanted to use a scene from *Queen Kelly,* when Norma shows her old film to Joe. I'd had such great hopes for *Queen Kelly*. This wasn't what I'd had in mind for it. On the other hand, I was struck by how wonderful the film was. If only I'd had Mr. Wilder as my director for *Queen Kelly,* how different it all could have been!

"Erich was full of ideas, mostly for making your film go over budget. In *Sunset Boulevard* he was only an actor, and Mr. Wilder understood how to listen to what Erich said, take something, and move on.

"I remember Erich's embarrassment when he was supposed to drive me as my chauffeur. He always acted as though there wasn't anything he couldn't do. Then, we had to be pulled by ropes, because he didn't know how to drive!

"Each day, we would receive more script. It was clear to all of us, it was brilliant. All of us believed we were making a wonderful film. Mr. Wilder never took his eye off the ball, but he was able to keep a lighthearted quality on the set.

"Edith Head was important in helping me find my character. She was a genius, and I loved working with her. She was small, as I am, and she understood the special needs of the small woman who needed to be big on the screen. The hat with the single white feather was my idea. It was important that the clothes I wore would seem a little out of date, as was Norma." (Head had been a costume assistant on *Music in the Air*.)

"Mr. Wilder asked me to contribute some of my own possessions for the house. I found wonderful stills of myself."

Miss Swanson poured herb tea from a Georgian silver pot. The sugar-free cookies were served on a hand-painted Tiffany plate. She said, "I'm going to tell you something funny.

"I was given a bit by Mr. Wilder, a Chaplin imitation. I'd done something like that in *Manhandled* in 1924. He had the wardrobe department bring out fifty bowlers so I could choose one. That was really funny, but then, the next day, he topped himself. I went on to the set with the bowler I had selected, and the crew and Billy Wilder were wearing the other forty-nine.

"Two days later, we did the scene of Norma and Max burying Norma's pet monkey. Mr. Wilder directed me to lift the shawl covering the monkey. I did, and the monkey was also wearing a bowler."

Wilder had played Richard Strauss's "Dance of the Seven Veils" as inspiration while writing *Sunset Boulevard* for the film, but for the actual score, he turned to Franz Waxman. "In Berlin," Wilder said, "I was his 'beard' when he wanted to go somewhere with his girlfriend. We worked together in Berlin and also in Paris, on *Mauvaise Graine*.

Eighteen years later, he gave me exactly what I wanted, and we worked on other pictures together until he died in 1967. I miss him."

John F. Seitz, the cinematographer, told British film historian Kevin Brownlow that Wilder and Brackett had wanted to do *The Loved One,* but couldn't obtain the rights. Seitz felt that the Evelyn Waugh novel influenced *Sunset Boulevard.*

"I shot *Sunset Boulevard* in about sixty days," Wilder said. "If only every picture could have gone so smoothly! I wanted Swanson, I got her. I wanted von Stroheim, I got him. I wanted DeMille, I got him. I wanted *Queen Kelly,* I got it. I wanted Paramount, I got it. Even when I didn't get the casting I wanted, it turned out to be right.

"I didn't know that *Sunset Boulevard* was going to be such a magnum opus when I was doing it. It worked. The films everybody scorns—you get up at five o'clock in the morning just the same."

In spite of some harsh criticism in Hollywood, *Sunset Boulevard* was nominated for eleven Oscars, of which it won three; for best story and screenplay, best art direction, and best score.

Von Stroheim was unhappy about his nomination, not that he didn't win, but that he was nominated as a supporting player. The nomination brought him many offers—to play butlers. Disgusted, he and his companion, Denise Vernac, went back to France, where they lived in a chalet just outside of Paris. There, he wrote and prepared projects that never happened, and acted in French films, until he died in 1958.

Wilder received no royalties from the Broadway musical play based on *Sunset Boulevard,* because the property belonged to the studio. Billy, Audrey, Nancy Olson Livingston and her husband, Alan, whom she had married after her divorce from Alan Jay Lerner, attended the openings in London, New York, and elsewhere as honored guests.

Afterward, Wilder said, "It'll make a good movie."

—Ace in the Hole—

"For a long time, when people asked, 'Which is your favorite film?' I answered, '*Ace in the Hole.*' I like that picture. I am proud of it. It's about the price of people's souls. It was not successful, so maybe I thought I had to like it more, because no one else did. Among my pictures, I think it was the runt of the litter."

Ace in the Hole would be the first film Billy Wilder produced and directed after his separation from Brackett. Lenore Hornblow, who knew both Wilder and Brackett socially, said that there never was any apparent animosity between them. She remembered several years after *Sunset Boulevard* having lunch with Brackett when Wilder entered the restaurant alone. "Charlie invited Billy to join us, and the two reminisced, laughed, and ate a lot. People don't laugh like that or eat so much unless they're happy to be together."

Wilder did not like to talk about his relationship with Brackett, usually dismissing the subject of their separation with, "The sparks just weren't flying anymore." There was more to it, however.

"The success of *Sunset* may have been part of our problem," Wilder said. "Where do you go from there? I had some ideas he didn't like, and he had some I didn't like.

"We had an argument, I don't remember about what. But we were sitting in the car, and it got louder and louder. It got pretty loud. We both got out of the car angry. Then I was working with somebody else, and we just never got back together again. But we stayed friends."

Nancy Olson observed a difference between the two men that she later came to think might have mattered:

"Billy was the European who had been through the extraordinary pre–Second World War Europe. It's unbelievable, that kind of experience, something Charlie and I and a lot of us had only an intellectual understanding of. We were totally protected Americans.

"Charlie Brackett was playful with me. He had a great sense of humor, different from Billy, but it was very much there. But it was more the New Yorker kind of humor. I remember he was always on the set with Billy. They got along very well and were totally unified on the set."

Ace in the Hole was the kind of theme Wilder wanted to explore, and Brackett did not. "We did not agree on much, " Wilder said, "but what we agreed on was more important than the long list of what we did not agree on. You have to know what you can argue about, safe argument territory. It's a question of something sacred. I wanted to approach different themes, to question things. I didn't quite have a hold on what I wanted to do, but I wanted to explore. We just couldn't agree on what these themes should be."

Brackett continued on in Hollywood, both as writer and producer, winning an Academy Award in 1953 for the story and screenplay for *Titanic,* which he coauthored with Walter Reisch and Richard Breen. In 1958, he was awarded an honorary Oscar for his service to the Acadamy of Motion Picture Arts and Sciences. He died in 1969.

———◄○►———

Before *Ace in the Hole,* Wilder had considered doing a comedy about a Mafia don being investigated by a Senate committee or a comedy featuring Charles Laughton. *Ace in the Hole* was inspired by a 1925 news story about a man who had been trapped in a cave. As the news got out, crowds gathered in a carnival-like atmosphere. The Lindbergh kidnapping trial, and a three-year-old girl trapped in a well also provided some story material. "Tragedies were exploited by the media and commercial interests, and the public participated too eagerly," Wilder said.

"*Ace in the Hole* was a failure here, but a success in Europe. I think my mistake was in offering the American public a shot of vinegar when they thought they were going to get a nice cocktail. It was a vinegar cocktail. The reviewers said I was too cynical, that no newspaperman would really act that way.

"I was feeling very downhearted, walking down Wilshire Boulevard when, right in front of me, somebody got hit by a car. A camera-

Billy and Audrey en route from a European trip on the Liberté *in 1951.* (Museum of Modern Art)

Ace in the Hole—*Kirk Douglas, a "suspenders and belt man," listens to William Holden, who isn't one, at Paramount between takes.* (Museum of Modern Art)

man comes running up out of nowhere. I said, 'We've got to help him.' The cameraman said, 'You help him. I've gotta get my picture in.' And off the guy went. Maybe I wasn't cynical enough when I did *Ace in the Hole.*

"Some people thought the Kirk Douglas character, Tatum, comes on too strong. One of my writers suggested we pick him up after he's been in Albuquerque a while and still hasn't found the story that will get him back to New York. I thought we could get the backstory out of the way early while showing his character, maybe with a little humor, by having him a tough guy who talks his way into a job on a newspaper that needs some new life.

"The head of Paramount did not like the title, *Ace in the Hole.* He wanted *The Big Carnival,* so that title was substituted at the last minute. They didn't ask me. When it didn't go well, they changed it back to *Ace in the Hole,* but it was too late. Pictures are like bridge. Once you've made your bid, you can't change it."

For *Ace in the Hole,* Wilder found new writing collaborators, Walter Newman, a young radio writer, and Lesser Samuels, a playwright. They were nominated together for the best original story and screenplay Academy Award, but Alan Jay Lerner won that year for *An American in Paris.* Accepting for him was his wife, Nancy Olson, who had been nominated for an Oscar herself the year before for her role in *Sunset Boulevard.* Lerner was in New York with his dying father.

Ex–New York reporter Charles Tatum (Kirk Douglas) takes a job on an Albuquerque newspaper in hopes that a sensational story will return him to the big time. When a man is trapped in an Indian cave, Tatum conspires with an unscrupulous politician to keep him there until the story can build to national proportions, which it does. When the man dies before being rescued, Tatum is revolted by the carnival-like atmosphere he has inspired, and disgusted by the man's faithless, hard-hearted wife (Jan Sterling). He is stabbed by the woman when he tries to choke her, and collapses at the newspaper office, dying with his story.

Kirk Douglas is one of Billy Wilder's "suspenders and belt" men. When Tatum notices that the publisher is wearing both, he says:

"I've lied to men who wear belts. I've lied to people who wear suspenders. But I'd never be so stupid as to lie to a man who wears both belt and suspenders."

Later, in a striking transition, Tatum walks into the camera, then walks out, dressed quite differently. His eastern suit is gone and he is wearing suspenders *and* a belt, indicating that he has been there much longer than he expected to be.

One of Wilder's best known, most characteristic lines is spoken by Jan Sterling when Kirk Douglas suggests it would be better for his story if she went to church to pray for her husband. She says, "I never go to church. Kneeling bags my nylons."

"It was Audrey's line," Wilder said proudly. "How would *I* know a thing like that?"

"I was really happy about being in a Billy Wilder picture," Kirk Douglas told me, "but it didn't go smoothly. I nearly killed Jan Sterling in that scene where I was choking her. I got too much into my part.

"I asked her why didn't you tell me I really was choking you, and she said it was because she couldn't speak because I nearly killed her. You can see it in the film. I'm glad I didn't hurt her, but she never forgave me. I felt I had to give her reason to stab me, and I guess I did.

"At the time, it struck me that my character was too unlikable. I'm not a writer, so I didn't know just how to do it; but I told Billy I thought the character needed something to get him more audience sympathy. He didn't see it my way, so I did the best I could."

"*Ace in the Hole* was too early," Wilder thought. "Somebody said, 'Showmanship is to know what the audience wants before the audience knows what it wants.' You can miscalculate.

"I thought producing would give me more control, but it actually gave me *less* control. Most of the time, I was too busy, except when there was nothing to do but wait. There was a lot of frustration, like weather. The producer can't produce the right weather.

"There was no tension with my collaborators. I couldn't get into an argument with them if I hit them over the head with a dangling participle. They tried too hard to be agreeable. Only Kirk Douglas disagreed about some stuff about his character, but he disagreed very politely. Maybe he should have been less polite."

Ace in the Hole was released in May 1951. The reviews were generally bad, and audiences stayed away. The picture won a best foreign film award at the Venice Film Festival, and in later years enjoyed a certain appreciation. It's a favorite of Woody Allen's.

Wilder said, "Maybe it'll get a hit on the fourth strike."

—Stalag 17—

On a trip to New York, Wilder saw a play about a World War II German prisoner-of-war camp. It was directed by José Ferrer and written by two former POWs, Donald Bevan and Edmund Trzcinski. Wilder persuaded Paramount that *Stalag 17* should be his next film.

He had been working on an idea with Norman Krasna about Laurel and Hardy type characters, homeless movie extras who slept in the Os of the HOLLYWOOD sign. "The Krasna thing just didn't jell," Wilder said. "It was going to take a long time, and you had to invest, or gamble time without knowing if your soufflé would rise or be scrambled eggs. *Stalag,* being a successful play, I could do it right away."

Charlton Heston and Kirk Douglas were considered for the J. J. Sefton character, but Wilder chose his friend William Holden. "Do you know that the only time I was Billy's first choice," Holden told me, "was in 1939 when he wanted me to play Henry Aldrich? Fortunately, Missy [Barbara Stanwyck] wanted me to be Golden Boy."

Coauthor Trzcinski, who played Triz in the film, was disturbed by changes Wilder and Edwin Blum were making to his play. "The writer didn't recognize the Holden character anymore," Wilder admitted, "with all his black market activities and betting on rats racing. As I remember it, I think he stopped speaking to me. If I'd been him, I would have stopped, too.

"Bill Holden pleaded with me to write him a line that would show his character was really anti-Nazi, but this guy was a completely unsentimental opportunist. Otherwise, he couldn't have been so successful at those rackets."

"A favorite gag of mine, which I was proud of, is when Otto Preminger's colonel makes his phone call to Berlin. That's a good joke, but I don't know how many people got it.

"The colonel wants to report to Berlin that an American officer suspected of espionage has been captured. He has his orderly put his boots on for the phone call. During the call, he clicks his heels for his superiors. After the call, he has the orderly take off the boots.

"Preminger missed a lot of lines, but he never missed a jar of caviar. He was a lot of fun to be with, and a fine director, but as an actor, he forgot lines. When I hired him, I told him every time he got his lines wrong, he owed me a jar of caviar.

"He may not have been the greatest actor, especially when it came to getting his lines right, but he was the world champion payer of debts. He missed a lot of lines, but he never missed sending a jar of caviar.

"He sent only the very best caviar. Now, *that* he did not have to do."

Preminger told me, "Billy was a stickler for every word, because they were *his* words. I did not direct the way he did. As a director, even though he came from Vienna, Billy directed like a Prussian officer. His manner was easygoing, and he was very good company and a fine director, but what he wanted with his words was rigid, absolutely rigid.

"I was happy to send him the caviar and the expense I didn't mind, but the real price I paid was Billy directed me too well, and many people thought I was the part I played, a Nazi. I am a Jew who had to run from Hitler." Not only was Preminger a Jewish refugee from Austria, but, like Wilder, he lost members of his family in the extermination camps.

"Once I became sick and collapsed on the sidewalk. Someone standing there loosened my tie and took it off. That's all I remember.

"At the hospital, they gave me my possessions. My favorite tie wasn't there. I thought, 'I'll never see that tie again.' Then, the next day, it arrived at my office in the mail with a note from the man who had taken it off when I was lying on the sidewalk. The note said, 'I thought you were great in *Stalag 17*. Thank you.' Imagine. *He* thanked *me*."

> When two escaping prisoners are killed, the barracks black marketeer, J. J. Sefton (William Holden), is suspected of being a German informer. These suspicions are reinforced when a new prisoner, Lieutenant Dunbar (Don Taylor), is taken away by the Germans after he has confided to his fellow Americans that he blew up a German munitions train. Sefton is beaten by the other prisoners.
>
> Sefton discovers the real informer, but waits to reveal his identity until he can help Dunbar escape from solitary confinement. Using the informer, Sergeant Price (Peter Graves), to create a diversion fatal to Price, Sefton then escapes with Dunbar.

"I loved the character of Holden in *Stalag*," Wilder said. "I missed him when he left at the end of the picture. When I wrote his last line, I missed him. People ask me, do I think he made it and got away? Yes."

Exteriors for *Stalag 17* were shot mainly at the Snow Ranch in Calabasas, California, interiors at Paramount. It was filmed during February and March 1952, and released in July 1953. The film was popular with audiences, critically acclaimed, and successful at the box office. Wilder was a Hollywood hero again. Wiped out were the box office deficits of *Ace in the Hole*. The U.S. gross of over $10 million covered the losses of the previous film, and audiences didn't remember the failure of *Ace in the Hole,* under that title or even its alias of *The Big Carnival,* because too few people had seen it. In Europe, too, *Stalag 17* was successful.

Wilder gave roles in the film to several former prisoners of war. These and some other POWs were invited to the Hollywood premiere and the supper party afterward. The picture was given for screenings and benefits to veterans groups, the American Legion, and American ex-prisoners-of-war organizations.

Stalag 17 was widely perceived and widely promoted as a comedy, being termed at one point by Paramount's promotion department as "a star-spangled laugh-loaded salute to our POW heroes," despite its treatment of torture, death, and war.

At the Academy Awards, Wilder was nominated as best director. He lost to his friend from German film days, *People on Sunday's* young assistant cameraman, Fred Zinnemann, who received an Oscar for *From Here to Eternity*. The best actor Oscar, however, went to a happy William Holden, who, having been told the Oscar show was running late as it always did, said simply, "Thank you, thank you," and left the stage.

—Sabrina—

 Wilder never hesitated to change a play, even one that had been successful, but in the case of *Sabrina,* the play opened while they were still writing the screenplay.

"A play for the theater and a picture for the screen are two very different things," Wilder said. "The biggest thing is you try out a play and change it as you are doing it, even after an audience sees it. It is never the same twice, anyway. With a picture all you can change is the audience. A picture will haunt you forever, even after you have become a ghost yourself."

Sabrina was plagued with difficulties. Problems started with the script, based on Samuel Taylor's play, *Sabrina Fair.* The play was about to open on Broadway with Margaret Sullavan as Sabrina Fairchild and Joseph Cotten as Linus Larrabee. Wilder wished to have Audrey Hepburn and Cary Grant in those parts, and began rewriting the dialogue with Taylor to fit their screen personalities. After they began revising, the play opened successfully, and Taylor became apprehensive about Wilder's changes.

After several arguments, Taylor quit and Wilder found another collaborator in Ernest Lehman, early in his remarkable Hollywood career. Lehman told me, "Every man working on *Sabrina* instantly fell in love with Audrey Hepburn, from the grips to Billy Wilder, and I was no exception.

"Billy wanted Audrey's character to have sex with Bogart while she's still involved with Holden," Lehman said. "I thought this went against Audrey's image, and it might have suggested she'd had an affair with the old baron in Paris. She does, after all, come back pretty richly dressed. Even her expensive French poodle has a jeweled necklace. So, I just couldn't let Billy make that mistake. We almost split up over it."

Years later, Wilder did not remember this discussion about the seduction of Audrey Hepburn as anything more than the normal "tugging on two ends of a taut rope," which is what Wilder said happens in a good collaboration.

"As I remember it, we pretty much convinced each other Audrey is an enigmatic mix of sophistication and innocence, and a lady in the best sense of the word. 'Lady' is a word we don't use so much anymore as what is admired in a woman. I haven't seen the picture in years, but now I agree that Sabrina would not be seduced as long as there was a chance she was going to choose David [Larrabee]."

Rewriting was necessary when Cary Grant said no and Humphrey Bogart said yes. Wilder played down the problems he is said to have had with Bogart.

"Too much is made of the idea that Bogart and I did not get along during *Sabrina*. Very early, Bogart got the idea that I liked Bill Holden more. Well, yes, I did. Bill Holden was one of my favorite people in the whole world.

"Bogart thought I loved dear, sweet, beautiful Audrey. Who could not? Audrey Hepburn was a unique creation. God kissed her on the cheek.

"Mr. Bogart was so unpleasant because he believed that we were a clique of three against him. He was both right and wrong. You might say Bill and Audrey and I had fun together, and you can't beat a bond of fun. And he was on the outside. Well, making a movie doesn't mean you get married. Bogart and I didn't hit it off. So what?

"Bogart was a needler. Bill and he didn't get along. But we worked it out and made a good picture. That's what's important, what the audience sees.

"In pictures, Bogart played the hero, which he wasn't. But when he

Sabrina—"You did not have to direct Audrey Hepburn, just give her a good lead," Wilder said of his leading lady. (Museum of Modern Art)

knew he was dying of cancer, he was the bravest person I ever knew. I went to visit him. Then he was the hero he played in all those pictures, and more."

Wilder said that he didn't notice the romance between Hepburn and Holden. "People on the set told me later that Bill and Audrey were having an affair, and everybody knew. Well, not *everybody!*

"*I* didn't know. I still don't know.

"I was with Bill and Audrey every day. They were both my friends. They didn't report anything to me. They were both wonderful people. If anything happened between them, I hope they found some happiness. They'd both had their share of unhappiness. They had great careers, but they weren't happy in their personal lives. Audrey had a very hard time in Holland during the occupation in World War II. In the picture, David didn't get Sabrina, and in real life, Bill didn't get Audrey.

"I miss them very much. I never expected to be missing *them.* They should have been missing me. It was all out of turn."

In her two films for Wilder, Audrey Hepburn played a fairy-tale princess playing a woman of the world, a variation of the Cinderella story.

"There could be no more perfect Cinderella than dear Audrey. She was adorable. She did everything with ease and grace. You did not have to direct Audrey Hepburn, just give her a good lead.

"Audrey was very thin. On camera, she looked fatter than she was. Sometimes she disappeared." Wilder shot more close-ups of her than were customary for him. He knew "the camera loved her."

Audrey Hepburn more than respected Billy Wilder. "I was in total awe of him," she told me. "I only wanted to please him. It seems I did.

"He is a darling, a great director and a gentleman. He is also a very good dancer."

Wilder agreed with her appraisal of his dancing. "I think of myself as pretty good. I have a natural sense of rhythm, and I enjoy dancing. I was going to show Audrey how Sabrina should dance in a scene, but she was a great dancer, much better than me. Her feet hardly touched the ground. She was floating. I didn't have to guide her. I forgot the camera, the set, I was transported to the ball."

Coincidentally, two of the favorite women in Wilder's life were named Audrey. "It was good in case I talked in my sleep."

The chauffeur's daughter, Sabrina Fairchild (Audrey Hepburn), has always been in love with one of the lords of the Larrabee manor, David (William Holden), but the wealthy playboy doesn't notice her until she returns from cooking school in Paris a beautiful, sophisticated young lady. Then, he is so smitten that his arranged marriage with a sugarcane heiress (Martha Hyer) is threatened, as is a Larrabee Corporation business venture dependent on sugar.

David's older brother, Linus (Humphrey Bogart), a bachelor married to the family business, attempts to save the merger by wooing Sabrina away from David, which he does so successfully *he* falls in love with her. David, sensing that the two have found true love, goes through with the family and corporate merger, and Linus takes Sabrina to Paris.

The next-to-last scene, in which David prevents Linus from abandoning the merger and losing Sabrina, had to be shot before an earlier scene, one which justified it, had been written. William Holden was leaving for the Pacific to shoot *The Bridges at Toko-Ri,* so all of his work in *Sabrina* had to be completed.

Audrey Hepburn's first appearance, wide-eyed in the tree with a full moon over her shoulder, is reminiscent of Puck in *A Midsummer Night's Dream.* It emphasizes her youth and innocence, as well as her Cinderella quality. The simple Edith Head dress is unnoticeable beside the contrasting Givenchy haute couture, but it establishes Sabrina's character and makes possible her outward change. A major transformation in her appearance is her French coiffure, after the French baron (Marcel Dalio) at the cooking school tells her that a ponytail is more appropriate for a horse.

Although brought up at the manor, Sabrina has viewed it only from the servants' quarters. She never feels social distinctions, though her father (John Williams) keeps telling her, "Don't reach for the moon, child." He compares life to riding in a limousine: "There's a front seat and a back seat, and a window in between." When she argues that the world has changed, he cautions her, "Nobody poor was ever called democratic for marrying somebody rich."

The opening "Once-upon-a-time" narration, spoken by Audrey Hepburn as herself rather than as Sabrina, sets the fairy-tale mood of the story. The Larrabee family is introduced in her voice-over as they pose for a family portrait. At the end of the fairy tale, Sabrina may be the lady of the manor and part of that portrait.

Sabrina has always liked older men—her father, the baron, Linus, even David. David's approach to life, however, is adolescent, although at the end it appears he might assume more responsibility in the company. In her way, Sabrina is adolescent, too, until she meets Linus. "I hadn't grown up," she realizes. "I just got a new hairdo."

Sabrina returns from Paris wearing Givenchy, Hepburn's own idea, though Edith Head won an Oscar for the costumes. On a visit to Paris, Audrey Hepburn had found her style in the clothes of Hubert de Givenchy, and they became lifelong friends.

Sabrina was filmed on location in Glen Cove, Long Island, in Manhattan, and at Paramount in Hollywood, September through November 1953, and was released in October 1954.

Wilder, who is knowledgeable about French cuisine, had one regret. He admitted that when they wrote *Sabrina* he didn't notice that Sabrina probably wouldn't be learning how to make vichyssoise soup at a Parisian cooking school. Vichyssoise was created in America. "I don't remember who wrote that line, but I should have caught it, especially if I wrote it."

Among those who admired *Sabrina* was Sidney Sheldon, who called it "an absolutely perfect film." Sydney Pollack admired the film so much that he remade *Sabrina* in 1995, with Julia Ormond as Sabrina, Harrison Ford as Linus, and Greg Kinnear as David.

—The Seven—
Year Itch

"Marilyn Monroe is what most people remember about *The Seven Year Itch*," Billy Wilder said. "She was not the kind of girl you would bring home to your wife.

"Marilyn told me right away that she didn't ever wear a brassiere. She needn't have mentioned it. I had no personal or professional objection.

"I would get very angry at her. For *The Seven Year Itch,* she was perfectly un-punctual. She never came on time once. Instead of studying with Lee Strasberg, she should have studied in Switzerland at Patek Philippe.

"She thought the way she looked entitled her to special privileges. It was true. But it didn't work with me, because I looked at her not as a man, but as her director. Well, most of the time. Anyway, she wasn't my type. She was more provoking than provocative. For me, personally, Audrey Hepburn was the embodiment of everything perfect in a woman. And she was punctual.

"When I look back over the years, I am not angry at Marilyn. She was someone you could get angry at, but not someone you could *stay* angry at. But I know if I were making a picture today and she was in it because I lost my mind and cast her, and she came late, I would get just as angry as before. Angrier. She wouldn't know her lines. Terrible. Then, on the thirtieth take, she would say it like no one else ever could.

"Working with her was like being a dentist, you know, pulling those lines out like teeth, except the dentist felt the pain. But no matter how much you suffered with Miss Monroe, she was totally natural on the screen, and that's what survived. She glowed."

This was Marilyn Monroe's twenty-fifth film, including two early uncredited appearances. One of her earliest pictures was *Love Happy,* the last Marx Brothers feature. Groucho told me that he personally selected her. "Very personally," he leered.

"They showed me a few girls, and asked me, 'Which one do you like best?' I said, 'Are you kidding?'"

Wilder considered Gary Cooper, William Holden, or James Stewart for the male lead in *The Seven Year Itch,* but after he saw the screen test of a young Walter Matthau, he believed he had the actor he wanted to play Richard Sherman, the summer bachelor of the Broadway hit. Playwright George Axelrod agreed, but 20th Century head Darryl F. Zanuck did not, and Tom Ewell, who originated the part opposite Vanessa Brown, was chosen.

Wilder saw the play before its Broadway opening and called Axelrod. The playwright was impressed that the great director himself was on the phone rather than an agent.

The Seven Year Itch was considered impossible to film because the Motion Picture Code did not accept adultery as a subject for humor. Wilder got around that by having adultery never occur in the film. Axelrod, who didn't wish to confuse or to compete for audiences, had stipulated in his contract that the film would not be released until the play's run had ended; but Zanuck paid him $175,000 in order to open earlier.

"Axelrod couldn't believe what was happening to his play," Wilder said. "On Broadway, the guy has an affair with the girl upstairs, but in the picture, he only gets to imagine how it would be to go to bed with Marilyn Monroe. And just the *idea* of going to bed with her has to terrify him, or it won't get past the censors."

Wilder's adaptation of George Axelrod's play paid homage to David Lean's *Brief Encounter,* which also featured the Rachmaninoff Second Piano Concerto. The summer bachelor story, a popular theme in French, Italian, and Spanish movies, was changed from an adulterous episode in a married man's life to a bittersweet fantasy of infidelity taking place in his imagination.

"The difference between a good film and one that is less than what it might have been in this case was a hairpin. I had this idea. The morning after, Tom Ewell's maid finds a hairpin in the bed. So, we don't *see* anything, but we *know* everything. That's how Lubitsch would have done it. But they wouldn't allow it. A picture that got down to one subtle hairpin, and we had to cut it out."

The Seven Year Itch is a film about adulterated adultery. "Everything has to be in the guy's imagination. That means it has to be in the audience's."

When editor Richard Sherman (Tom Ewell) becomes a summer bachelor, he imagines all of the mischief he can get into, and resents that his wife isn't at all worried. Then, the girl upstairs (Marilyn Monroe) makes herself available, but he can't go through with a real seduction. Meanwhile, after he imagines his wife (Evelyn Keyes) having an affair with an old flame (Sonny Tufts), he rushes to visit her.

The famous scene with Monroe standing over the subway grating proved unsatisfactory after it had been shot on location, and it had to be reshot at 20th Century Fox in Hollywood, requiring forty more takes. In New York, Marilyn Monroe's skirt had blown up over her head, and the crowd noise was too loud.

"I asked the crowds to be quiet," Wilder said. "Nothing. Just the same noise. Then, Marilyn Monroe put a finger to her lips. Absolute silence."

In her New York dressing room, before she went out to do her scene, Monroe checked her panties and realized that in a certain light, it was possible to see through them, so she put on a second pair. Wilder called this a "two-panty shot."

In the bright glare of the arc lights, however, it was still possible to see through her panties. These New York shots were not used in the film. "This footage immediately disappeared," Wilder said, "but one day, I'm sure some film scholar will dig it up.

"When we shot it on Lexington Avenue in New York, the wind was hot on the grille, and ten thousand people were waiting for Marilyn, and watching. Unfortunately, one of them was her husband, Joe DiMaggio, and he didn't like what he saw or what everyone else was seeing." (Others present made estimates of closer to only two thousand people.)

"I would've been upset if *I* had been her husband, and there were also a lot of comments being called out. This *was* New York. We did take after take after take after take.

"I heard later it was what ruined the marriage. I think there had to be more wrong with their marriage for them to get a divorce. I think DiMaggio had ambivalent feelings. He wanted to marry Marilyn Monroe, and then he didn't like her being Marilyn Monroe, except for him. I don't know if he was jealous of other men looking up her skirt or jealous of her getting more attention than he did. Probably both."

Monroe's marriage to Joe DiMaggio ended during the shooting of the film, which lasted from September through November 1954.

Millions of people had already seen more of Marilyn than her bare legs before DiMaggio married her. She was cover girl and centerfold nude of the first issue of *Playboy*. "All I had on was the radio," she said proudly. The famous nude calendar photo of Marilyn was on a single page in the center of the magazine in color. This was the predecessor of the *Playboy* Gatefold Girl. Hugh Hefner gave her credit for contributing to the instant success of the magazine. In advertising *The Seven Year Itch,* the famous photograph of Monroe with her skirt blowing up was used for a fifty-two-foot-high billboard cutout that towered four stories over Times Square.

DiMaggio escorted his ex-wife to the film's premiere on June 1, 1955. It happened to be her twenty-ninth birthday. She was late for both the premiere and her birthday party.

Marilyn Monroe retained a warm feeling toward Joe DiMaggio which, though they were married only nine months, endured until her death.

Shortly after the divorce, she went to New York to study with Lee Strasberg. One day, she left the Actors Studio with publicist and friend John Springer to go to lunch at Gallagher's restaurant. "There was a crowd waiting outside the Actors Studio when we left," Springer said, "and it wasn't me they were waiting for. They were screaming, 'Marilyn!' They wanted autographs. Some of them were able to get cabs, and they followed. A few fans jumped on their motorbikes."

The Seven Year Itch—A *"two-panty shot"* of Marilyn Monroe. (Museum of Modern Art)

Sitting in Springer's favorite booth at Gallagher's, Monroe looked up and just above her head was a photograph of DiMaggio. "My love," she said. She kissed her fingers and touched the lips of the photograph. Then, she rose and caressed DiMaggio's face in the photo.

"What a lucky place to sit," she said to Springer.

As they studied the menu, a man came over and said, "Hi, John." They looked up. It was Henry Fonda. "I really came over to meet Miss Monroe," Fonda said. They were joined by Myrna Loy, who had been eating lunch at another table. Not having heard Fonda's words, she said, "I've come over to meet Miss Monroe."

"When they left," Springer said, "Marilyn was so thrilled. She sighed and said, 'They are *real* stars.'"

Marilyn Monroe and Tom Ewell worked well together during the filming. Ewell was impressed by her seriousness and dedication, and she said of him, "Only Tom Ewell could do it that well."

In December 1954, after the film wrapped, Monroe went back to New York incognito, traveling as Zelda Zonk because, as she explained, she didn't want to attract attention. Her purpose was to study at the Actors Studio with Lee Strasberg in order to became a "real" actress. "She was already a real actress," Strasberg told me, "but she didn't know it."

In New York, Monroe met Arthur Miller. Shortly afterward, they were married.

People who worked with her complained that she kept them waiting. She knew it was true. She understood how her co-workers felt about it, but that didn't help. When Strasberg talked with her about this, she responded wistfully, "I've been waiting all my life."

For his part, Wilder never got over that hairpin. "Unless the husband, left alone in New York while the wife and kid are away for the summer, has an affair with that girl, there's nothing. But you couldn't show that in those days, so I was straitjacketed. I wish I could have done *The Seven Year Itch* later, because it was a good property to do without censorship. Just one hairpin."

—The Spirit—
of St. Louis

Before the Film Society of Lincoln Center gala tribute to James Stewart, there was a cocktail party, and someone standing in the small group gathered around the guest of honor asked which of his films were his favorites.

Stewart answered *The Spirit of St. Louis* and *The Man Who Shot Liberty Valance.*

"And between those two, which was your favorite?"

"*The Spirit of St. Louis,*" Stewart answered without hesitation. "In *Liberty Valance,* it looked like I had the title part, but it didn't turn out that way. In *Spirit,* I didn't have the title part. An airplane did.

"I think the part I played in *Spirit* was the one I most wanted to get, ever. I don't think it was a highly appreciated picture, but I appreciate it. And I got to work with Billy Wilder.

"The trouble was, I think, most people thought they were going to see a movie about Charles Lindbergh, when it was really about the flight he made across the Atlantic in the *Spirit of St. Louis.*"

Wilder approached the subject of Charles A. Lindbergh from a different perspective than that of most people in 1956. "You cannot imagine now what the name Lindbergh meant to us in Europe in 1927."

The story treats the events leading up to Lindbergh's famous flight and the flight itself, interspersed with memories of his life, as he struggles to stay awake over the North Atlantic.

On May 19, 1927, twenty-five-year-old Charles A. Lindbergh [James Stewart] spends a sleepless night in a Garden City, Long Island, hotel room. He recalls days as a mail pilot and flight instructor, and how he persuaded some St. Louis businessmen to back his entry into the transatlantic flight competition.

Because other pilots are eager to claim the $25,000 prize, Lindbergh inspires the small Ryan Aircraft Corporation to build the *Spirit of St. Louis* far ahead of schedule.

On the morning of the flight, a small crowd is on hand, among them a young woman from Philadelphia (Patricia Smith) who gives Lindbergh her compact mirror so he can read his compass reflected in it.

Taking off successfully in the mud and rain, he faces the challenge of staying awake for forty hours after not having been able to sleep the night before. Lindbergh's only companion for a time is a fly, with whom he converses. He recalls his youth in Minnesota, buying his first plane, and barnstorming with a flying circus.

Over the North Atlantic, he struggles not only to stay awake, but to stay on course and reach land before the plane runs out of fuel.

Sleep finally overtakes him, and his plane spirals downward; but just before he hits water, the sun, reflected in the young woman's mirror, awakens him. Though able to recover altitude, he has lost his bearings.

After a moment of uncertainty, he recognizes the coast of Ireland. He reaches France and follows the Seine to Paris, managing to restart his engine when it stalls. He again becomes disoriented when the lights of Paris at night serve only to confuse him. Though not religious, he prays, and is able to find Le Bourget airfield.

Lindbergh is greeted by a crowd of 200,000 cheering people. Later, alone in the hangar, he shares the moment of triumph with his leading lady, the *Spirit of St. Louis,* before returning to a hero's welcome in America.

In *Hold Back the Dawn*, Charles Boyer had refused to speak with an insect because, as he told Brackett and Wilder, "It is not logical." Talking about his scene with an insect in *The Spirit of St. Louis*, James Stewart told me, "I like it fine talking to flies. They don't talk back. This fly came in handy because if I just talked to myself, people might have thought I was crazy. Anyway, he just took a quick hop, getting off as soon as he could.

"I couldn't imagine myself telling Billy Wilder how to write or how to direct. He's one of the best who ever was. I'm just an actor. I was pretty glad to have that part, and I only wanted to do my best."

Since there are long periods of visual action in the film with little dialogue, Franz Waxman became one of Wilder's most important collaborators on this film. His score, however, wasn't nominated for an Oscar; but then, 1957 was the year *The Bridge on the River Kwai* won most of the Academy's honors, and another Wilder picture, *Witness for the Prosecution* was more noticed critically than *Spirit*. Louis Lichtenfield's special effects for *Spirit*, however, did receive an Academy Award nomination.

Billy Wilder mentioned a "far-fetched" theory he had heard about Lindbergh. "I was told by someone who *could* have known that Lindbergh was really a spy for the U.S. when he went on his trip to Germany just before World War II. What a great movie story that would have been!

"It would have made sense out of how a man like that could go so wrong. But if he went to Germany to spy, why didn't he ever say so? I don't know. He was a very stubborn guy. I knew him, but you couldn't know him well, because he was very touchy.

"What happened to his son, that had to change him, and what happened after that, all that stuff with the press. I was thinking about the Lindbergh kidnapping trial when I made *Ace in the Hole*. It was what the press did to Lindbergh and his family after the murder of his little boy. The newspapermen helped make the trial into a big carnival.

"I remember once when someone from some newspaper asked me how did I feel when I learned my mother had died at Auschwitz. Can you believe it?"

Anne Morrow Lindbergh, the widow of Lindbergh and a fine writer, spoke with me about her husband's attitude toward World War II:

"He had a strong feeling about war. He understood what it would mean to large numbers of young men and to the people who cared about them and could lose a son, as we had.

"When my husband saw that he had been wrong in his judgment of Hitler and the Nazis, he completely reversed his position and entered the U.S. war effort. He made a considerable contribution, but he wasn't allowed to change his mind by the press or by history."

———◇———

The Spirit of St. Louis received good reviews when it opened in April 1957, but audiences stayed away. The poor box office was attributed to lack of interest in Lindbergh and to his not being known by a different generation. Wilder was puzzled.

"I thought about it afterwards. What did we do wrong?

"I think we did not choose the right title. It was suggested Lindbergh's name had to be in the title. When we made the picture, not enough people knew what the *Spirit of St. Louis* was. When the audience is expecting something else, it takes them time to understand what they are seeing, and they can resent it. It is better if the audience has been prepared.

"Maybe I shouldn't have told the audience at the beginning of the picture that the flight was successful. But I thought they already knew.

"Steven [Spielberg] told me he liked *Spirit*. He could appreciate what we went through to get some of this. A director sees films in several ways. He sees them as a director, what he likes, what he doesn't like, what he would have done or wouldn't do. But it's not easy to forget and just be entertained.

"You turn off as a director when you see something so bad it isn't worth seeing. When it is so good you are transported, you have to go back and see it again. I had to see *Schindler's List* more than once."

The filming of *The Spirit of St. Louis* lasted from August 1955 through March 1956. The long production schedule was because of the need for so many exterior locations—the Santa Monica Airport, Long

Island, Manhattan, Guyancourt near Versailles, and the North Atlantic along Lindbergh's actual flight path.

"*Spirit* was the toughest picture I ever made. Not only was it an exacting period piece, but shooting the aerial scenes was especially tiring and, after a while, boring. We had to use two planes for each one shown on the screen, one for the ground, the other for the air. It took hours for anything to happen. The replica we had built of the *Spirit of St. Louis* cost many times what the original *Spirit* cost. I think there were more actors and extras than D. W. Griffith had for *Intolerance*.

"We spent a lot of time shooting aerial circus stunts we didn't use. Jimmy Stewart bet me $100 that I wouldn't do one of them myself. Maybe he wanted a new director. Anyway, I won the bet and bought the crew a keg of beer, and I included Stewart.

"I am not an outdoorsy director. My idea of a good outdoor scene is a balcony of the Paris Ritz built by [Alexander] Trauner in the studio."

King Vidor had believed he was going to be the director of this film until he wasn't. He told me the tale.

"You know, it's funny how in life, for some reason it's the one that got away that you always remember—a fish, a girl, a film. The film that got away from me was the one about Lindbergh that was based on his book. I'd always really admired Lindbergh. He was the one person I most wanted to meet. Then the chance came to meet him.

"I got right on a plane to New York, and I cried in the lobby of the Pierre Hotel when I read that book.

"I was introduced to Lindbergh, and we got along just great. The two of us spent a lot of time together. Lindbergh and I ate a lot of Chinese food, which was what he liked.

"It was interesting the way no one ever recognized him. He'd been the most talked about man in the country, in the world. But no one recognized him, not even once. He just wasn't a visible celebrity without his aviator's cap and goggles. But he didn't mind. He said he preferred it that way. I guess he'd had enough.

"We talked mostly about the picture I was going to make from his book. I pretty much had the whole picture worked out, and we had a gentleman's agreement. I *thought*.

"Then, one day Leland Hayward, agent–producer extraordinaire, appeared. He offered Lindbergh more than I'd planned to spend on the entire film. And Lindbergh just signed.

"I didn't hear from Lindbergh. He seemed to have lost his big interest in Chinese food. I called him. He said sort of apologetically, 'I did it for my family.' Then he said brightly, 'Couldn't you just do it with Leland Hayward?' Now, of course, Leland Hayward was working with Billy Wilder. My first thought was, Lindbergh doesn't know much about business. My second thought was my first thought was wrong. Here was Lindbergh getting rich while I'd just wasted my time and enthusiasm and money.

"They made the picture with James Stewart, which was just the opposite of what I had in mind. Jimmy Stewart was in real life a general in the air force. He represented something quite different. He was a person who knew how to get along within the mainstream and to rise to the top. Lindbergh was a person who was always something of an outsider, always a little out of order, not quite fitting in, more of a loner and an individual than a leader.

"Younger was important, too. At that time Stewart was too old for the part. But even more important, I felt he had to be an unknown. Stewart brought too much of Jimmy Stewart with him. It was such an established identity, and all those pictures he'd made before came with him to the part. I couldn't believe I was seeing Lindbergh. Afterwards, I don't think Lindbergh was exactly happy about the picture, but then he had all that money.

"With anyone else, I would have produced a contract and had him sign it. My lawyers would have been talking with his lawyers. But you couldn't do that sort of thing with that kind of man. You couldn't be so small as to ask for a signature on the dotted line from a man like Lindbergh, the hero. I'd been hero-struck by Lindbergh, and I'd confused the public hero with the private man.

"So that was how I happened a year later to be sitting in a movie theater in Westwood watching a film of the life of Lindbergh and reading the credit, 'Directed by Billy Wilder.' "

—Love in the—
Afternoon

"To film in Paris seems wonderful," Wilder told me, "but it is torture. It is no holiday, believe me. To be locked up in the studios and not to be able to walk in the streets and breathe the air, look in the shop windows, drink coffee in a café is like being a pianist in a bordello. It seems you are the only one who isn't making love.

"When I was shooting the crowd scenes for *Spirit* at Guyancourt, I met Alexander Trauner. He said to me, 'What are you doing here? This is second unit stuff. You should be at Maxim's enjoying a Grand Marnier soufflé.' He was almost right. I prefer chocolate soufflé."

With *Love in the Afternoon,* the Hungarian-born Trauner began his long association with Wilder, as did I. A. L. Diamond. Wilder described how he met Iz:

"There was a monthly Screen Writers Guild magazine with some news about the guild. In it were some funny pieces, which I liked. A name I always saw with these pieces was I. A. L. Diamond. I always look to see the writer's name with anything I like, and you couldn't miss a three-initial name like that. I inquired about him, and he came to my office. We talked for about half an hour. We went to lunch. We stayed together for more than thirty years."

Wilder knew that he wanted Audrey Hepburn as Ariane for *Love in the*

Afternoon, but Gary Cooper was not his first choice for Frank Flannagan.

"I wanted Cary Grant for Flannagan, but I always wanted Grant for anything. It was a disappointment to me that he never said yes to any picture I offered him. Nothing personal. Intuitive. He didn't explain why. He had very strong ideas about what parts he wanted."

Audrey Hepburn told me that Wilder selected Gary Cooper as a person with whom to be in Europe because they shared similar tastes. "He and Billy Wilder were connoisseurs. They talked about food and wine and clothes and art. I was never included in that rapport. I have the greatest respect for Mr. Wilder, but I don't know him personally, really well. I couldn't speak with him in the way I could with King." King Vidor had introduced me to Audrey Hepburn.

I. A. L. Diamond remembered that they started writing the character with Cary Grant in mind, "but as we were writing, Gary Cooper became more evident."

An obviously posed picture. Wilder never sat still and I. A. L. Diamond rarely typed during their story conferences. (Museum of Modern Art)

Maurice Chevalier was brought to Wilder's attention by their mutual friend, the agent Paul Kohner. He had asked Chevalier if he would like a major part with Audrey Hepburn and Gary Cooper in the next Wilder film. Chevalier replied, "I would give the secret recipe for my grandmother's bouillabaisse to be in a Billy Wilder picture."

He and Gary Cooper had been two of the biggest stars at Paramount during the early 1930s. This was the first time Chevalier had not played a romantic lead, while Cooper was still playing leading men.

A mysterious young woman (Audrey Hepburn) comes into the life of industrialist Frank Flannagan (Gary Cooper), but she will rendezvous with him only in the afternoons. He hires a private detective, Claude Chavasse (Maurice Chevalier), to find out who she is.

She turns out to be Chavasse's own daughter, Ariane, a music student who became so intrigued by her father's file on Flannagan that she had to meet the notorious womanizer. Told that Ariane is now very much in love with him, Flannagan plans to leave Paris without her, but cannot. He loves her, too. At the station, as Ariane runs along the platform beside the train, he sweeps her up onto the train and into the coach with him.

In the U.S. version, Maurice Chevalier announces in a voice-over that Ariane and Flannagan are now serving a "life sentence." They are married and living in New York. Billy Wilder didn't like this ending, but he had to add it in order to satisfy those who considered *Love in the Afternoon* an immoral picture.

In the original ending, after Flannagan has lifted Ariane up from the railroad platform and taken her to his compartment, he calls her by her name, Ariane, for the first time, "and that was the real end," Wilder said.

Audrey Hepburn being swept up by Gary Cooper is one of Wilder's most famous images, almost as famous as Marilyn Monroe's blown-up skirt in *The Seven Year Itch*. This was not the first time in a film, however, that Ariane had been swept up by her departing lover. *Scampolo,* the 1928 German-Italian film based on the *Ariane* novel, has a similar scene, and Wilder was one of the writers of the 1932 German remake, *Scampolo, ein Kind der Strasse.*

Gary Cooper plays a role similar to his character in *Bluebeard's Eighth Wife.* Michael Brandon has been married seven times, and Frank Flannagan only five times. Both characters are stylish cads, and *Love in the Afternoon* is the reverse of *The Taming of the Shrew,* as was *Bluebeard's Eighth Wife.* It treats the taming of the stylish cad.

After a poor showing by the film in the United States, Allied Artists sold their European rights, and then it was successful in Europe. Based on a French novel, the story had appealed to Diamond as well as to Wilder. Like Wilder, he was not born in the United States, but had come to New York from Romania when he was a boy.

Audrey Hepburn made this picture immediately after *Funny Face,* which was also filmed in Paris. In *Love in the Afternoon,* her wardrobe was designed by Hubert de Givenchy, as it had been, in part, in *Sabrina.*

In *Funny Face,* she had played opposite another much older man, Fred Astaire. She was twenty-eight at the time, but the Ariane character was perhaps as young as eighteen. Some critics complained that Gary Cooper, at fifty-six, was too old for the part. "The day I signed Gary Cooper for this movie, he got too old," Wilder commented.

"Everyone said he was cast against type, but it *was* his type—his real-life type. Mr. Cooper was an elegant man, and I was influenced by the real Gary Cooper. Women loved him.

"I was interested to observe his technique with women in real life. He did not have a 'line.' He said very little. He listened to every word *they* said, and that is what charmed them, a man who was charmed by *them.* I saw this. The audience saw him as the epitome of the strong, silent, western hero."

———◄o►———

As in other Billy Wilder films, props play important small roles in *Love in the Afternoon.*

When Flannagan is leaving, he gives generous tips to the people who have served him. To Ariane, he says, "I wish Cartier was open." But she only wants the carnation from his lapel. It is discovered in the ice-

Love in the Afternoon—"The day I signed Gary Cooper for this movie, he got too old," Wilder complained. Cooper was fifty-six and Audrey Hepburn, twenty-eight, playing perhaps as young as eighteen. (Museum of Modern Art)

box the next morning by her father. Then, each time Flannagan leaves, Ariane continues the ritual of taking his carnation.

Wilder described the cello case as "her chaperone." She sets it against the wall outside in the hall with Flannagan's overflow luggage whenever she enters his hotel suite. At the end, when she is on the train with Flannagan, the case is left with her father.

Ariane's cello case also holds a borrowed white ermine fur coat. When the coat falls from her shoulders to the floor, her resistance is falling away, too.

The anklet Ariane wears was originally a key chain for her cello case. It accentuates the artificial, transparent efforts of the youthful, innocent Ariane to persuade Flannagan that she is a girl of the world. Barbara Stanwyck's anklet in *Double Indemnity* is a brazen challenge; Audrey Hepburn's is a demure invitation.

Do Flannagan and Ariane make love in the afternoon? On the first occasion, she comes early for a 4:00 P.M. date and stays until 10:00 P.M., and at the end of the evening, she's seen fixing her hair in the bathroom. This would seem to indicate that they did.

There are many references to songs and music, and to musicians. Ariane is an orchestral cellist. A Gypsy orchestra sets the mood for Flannagan's seductions. The waiters always have a martial drum rhythm to accompany their parade to Flannagan's room. Ariane hums "Fascination," the seduction song. In the long opera house sequence, much of the *Tristan und Isolde* prelude is played. Appropriately, that opera is about a casual relationship that grows into undying love, and is set in Ireland, Flannagan's ancestral home.

Flannagan's lovely brunette companion at the opera is Audrey Wilder, who in this film makes her second and last appearance in one of her husband's films.

Matty Malneck, Wilder's friend from their Paul Whiteman days in Vienna, wrote three songs for this film. He would contribute, as well, to *Witness for the Prosecution* and *Some Like It Hot*.

Wilder asked director William Wyler his opinion of the film. "Willy was my friend, and he told me the truth the way he saw it. He said, 'At the end, I don't think Audrey Hepburn should be talking to Cooper. She should run along the train in silence.' He was right. But there was nothing I could do. Her lips were moving, and I couldn't go back to Paris and reshoot it."

Audrey Hepburn disagreed. "Oh, I thought that was brilliant, the way he had me talking. I adored that. It's my favorite part of the film."

Wyler may have subconsciously remembered the image of Carmen Boni running alongside the moving train while Livio Pavanelli tries to decide whether he should scoop her up or not in Augusto Genina's 1928 *Scampolo*. She didn't say a word; but this wasn't a decision then. *Scampolo* was a silent film.

—Witness—
for the
Prosecution

Billy Wilder, speaking about Marlene Dietrich many years after *Witness for the Prosecution* was made, told me, "Marlene Dietrich was an aristocrat who had to leave her title behind, but she took her nobility with her.

"I directed the picture because Marlene asked me to, and I liked the story. Very Hitchcock. She wanted to play the part of the murderess, and if I was directing, she was more likely to get it. She liked to play bad girls because they were more interesting than good girls, and she preferred real-life love scenes to the ones on the screen. In pictures, kissing embarrassed her, but I do not think so in real life."

Producer Arthur Hornblow, Jr., had approached Dietrich about playing Christine, but his producing partner Edward Small, who had bought the film rights to Agatha Christie's long-running play, was not certain that she was right for the part. He did, however, readily accept Hornblow's suggestion for a director, Billy Wilder. It was Hornblow who had given Wilder his first chance to direct in Hollywood.

"Billy wanted Marlene Dietrich," Lenore Hornblow told me.

"Marlene was coached how to speak cockney by Noël Coward, who was a close friend of hers. He came to the set.

"She made a marvelous mushroom soup. Billy was absolutely crazy about it. She would drop it by his home for him in a covered pot with a copper lid on it. The first time it arrived, Billy was very pleased, and he and Audrey planned to have it as the first course of their dinner.

"When Audrey went to heat it, she saw that there was only a very small amount, not enough for two, only enough for one bowl.

"She served the mushroom soup to Billy, who offered to split it with her. Audrey said, no, she didn't like it as much as he did, and she said, 'Marlene meant it for you.' After the one-bowl delivery, Audrey probably liked it even less, and it didn't end there. Whenever the pot got left off with its contents of mushroom soup, there was always just enough for one bowl.

"I tried to explain to Audrey that I didn't think Marlene did it deliberately, but it was just that Audrey didn't exist for her. She said, 'Does that make it better?'

"I suggested to Marlene that Audrey wasn't going to like her, and why didn't she just leave more, say, enough for two bowls. But though the deliveries continued from time to time, there was always just enough for Billy."

<hr />

Wilder's first choice for the male lead in *Witness* had been Kirk Douglas, but he decided Douglas was "too hard-boiled." Tyrone Power was reluctant to take the part because he would not be the true lead, but Hornblow talked him into it, stressing the quality of the play and the opportunities it offered an actor. Small's offering Power a higher salary and a three-picture deal also helped.

Lenore Hornblow told me, "It was the happiest set I was ever on. There are always problems on a set; jealousy, love affairs, the ones who think someone else is being favored by the director and is getting more close-ups, this one doesn't like that one. That's regular. It's always a mess.

"But not on this set. Billy and Tyrone and Charles Laughton loved each other. They got along so well that after the film, the three of them went off together to Bad Gastein.

"It's hard to remember events from that film because it was so happy. The bad things stand out in memory and make more interesting stories. We were in London for exteriors in August, and the only thing that happened that wasn't good was it rained more that summer than it has since the time of Alfred the Good.

"Mostly *Witness* was done on the Goldwyn lot. Trauner's Old Bailey was the most wonderful set. I don't think anyone could have told the difference between the court on the set and the real thing.

"I had a passion for Agatha Christie, and we were in London at the Connaught, and Arthur called her. She said, 'Come and have tea.' Did he say, 'My wife, Lenore, is your greatest fan. May I bring her?' Not at all. He said to me, 'It's business.' He was a very professional man.

"Then, the worst of it was he came home and told me she had said,

Witness for the Prosecution—*Charles Laughton, Marlene Dietrich, Tyrone Power, and Billy Wilder relaxing between takes.* (Museum of Modern Art)

'Why didn't you bring your wife, Mr. Hornblow?' And worst yet, they had a delicious tea, my favorite meal, at her home. I never got to meet her.

"After the film, she wrote a wonderful letter to my husband about how happy she was with the movie." Wilder received a similar letter.

"She said, 'This is the first time anything of mine has been done properly,' because she always hated what they did.

"A lot was changed and a lot was added to make it a full evening's movie, which obviously moves much faster than the play. You are restricted by the stage milieu. A play has certain rules and certain limitations. In the films, you can expand. On the other hand, since you can do everything you want to do, that makes it so much more difficult because the choice is so enormous."

Wilder, who had always admired Charles Laughton, chose him for the part of Sir Wilfrid Robarts, "the champion of the lost cause." Alfred Hitchcock had disliked working with Laughton for the same reason Wilder loved working with him. He had so many ideas.

"Laughton was one of the best actors I ever worked with," Wilder said, "and I've worked with a lot of very good actors. He would come by my office at Metro at the end of the day, after we had finished shooting, and he would say, 'I have a few ideas. Could I show you what I have in mind?' This is, like, six o'clock in the evening. By nine o'clock, he is still at it. I guess some directors would have not liked that too much, but I was impressed. Jack Lemmon does the same thing, only he does it in the morning before shooting, and not for so long."

It was Laughton who suggested casting his wife, Elsa Lanchester, as Miss Plimsoll, the punctilious nurse, who is not in the stage play. Wilder created the part for the film.

The first treatment was begun with writer Larry Marcus. Lenore Hornblow remembered Marcus as being "so nice, but too much in awe of Billy." Then, Arthur Hornblow asked Harry Kurnitz, a successful screenplay writer as well as the author of detective novels, to leave Paris and come to work with Wilder.

While convalescing from a heart attack, barrister Sir Wilfrid Robarts (Charles Laughton), defends a man, Leonard Vole (Tyrone Power), accused of murdering a wealthy widow (Norma Varden) for her money. The chief witness for the prosecution is the man's German wife, Christine (Marlene Dietrich), who can testify against her husband because her marriage to him is not legal.

Christine's testimony, however, is discredited by love letters to another man in which she outlines her plan to falsely implicate Vole in the murder. Vole is found innocent and released.

Triumphantly, Christine admits to Sir Wilfrid that she was the mysterious cockney woman who sold him the letters discrediting her own testimony, and that Vole *was* guilty of the murder. Vole appears in the courtroom with a young woman (Ruta Lee), saying he is going away with her. Enraged, Christine stabs him. Despite his bad health, Sir Wilfrid makes plans to represent her defense.

Norma Varden, who played Mrs. French, appeared in *The Major and the Minor,* and had an important small role in Hitchcock's *Strangers on a Train,* in which Robert Walker almost strangles her to death at a party. "She was great," Wilder said, "and part of a whole slew of character actors which have disappeared that made pictures enormously enjoyable, pinch hitters who could hit homers. You have your stars, which have mostly disappeared, too, and then that little vegetable on the side. I'm talking about small-part actors.

"Where would we all be without those bits, sometimes noticeable, sometimes not, that all the others play off of? Sometimes the lead actors and the picture depend on how well these bit players do their jobs, but they don't get recognized. There ought to be a best-bit award for the best small-part actor."

Billy Wilder was the first director to sign with the Mirisch Brothers' new production company, and *Witness for the Prosecution* was his first film for them. They worked out of the Samuel Goldwyn Studios and had a distribution arrangement with United Artists. Wilder's last film with the Mirisches was *Avanti!* in 1972.

—Some—
Like It Hot

 "When you are acting in movies," Tony Curtis told me, "there are those moments you can't forget. I cannot forget being under Marilyn Monroe.

"One day Billy came up to me and said, 'I've got something for you, Tony. I don't know if you can do it or not. You're gonna have to be kissed by the Monroe.'

"I said, 'I'm up to it.'

"He says, 'Are you sure? You won't be swallowed up?'

"I said, 'I'll do my best. To get swallowed up.'"

Curtis, however, had already been "swallowed up" by Monroe.

"I knew Marilyn, in the biblical sense, before anyone in the picture business knew her in any sense. I got into the movies in '48, and I met her less than a year later, in '49, when she was this sweet kid hoping for a break. She and I got together sexually.

"We had some good weeks together. She was so attractive, I don't think any guy could be a good lover with her, if you know what I mean. Maybe her husbands got used to the way she was. If not, poor Marilyn, because she never got much out of it.

"It worried me that working together might be awkward because I hadn't called back. I was also worried she might not remember me, though girls usually did.

"She said, 'Hello, Tony. Have you still got it?'

"I didn't know exactly to what she was referring. She said, 'Have you still got that green convertible?'

"I had a green Buick convertible we used to make out in.

"I said, 'No, I sold it.'

"We got along just fine making *Hot*.

"When I first got my dress and makeup, and I was testing the guise, I invited her to go to the ladies' room with me. She did. She thought that was funny. Marilyn Monroe was a good sport."

———◦———

"Before it was made, *Some Like It Hot* was considered too controversial to be a comedy," Wilder told me. "It had cross-dressing, inferences of homosexuality, and all those murders.

"I remember talking to [David] Selznick. He was a very smart man and a marvelous producer. I told him a little bit about *Hot*.

"He said, 'The Valentine's Day Murder? You're crazy. You mean real machine guns, and blood, in a comedy? It'll be a total failure.'

"I said, 'Well, I think I'll try it anyway.'"

Early casting ideas for *Some Like It Hot* included Danny Kaye and Bob Hope. Frank Sinatra was also discussed. The most difficult part, according to Wilder, was that of Sugar Kane.

"She was the weakest part and also the most important. I knew I had to get a very strong actress to play Sugar, a real star, and that was a big problem. She had to bring something with her that we could not just convey on paper. I considered Mitzi Gaynor, who had just come off *South Pacific*. Then, I got this letter from Marilyn Monroe telling me how much she enjoyed working on *Seven Year Itch,* and how she hoped we could work together again. Of course! She would be the perfect Sugar. I sent her an outline of the script.

"I didn't send her much, though, because I think it's bad to tell the actors, 'I'm writing this for you, and only you can play it.' They don't like that. I just say, 'I know you can interpret this part because you can play anything.' They love that.

"I also didn't want Miss Monroe to think she was being typecast. She wanted to believe she was an actress, not just a star, a personality. Nobody could play her the way she could. I wanted her to feel good, but not so good she would be impossible during the filming. There was always a delicate balance which had to be maintained in handling her. You did it the best you could, and the thing you knew was you would fail. You would tip the balance wrong, and then you would pick up the pieces, not of her, but of you.

"I also needed a good actor, and he had to be good-looking enough to have Miss Monroe fall for him. The handsomest actor I knew who was just right for the part was Tony Curtis."

"I love that," Tony Curtis told me. "I would've done anything with Billy. I didn't need to know the part or the story, just that it was Billy Wilder. We got to know each other at Paramount when I was doing *Houdini* and he was doing *Stalag 17*. My looks had some special attraction for him. I would see how he looked at me, and I understood what it was.

"He was Austrian, and I was Austrian. I was a Hungarian and Austrian, a Hungarian-Austrian Jew. The handsomest of men. And I think the fact that we were related like that gave him a lot of pleasure.

"I was so young, twenty-two, when I met him. He scared me to death. He had such a *der überstandaten Führer* look about him. An *überstandaten Führer* is like a sergeant, a blown-up minor soldier in the army. I called him that for years, and he loved it.

"He also loved talking about all the girls I went out with. The first question he'd ask me in the morning when I got on the set was, 'Well, who did you do it to last night?'

" 'The girl at the bar.'

" 'That girl? I never thought anybody'd get to her!'

"I kept track for him! I won't say he enjoyed it vicariously, but you know, he liked my looks and he liked the idea that I was having a good time as a man. It was hard in those days, because there were very few of us guys around that were dedicated to the woman condition. I really liked women. So, that was a pleasure for him, too, and he thought it was entertaining."

Tony Curtis recalled being approached by Wilder to play the parts of Joe, Josephine, and the millionaire playboy:

"Harold Mirisch was running a movie one night at his home, and I was invited. Mirisch says, 'Billy wants to talk to you about a movie. Come in a little earlier.' Well, I got so excited, I couldn't see straight.

"So I got to the projection room of Mr. Mirisch's house, and there was Billy. He says, 'I'm gonna make a movie about two guys, and have them dress up like women to escape from being killed. They're two musicians, a saxophone player and a bass player, and they escape town, only dressed up like girl musicians, and go out to the South, to a fancy hotel in Florida. How does that sound?'

"I said, 'You mean you want me for one of the parts? Oh, Billy!' I started to cry.

"'Take it easy. I'm gonna get Frank Sinatra and maybe Mitzi Gaynor to play the other two parts.'

"'You get anybody you want.' About four days later, I ran across Billy. He said, 'I'm not gonna use Frank. He's gonna be too much trouble, and Mitzi Gaynor is not just what I want. But I saw an actor, you know him, Jack Lemmon? I'm gonna have him play the other part, and I'm gonna get Marilyn Monroe,' who I think was then having a lot of trouble functioning, and for that reason nobody wanted to bother with her. And that's how Billy put *Some Like It Hot* together. That made me feel so good, to be right in on the ground works of that picture.

"The reason he didn't want to use Frank was he wanted Frank to be the Daphne role, but he wasn't sure Frank would be able to play it. Frank was a little bit cantankerous, and Billy didn't want to take a chance on that, with the big chance he took on Marilyn. He accomplished that, but he knew she was gonna be trouble for him. And she was quite troublesome."

I. A. L. Diamond told me the real reason Frank Sinatra was not in *Some Like It Hot:*

"With the films that turn out the way you hoped, you can always find some element of luck. The luck sometimes is something you *don't* get. The studio wanted Sinatra and thought he could play both parts when he couldn't play either one.

"Billy made a lunch date with Sinatra, and he went and waited and

Some Like It Hot—*Tony Curtis said he had something more ladylike in mind for his female character than Jack Lemmon's "ditzy three-dollar trollop."* (Anthology Film Archives)

sat there, and sat there, and Sinatra never showed up. He stood up Billy. Now, *that's* luck."

One night at Dominick's restaurant in Los Angeles, Wilder approached Jack Lemmon. Lemmon remembered the moment very clearly, decades after he had forgotten what he had for dinner that night:

"I didn't know Billy very well at the time. We'd met at some social events. It was a little checkered-tablecloth joint. Anyhow, he sat down at my table and he said, 'Now, look. I've got this script here. You and the other fellow there with you, you are both musicians, and you witness the St. Valentine's Day Massacre. So now what you've gotta do is dress up like women and join an all-girl orchestra, because they know you've seen the murders, and they may come and kill you. For 85 percent of the picture, you're gonna run around in drag. So, you want to do it?'

"I was dumbstruck. I said yes. It was, after all, Billy Wilder."

Billy Wilder told a shorter version of this story. "I went up to him and I said, 'Would you like to be in a movie I'm going to make? You get to play a woman,' and he said, 'Yes.' I said, 'Are you sure? Being a woman is drafty.' He still said yes.

"Lemmon, I would describe as a ham, a fine ham, and with ham you have to trim a little fat.

"Joe E. Brown had been out of sight for quite a while. When I saw him at a Dodgers game, I thought he would be perfect as Osgood. That was one time where 'somebody's perfect.' He was also a part-owner of the Pittsburgh Pirates, so I got a lot of inside information about trades while we were making Hot.

"I wanted some people from the old gangster pictures, like Eddie Robinson, who I couldn't get. But George Raft, Pat O'Brien, George E. Stone, and some others were available, and they were important for the look of it.

"After Marilyn saw the black and white test for Some Like It Hot, she said she wanted the picture to be shot in color. I told her, 'You will be aware of the makeup. It will come out blue for the boys because of their beards.' I reached her. She bought it. She liked color better. But black and white was right for this picture. It works.

"Diamond and I got the idea from Fanfaren der Liebe [Fanfares of Love, 1951], a German remake of an old French film, Fanfares d'Amour [1935]. Two desperate musicians will do anything to get work. They put on blackface for a jazz band. They dress up like Gypsies for a Hungarian cimbalom group. They disguise themselves as women for an all-girl orchestra and romantic complications follow. We set our film in Chicago and Miami during the Roaring Twenties because prohibition, bootleggers, speakeasies, gangland killings, Florida millionaires, jazz, and flappers are such a good background."

For Diamond, "the humor in the German movie was rather heavy-handed and teutonic, though the basic idea was good. We needed stronger motivation and more complications. It was Billy who got the idea for linking our two desperate musicians with the St. Valentine's Day Massacre. He got it one morning while he was driving to work to meet me. Billy got a lot of his ideas driving."

"When we started working on this picture," Wilder added, "I said to my friend, Mr. Diamond, we have to find the hammerlock of the story. We had to find the ironclad thing in which these two guys trapped in women's clothing cannot just take off their wigs and say, 'I'm a guy.' It had to be a question of life and death. We introduced the Valentine's Day Massacre as part of the plot, so if they get out of the women's clothes, they will be killed by the Al Capone gang or whoever it was. How could these guys ever feel safe again with the gang knowing they were witnesses? That was the important invention that made everything else possible."

"We couldn't think of a title we liked," Diamond said. "At first, we were considering *Fanfares of Love* as a title. Then we came up with *Not Tonight, Josephine,* and finally *Some Like It Hot.* We put it in the script. Mr. Curtis says to Miss Monroe when he first meets her on the beach as the millionaire, 'I guess some like it hot, but I prefer classical music myself.' They told us that some years before the same title had been used for a Bob Hope film, so we had a secondhand title. Then, they told us it wouldn't be a legal problem."

Wilder added, "Our *Some Like It Hot* is the one everyone remembers, and not because of us. Everyone was *very* good."

> Two musicians, Joe (Tony Curtis) and Jerry (Jack Lemmon), witness the St. Valentine's Day Massacre and have to flee Chicago disguised as women in an all-girl band. In Florida, Joe romances one of the girls in the band, Sugar (Marilyn Monroe), pretending to be a millionaire, while also being her best girlfriend, Josephine. Meanwhile, Jerry, posing as Daphne, is romantically pursued by a real millionaire, Osgood Fielding III (Joe E. Brown), who proposes marriage, and Jerry, as Daphne, considers accepting. When the Chicago mob has a convention in Miami Beach, Joe and Jerry have to flee again, this time with their new romantic partners, Joe with Sugar, Jerry

with Osgood. When Jerry reveals that he is a man, Osgood replies, "Well, nobody's perfect."

What may be the most famous last line in any film wasn't always intended by Wilder and Diamond to be the last line. At the end, Jack Lemmon's lips move in a final silent muttering. "There was going to be some throwaway line, like, 'Aw, what's the use,'" Diamond told me, "back in the early days, when we thought Lemmon's character should have the curtain line, before we knew what we were going to do, before we knew what we really had. At the end of their last scene together, Joe and Sugar had to disappear in a passionate clinch on the floor of the boat so we couldn't see them. That was because Monroe couldn't be there for the final scene. As it turned out, it was much more effective just having Osgood and Jerry alone."

—◇—

One Saturday, while I was staying at Groucho Marx's Hillcrest home in Los Angeles, writing a book about him, an unshaven Jack Lemmon arrived for lunch. Lemmon apologized, explaining that it was his matinee day. His part in the play *Juno and the Paycock* at the Mark Taper Forum, in which he was appearing with Walter Matthau, necessitated his unkempt appearance.

"I hope you won't mind my dirty fingernails," Lemmon said, displaying them for us as he sat down at the table with Groucho and me. "It's so I can be in character for the people in the first few rows. I always go into my garden and make my fingernails dirty."

His part was important to him in that special way film actors feel about their stage appearances, especially in Los Angeles, where the audiences are so often made up of their peers. He said that ordinarily he wouldn't have eaten lunch before a matinee, but he had made an exception for Groucho.

Lemmon talked about the physical ills and accidents that had plagued Walter Matthau during the run of the play. They were sharing one tiny dressing room. Lemmon was excited about the visit of Sean O'Casey's widow, Eileen, who had come to Los Angeles to attend the opening.

"They served wine," Lemmon said, "and she could really put it away."

The conversation turned to *Some Like It Hot,* a favorite film of Groucho's. Lemmon told us that Wilder and Diamond had written *Some Like It Hot* as they went along. "I'd seen sixty pages that knocked me out, but Billy and Iz didn't come up with the last scene until we were almost ready to film. Well, they had to have it, because they needed it for the next day.

"I think it was Iz who thought of it, and Billy wasn't very enthusiastic, and Iz wasn't either. When they shot it, they liked it a whole lot better. And then, they liked it better and better, and now, it's a classic, maybe the greatest line ever."

Though Lemmon didn't realize it, the line had actually been thought of several months earlier. Wilder hadn't shared the line with Lemmon, because it wasn't yet decided what the final line or even the final scene would be.

"The Pullman berth party is my homage to the stateroom scene in *Night at the Opera,*" Wilder said, "though no one could have done it better than the Marx Brothers. When the bullets fall out of the gang's trousers in *Some Like It Hot,* I am doing another homage to them, to that great scene in *Animal Crackers* when the silverware falls out of Harpo's sleeves. I wish I could have made a Marx Brothers picture, and I talked about it with them, but it's one of those never-was films. I've got a headful of those."

———◅◦▻———

"You know when my leg goes up in the air when Marilyn Monroe is kissing me?" Tony Curtis explained. "That was my little ad-lib. And, you know, I was very scared about it.

"We were under an extraordinary amount of pressure and tension when we were doing that scene. This was near the end of the movie, and Marilyn was very recalcitrant. Some days she wouldn't come in, some days she would. She had everybody frightened to death—*to death.* All she had to say was, 'I don't want to do it,' and the walls would fall down. They were treating her so delicately.

"Right in the middle of that kissing scene, after she grabbed me and laid on me for a while and rubbed herself up against me, she stopped and looked down at me. I said, 'Oh, God, here it comes!' She was gonna jump off me and say, 'I can't do it!' and leave. And that's what it was like. I liked her a lot, and we had a good time, but you know, that's working for the ax man, the executioner, because all she had to do was say, 'Listen, I don't like it,' or whatever, and she'd run off the set.

"Billy said to me, 'I wanted to play your part in that movie.' I knew why, too. Marilyn was very uninhibited. When she laid on me, she really straddled me. She was grinding away and really tight against me. She could feel that I was having an erection, and she would stop and look down at me with a kind of 'I gotcha.' I didn't know what to do. I mean, she acknowledged it. I didn't react or respond. I just let her know she could do it to me! And she liked that. There was nothing salacious about it. She knew she could still do it to me.

"Billy kept saying, 'Do what you're doing, she loves it.' And I said, 'Billy, I'm doing the best I can.'

"Before we shot the scene, I went to Izzie Diamond and I said, 'Izzie, would it be all right if I lift my leg up in the air while she kisses me?' and Iz says, 'Do it.'

" 'You'll tell Billy?'

" 'No, I'm not gonna tell Billy.'

" 'Okay, but if he asks you, you tell him I told you.' Iz didn't answer, but I wanted to be very aboveboard with everybody. And Billy liked it."

The theory behind the seduction was Wilder's:

"The scene on the couch. I made *her* the seducer, Marilyn Monroe. He tells Sugar how it will not work. Sex does not work for him anymore. He had tried every kind of girl, and nothing happened after the initial heartbreak which had produced his condition. So, she wants to take the offensive. That makes men in the audience feel better when a girl like Miss Monroe is taking the offensive. She has a lot of confidence in that department, and she goes farther and farther. That's sexy. Sugar does all kinds of things, and still he seems to be impotent, but of course he isn't. The scene plays. The whole picture plays."

Jack Lemmon told me about the unexpected effect dressing like a woman had on him:

"I found myself thinking like a woman. I think Billy understood all that, that dressing like a woman would have that effect. I am particularly susceptible to parts I play. I found myself starting to worry about having security, just like Daphne.

"Billy probably wouldn't like this at all if he knew I said this about him, but he would have made a great psychiatrist. He even came from Vienna. He always understood what made us tick.

"I found I had to think twice about a part I took, because I got so deep into my part, especially as it went on, that if my character was having a nervous breakdown, I started to have one.

"We were doing drag in a different America. I figured we were making a classic blockbuster, or a flop.

"We spent hours with makeup. We couldn't afford to have our beards show through. We both had heavy beards. The most difficult thing was walking around in high heels. And costumes. We were very cooperative, but we did put our feet down when we wanted better dresses. They wanted us to select off-the-rack stuff from the costume department. We said we wanted dresses done by Orry-Kelly, who was doing Monroe's costumes."

Tony Curtis agreed. "I didn't want to look like Loretta Young. You know, those high-waisted things, and I wanted a new designer dress of my own, not one of those used things. I went to Billy, and I told him that Jack and I wanted Orry-Kelly dresses, too. He said, 'Okay.'

"Finding the right bra wasn't easy. I was a 36-D.

"We had to hold our arms, palms down, so our muscles didn't show, which was a bigger problem for me than for Jack. I'd played a boxer. We had our legs and our chests shaved, our eyebrows plucked, got false eyelashes. Our hips were padded.

"The day came when we did our clothing test, dressing up like women. We had two dressing rooms alongside each other on the set, and I got dressed in this woman's outfit. I was embarrassed. There wasn't that easiness in the '50s that there is now. Well, I guess I still feel that way. I could never feel comfortable dressed like a woman.

"You're the only person I've ever told this to," Curtis confided. "I didn't want to come out first. I wanted him out first, to see what Jack would be like, what kind of woman he would be, what he would enjoy doing. Then, I see Jack come dancing out of his dressing room, and he looked like a three-dollar trollop. You know, skipping along, talking in a high voice. I said, 'Oh, shit, I can't do that.'

"But I knew what I *could* do. I came out exactly the opposite. Restrained. I had to be a lady, very grand, like my mother or Grace Kelly, Eve Arden. I held my head up, straight and high, and never went for those low-down jokes.

"There had to be that contrast. I was really happy to see Jack's three-dollar trollop turn up. Ditzy all over the place. A broad playing it broad. And you see, that kind of symmetry or chemistry, or whatever you want to call it, made our relationship so solid. It wasn't like I gave him a choice. I didn't do anything. I just watched him first.

"That relationship paid off, because in the film it pays off."

Jack Lemmon remembered being concerned about how he and Tony Curtis would look in their women's makeup. "Would it be believable? Could we fool anybody? We spent a week going through a series of makeup tests with different size lips with lipstick and with assorted wigs. We were going crazy. When we got what we thought was the right makeup and wigs, Billy said, 'Okay, now you've got to go to the ladies' room.' We were on the Samuel Goldwyn lot at the time.

"'What?' we said in unison.

"'We're gonna find out if this acts or not. Go to the ladies' room!'

"So, traipsing into the ladies' we went, and, boy, oh, boy, the flop sweat was really flying. I was scared to death. I've never been so embarrassed.

"All the women going in and out accepted us. Nobody gave us a second look. Nothing. They just thought we were extras or bit players doing a period piece. But they thought we were women! We came out, rushed back to Billy, and told him that not one woman paid any attention.

"He said, 'That's it! Don't change one thing. That's exactly the way you want to look.'"

Tony Curtis, however, was not satisfied. "When Jack said, 'We made it,' I said, 'No, it's just because we're so ugly, they didn't even notice us. They couldn't stand looking at us.' I said we should go back to makeup.

"We were given more eye shadow, more mascara, and higher heels. I had my boobs enhanced, as they say, and Jack had his rump reupholstered."

The pair revisited the ladies' room in another test. This time when they walked in they were greeted. "One of the girls said, 'Hi, Tony.' I said, 'Let's go, Jack', and back we went to the original makeup."

"The first time I saw Jack and Tony dressed as women," Wilder said, "I felt wonderful. But Tony Curtis was bashful. He didn't want to come out of the dressing room. After a couple of days, he was fine with it.

"From my young days seeing shows in Europe, I remembered Barbette, the great female impersonator. I figured Barbette would be the perfect teacher for the guys. The only thing I worried about was, he would teach them *too* well, because they couldn't be *too* good as women, but should be kind of clumsy and awkward, so the audience is in on the joke and pulling for them. Perfect wouldn't get the laughs because perfect is not funny. Part of the secret was the boys never camped it up."

Curtis said he learned how a woman is different from a man.

"Barbette showed us that a woman puts one foot in front of the other and that's what makes her hips move the way a woman's hips move. No man walks like that. He said, 'Tighten up. Keep the cheeks of your ass tight,' which you did anyway if you were in the navy. Barbette was very finicky, and I didn't really enjoy my how-to-be-a-girl lessons.

"A reason I was angry at Marilyn Monroe was that when we had to stand around and wait, I was wearing high heels and my feet hurt. At first, we were going to wear two-inch-thick heels, but as we really got into it, we decided to go for it, all the way—three-inch heels. Tubs of ice water were put on the set for us to soak our feet in when we took off the high heels.

"Standing around like that, waiting for Marilyn to get in the mood, was not just hard on the feet, but on the bladder, too. You had to piss, but it was impossible to do it with those metal jock straps they fitted on us. I never had any trouble, but it bothered Jack a lot. He said, 'Why in hell don't you ever have to take a leak?' He complained to Billy, too, but Billy only said, 'Don't drink too much before you go to makeup.'

"I had a secret. I had rigged up a relief tube, a little funnel and hose device that allowed me to relieve myself without going to the john. It was of my own design, and it worked so well, I considered patenting it. I finally told Jack about my invention, even offered to make one for him, but he was too conservative in that respect."

Jack Lemmon never remembered seeing Wilder truly unnerved, except by Marilyn. "We were doing this scene, and all she had to do was to walk into the room, open a bureau, and say, 'Where is that bourbon?' Four little words."

Wilder estimated that he did almost eighty takes to get those four words. "We had a lowboy there with many drawers, and I put into every drawer notes with the words, 'Where is that bourbon?' After take sixty-three, I took her aside—we're in the second day already—and I said to her, 'Don't worry about it, Marilyn. We'll get it.' She just looks at me like she doesn't know what I'm talking about and says, 'Worry? About what?'"

Lemmon remembered that scene from a different perspective. "Billy told Tony and me that we'd better get it right *every* time because the first time Marilyn got it right, that would be the one he'd print, no matter how *we* were.

"There was the scene I always remember with the bourbon bottle. Marilyn had one line and she couldn't remember it. On about the seventieth take, Billy started to say something, and I don't think he got any farther than just saying, 'Marilyn,' when she cut him off and said in her little girl way, 'No, no. Don't talk to me. I'll forget how I want to play it.'

"Well, Tony and I didn't dare look at each other. We might have gotten hysterical."

Jack Lemmon admitted to me that he was affected by "emanations of unhappiness" from Marilyn Monroe. "She was so unhappy, you could feel it. Her unhappiness was so tangible, it was catching. I'm a suggestible person, and sometimes I caught it from her myself.

"Waiting for her on the set made me angry sometimes, but I never let it show. She would be in her trailer, and she wouldn't come out for a few hours until she felt ready. I said to myself, it was a worse problem for her than it was for me.

"While we waited, we took off our high heels to help our swollen feet, and then when she got around to dropping by, we couldn't get our feet back into our shoes."

Wilder said, "I had no problem with Monroe. Monroe had problems with Monroe. She was at all times slightly unraveled. She had great difficulties in concentrating. Something was always biting her, eating away at her. But, when it was all done, and my stomach got back to normal, it seemed well worth the agony of working with her. I even thought about doing it again. It's that old story that I've been saying for years: If I wanted someone to be on time, to know the lines perfectly, I've got an old aunt in Vienna who's going to be there at five in the morning and never miss a word. But who wants to see her?"

Lemmon never established the kind of relationship with "the Monroe" that Tony Curtis had. "Marilyn had a fatal flaw," Lemmon said. "She didn't believe it would last, and she had to have it—the success, the fame, all the attention. She squeezed life too tightly."

"There were stretches where she was as good as anyone," Wilder remembered, "a marvelous comedienne. But you had to get the right mood swing. I didn't like being dependent on her moods. I could never understand what made her tick. It wasn't her heart.

"But I listened to her suggestions. When Sugar made her entrance on the train platform, she complained she needed some business. She didn't feel that just walking down the platform was enough. That's when I got the idea to have the steam hit her undulating derrière. It was perfect for her first scene, and she loved it.

"She knew where the laugh was. It was her intuition. When she delivered a line that was supposed to get a laugh, she always got the delivery right. The only suspense was, would she remember the line so she could deliver it right?

"You could always count on her—to be late. You could set your watch by it. There would be a few hundred people waiting, among them her costars, and me, and she would finally arrive and say, 'I lost my way on the way to the studio. I'm sorry.' Seven years of going to the studio, and she lost her way. In the beginning, I didn't believe she was telling the truth. Then, worse. I believed she *was* telling the truth."

Curt Siodmak, who had worked with Wilder in Berlin, told me

about his opportunity to observe Marilyn Monroe when he visited his old friend on the set of *Some Like It Hot.*

"It was the day of the train sequence. Tony Curtis and Jack Lemmon were waiting to be called for their scenes. They were enjoying themselves very much as women dressed in their disguises. Billy was talking intently with Marilyn Monroe, who was more than pretty, and you could see that special quality that makes a pretty girl a star. She listened for a while, and then she seemed to get tired of listening, bored, a little annoyed. She interrupted him.

"I remember when nobody knew him and he was just a reporter spending his time with us at the Romanisches Café, and he didn't know how he was going to afford his next cup of their delicious coffee. Way back then, he didn't like to have anyone interrupt him, and we didn't.

"So, Marilyn Monroe, petulant, interrupted him: 'Mr. Wilder, I wish you would not explain that scene to me. It interferes with my conception of it.' The actress looked over at someone. There, a woman was nodding approvingly. The actress had received the approbation that counted. I learned that this woman was her acting coach, Paula Strasberg, the wife of Lee Strasberg of the Actors Studio. Marilyn Monroe looked very pleased with herself. She had the power, and she knew it. A star could shut things down, and a director couldn't win, especially after they had been shooting for a while.

"So, Billy had to take it. But what surprised me was he didn't seem angry. I guess he had learned better how to hide his feelings. When I'd known him in those days before he made *People on Sunday,* nothing could have induced him to hide how he felt. He was a choleric personality, like my brother, Robert, a reason the two of them couldn't get along for any length of time. I was shocked, so I asked Billy, 'How can you take that kind of thing from her?'

"Billy wasn't angry. He even smiled. 'Because Miss Monroe has a brain of cheese, tits of steel, she is very good in her part, and I am getting paid a quarter of a million dollars.'"

Wilder was not happy to accept Paula Strasberg's constant presence on the set, but Marilyn had insisted. "The Strasbergs didn't do Miss Monroe any good, but she worshipped them like a religion. She put her total trust in them. I was talking to Miss Monroe, and she was looking the other way to see the look on Madame Strasberg's face.

"I tried to make some contact with Madame Strasberg, to establish some rapport, but she had a permanently disapproving face. Marilyn said she had given her the right of approval, but it was more like the right of disapproval."

Lee Strasberg told me that Monroe respected Wilder and said he wasn't like the others. He treated her "with respect," she reported, and "he never made a pass." Usually, she complained, "I'm not a character. I'm a prop."

"Some Like It Hot will be a picture of mine people will see for as long as prints last, not because of me, but because of Miss Monroe," Wilder said.

"She always looked nervous. She always seemed nervous. She always *was* nervous."

"Paula Strasberg was the most important person in Marilyn Monroe's life," I. A. L. Diamond commented at a lunch with Billy Wilder and me. "It wasn't Joe DiMaggio. It wasn't Arthur Miller."

"And it wasn't me!" Wilder added.

Diamond's comment was truer than he knew. When Marilyn died only a few years after making *Some Like It Hot,* she willed most of her estate to Paula Strasberg. When Paula died, the inheritance passed on to Paula's husband, Lee Strasberg, who remarried. On his death, the Marilyn Monroe properties were inherited by his second wife, Anna, who had never known Marilyn.

Anna donated Marilyn's undergarments, her bras and panties, anonymously to charity thrift shops. In 1999, an auction of Marilyn's property at Christie's brought millions, part of which Anna donated to charity.

In that auction was Marilyn Monroe's own script for *Some Like It Hot,* with her handwritten notes in the margins. In her notes, as she often did, Marilyn referred to herself in the third person.

————◦————

"We were shooting the scene with the machine gunner popping out of the birthday cake," Curtis said, "and I decided to relieve the tension with a little entertainment for Billy.

Some Like It Hot—*Between takes, Tony Curtis tells Marilyn Monroe something that is probably too hot for* Hot, *and Billy Wilder agrees.* (Museum of Modern Art)

"I got this stripper with phenomenal tits, gigantic, and she popped out instead of the man, and shot right over to Billy and kissed him. Was he surprised!"

Wilder said that Curtis's imitation of Cary Grant wasn't his idea, but came from Curtis.

"I said to Mr. Curtis, 'You must do some kind of different voice, so the audience can believe Sugar doesn't recognize you.' He comes right back, not missing a beat, and says, 'I can give you Cary Grant.' Then, he goes right into Cary Grant, who is a friend of mine. I said, 'Terrific,' and I kissed him. It was as close as I got to having Cary Grant in one of my pictures. Later, at our wrap party, he got a *very* big kiss from Miss Monroe, which he enjoyed more."

Tony Curtis told me, however, that the kiss that meant the most to him was Billy Wilder's. It meant even more because Jack Lemmon had just received a best actor Oscar nomination for *Some Like It Hot.* Curtis was proud of his performance and disappointed that he was overlooked for a nomination.

"Tony Curtis gave me Cary Grant because he knew I always wanted to get Grant for a picture," Wilder said. "Cary Grant went to see *Some Like It Hot,* and he liked the imitation of him."

Curtis said, "Cary Grant once told me that to work in movies, you've gotta be so artful, it looks artless. That made such a profound impression upon me, I never forgot it. I work in an artless world. Everything must look like an improvisation. It must not look like I've prepared doing anything. How many movies have you seen where you know what's going to happen? I like to walk into a scene completely unnerved, and for people to be unprepared for what they're gonna see. That's what I did with Joey, the character I played. And that was really a good, strong counterpart for whatever was going on around me.

"There I was doing scenes with Jack Lemmon, who would come into work all dressed up, and standing on the sideline was Marilyn Monroe and me, and Jack would go say, 'It's magic time!' And Marilyn Monroe would shake her hands, to relax.

"Mrs. Strasberg, all in black, like an ever-present specter, would follow Marilyn around, whispering in her ear so we could all hear, 'Relax!

Relax!' It was very unrelaxing for everyone else, but Marilyn seemed to eat it up. She was hungry for every Strasberg word.

"Each time I thought, one more 'magic time!' or 'relax!' and I'd have a nervous breakdown, maybe laugh hysterically, even though it wasn't funny.

"But I never broke down. I had those three excellent parts: Joey, the gonef; I had the millionaire that I loved; and I loved the woman that I played. These three characters are so distinct because of Billy. He had a sharp, clinical eye for what the human condition is.

"At that time, I felt I owned the world, or whatever part of it I wanted. Jack and I were two young guys, hot to trot. We loved what we did, and we were always doing our best because it was what we wanted to do. Nothing seemed impossible. Jack would pitch me a line, and I'd field it over my shoulder. That was how we were in those days. We were serious about our work, but we knew how to play.

"Marilyn did not know how to play. She was younger than us, but she just didn't know how to play. She never learned how. She had lost her childhood, so she never learned how to be a grown-up.

"I think a lot of the trouble we had with her was because she was afraid, a little girl lost. She always seemed tense and intense, afraid of a shadow, especially her own.

"Sometimes she would talk this funny baby talk, but a girl who looked like that had to know a lot. You might say she had a voluptuous naïveté. I think what she was afraid of was of losing what she had. Getting older is different for a woman."

One of the things Diamond had disliked about the German film was its showing on-screen of the makeover in an attempt to be funny. "Billy didn't waste the time showing how they change clothes." Wilder referred to this concept as "the power of omission."

"We have Tony Curtis phoning his agent," Wilder said, "but disguising his voice like a woman so they can get the job in the girls' orchestra. Cut. Next, from the rear, we see two women walking down a railroad platform, but their legs are hairy and they are having trouble with the high heels, especially Lemmon. No need to show how it happened, just cut.

"We don't see the guys becoming girls. That would be boring and wastes time and film. What probably happened was the guys knew some girls and borrowed a few *schmattes*—rags, that is. If we involve ourselves in how did they get the dresses, then it's fifteen minutes of boredom, and it's less convincing than the audience's imagination.

"I did not invent this technique; it was Laurel and Hardy. In one of their silent two-reelers, they get rich during Prohibition making booze in the bathtub. Laurel gets scared and says, 'This is very dangerous,' but Hardy says it's perfectly safe. Cut.

"They are now both behind bars in striped suits. They didn't need any scenes getting caught and being sentenced, just cut from the idea to the reality. And it worked.

"Sydney Pollack, one of our best directors, understood what *not* to put in when he did *Tootsie*. Dustin Hoffman makes up his mind he's going

Some Like It Hot—Jack Lemmon's famous next-to-last line, "I'm a man!" just before Joe E. Brown tops it with "Well, nobody's perfect." (Museum of Modern Art)

to become an actress, and then, suddenly, he's walking down the street dressed like a woman. No need to show how it happened. Just cut."

———◄○►———

Some Like It Hot wrapped late in early November 1958, $500,000 over budget. After two unpromising previews, the producers prevailed upon Wilder, who had the right of final cut, to make some small cuts. He took out one short scene in the Pullman car. Jack Lemmon climbs up into what he believes is Marilyn Monroe's berth. He admits to her that he is a man, only "her" turns out to be Tony Curtis.

The film opened in March 1959 to excellent reviews, but small audiences. It picked up, however, and became one of the most profitable films of 1959, earning $15 million. Of its six Oscar nominations, Orry-Kelly won for costumes. Among the nominations were best direction, best adapted screenplay, and best cinematography.

Some Like It Hot was the basis for the 1972 David Merrick Broadway musical, *Sugar,* which was based on the Wilder-Diamond script.

"What happens after Joe E. Brown says, 'Nobody's perfect'?" Wilder said. "People ask me that. The American public wasn't ready for that in 1959.

"*Some Like It Hot* is a picture I sometimes wish I had saved and made later. It was a daring theme for its time, two boys dressing up as girls. Ten years later, we could have been bolder. But the picture was too successful for me to do the subject again. And I'm glad I did it, just the way I did."

Tony Curtis visited the ninety-five-year-old Billy Wilder. "I went to see him, the day Jack [Lemmon] died. I didn't know until I got up there. I looked at him, and he kept peering at me.

"He said, 'You look forty-six.'

"He'd heard everything. He didn't need any input anymore.

"Somebody called and they wanted a Lemmon quote from him, and he said, 'Tell them he was the greatest, finest actor in the movies.'

"I would like to have worked with Billy again. I'd like to have done *The Apartment,* which Jack Lemmon got. Billy said, 'You're too good-looking for the part.' What was it they said? 'That's how it crumbles, cookie-wise.'"

AN ALTERNATIVE ENDING FOR SOME LIKE IT HOT

At lunch with Billy Wilder and I. A. L. Diamond, Wilder described an
ending for *Some Like It Hot* that he and Diamond had worked on even
before they completed the first draft of the script, an ending that might
have been. I wrote down what Wilder said and showed it to Diamond,
who filled in a few words.

DISSOLVE TO:
EXT. A HAVANA NIGHTCLUB—NIGHT
1920s AUTOMOBILES arrive and depart outside a Spanish-name
NIGHTCLUB. Uniformed DOORMEN greet GUESTS in tuxe-
dos and evening gowns. Latin American—style MUSIC is heard
playing inside.
INT. THE NIGHTCLUB—CONTINUING
COUPLES are dancing to a Latin beat, a big BAND is playing on a
bandstand, DINERS are sitting at tables in the foreground, and in
the background, PEOPLE are playing gambling machines.
SUGAR KANE steps up to the microphone and starts singing in
bad Spanish.
JOE and JERRY, out of drag, are playing in the band. Joe is obvi-
ously still in love with Sugar, but Jerry looks bored by his new émi-
gré status.
Suddenly, Jerry is no longer bored, but shocked at something he
sees. He stops plucking his double bass.
Among those entering the nightclub is a familiar figure,
OSGOOD, in a tuxedo, a tall blonde on each arm. As he nears us,
Osgood's face lights up. He has seen Jerry.
CLOSE—Jerry's dismayed reaction.
CLOSE—Osgood's wide smile.
FADE OUT

THE END

—The Apartment—

"Some people say it's my best comedy, but with *The Apartment,* I never set out to make a comedy. I don't consider it a comedy. But when they laugh, I don't argue."

The Apartment is one of the films of which Billy Wilder is most proud. "One of the few I wouldn't go back and change. I edited it in a week.

"I went around for several years with the idea for *The Apartment* in the back of my mind. Already, from the time I first arrived at Paramount, I had the ideas that became *Sunset Boulevard* and *The Apartment.* But it wasn't their moment. These ideas, these themes, I believed, belonged to a later time when the audiences were ready for them. Everything in life has to have its moment."

Billy Wilder talked with I. A. L. Diamond and me about how *The Apartment* happened, or as Billy Wilder said, "how it got activated."

"*The Apartment,* I remember the genesis of it very, very vividly," Wilder recalled. "I saw a picture of David Lean's called *Brief Encounter,* based on a play by Noël Coward, and in that picture Trevor Howard was the leading man.

"A married man has an affair with a married woman, and he uses his chum's apartment. I always had it in the back of my mind that this friend, who just appears in one or two scenes, who comes back home and climbs into the warm bed the lovers just left, this man who has no mistress of his own, I thought he would make a very interesting character.

"Years later, after Iz and I had finished *Some Like It Hot,* we wanted to make another picture with Jack Lemmon. So, I dug this thing out, and we just sat down and started to talk about the character, started the structure of the thing, started the three acts, started the other characters, started to elaborate on the theme, and then when we had enough to tell the story, we just suggested it to Mr. Lemmon and to Mr. Mirisch and to Mr. United Artists. That was about it." Wilder turned to Diamond. "Is that the way you remember it, Iz?"

Diamond never interrupted Wilder. He could always differentiate between a comma or a genuine period in Wilder's thinking and speaking, and recognized a question that was purely rhetorical.

"We had the character and the situation," Diamond said, "but we didn't have a plot until we remembered a local scandal here. An agent, Jennings Lang, was having an affair with a client, Joan Bennett, and he was shot by the woman's husband, Walter Wanger, who was a big-time producer. But the interesting thing was that the agent was using the apartment of one of the underlings at the agency. That was what gave us that relationship, somebody who was using the apartment of a low employee in his big company. That gave us our plot.

"I also remember some construction problems. There was one point in the second act where Billy kept saying, 'The construction is humpbacked.' What he was saying was that we were faced with two exposure scenes back-to-back. There was one scene where Fred Mac-Murray's secretary gives away to his wife that he was having an affair, which was immediately followed by a scene where the guys who had been thrown out of the apartment give away to the girl's brother-in-law that she's staying with Lemmon. Those scenes came back-to-back, and Billy kept saying, 'It's humpbacked,' but it was the only way we could arrive economically at the third act, so we were just stuck with that construction. So, there are two exposure scenes back-to-back, which is not the neatest construction in the world, but it was the best we could do."

"Nobody notices that anymore," Wilder said, "because neat constructions are out; third acts are out; payoffs are out. Jokes don't have toppers; they just have, I guess, an interesting straight line and let the audience write their own toppers. We have to face we come from a different style of filmmaking.

"If you look at a comedy now, it's not constructed at all. What makes it successful, I guess, is that it's slapped together with verve and overt language and naked behinds and God knows what. It's that kind of super-gusto, kind of sex chutzpah, you could call it, that makes it come off. If you come now with the tight complex construction I've been doing for so many years, it is being frowned upon. But that's the way we've been doing it and that's the way we're going to do it until they take the cameras away from us. Maybe they *have* taken the cameras away.

"You try to make your comedy say something serious, naturally, but if you can just make people think, even for a little while after the movie, then that's wonderful. Maybe there is a little talk about it where they work or with people at parties. That is when you score your biggest success.

"*The Apartment* had a bit of sadness, too, but some critic called it 'a dirty fairy tale.' If people listen to the dialogue, they will know how Lemmon, a decent guy, gets involved in these things. He did not volunteer his key and say, 'Anybody who wants to shack up in my apartment, here it is.' Not at all.

"The first guy says, 'My wife and I have got tickets to *Fair Lady,* and we have to change our clothes. But we live on Long Island. Can we use your apartment?' Then, another guy comes, and the bed is a little bit unmade, right? It just sort of snowballs, and he cannot stop it. He's basically a decent guy, but I think each time, a little corruption sets in."

———◦———

At the American Film Institute Life Achievement Award to David Lean, everyone rose as the guest of honor entered the room, in a wheelchair. Wilder said to me, "I'd never do this in a wheelchair. I don't like sympathy. I'll be at home when that happens, and no one will see me."

Lean was far from the high-energy, strong figure he had been when I met him only a few years before at the Savoy Hotel in London. His

enthusiasm then was great, as he spoke about the films he was planning. His disappointment and frustration were also extreme when none
of those film projects materialized. Several had come close, each taking
its toll as his hopes rose, then fell even lower. The impression was that
suddenly he had aged greatly in a business in which no one could afford
to age at all.

In accepting the invitation to be the AFI's honoree, Lean had nurtured the hope that the high visibility it afforded might help his current
film project, *A Passage to India*.

At the private party afterward, Lean's face lit up when he saw
Wilder. Lean's first words to him were, "I've got work!"

"Do you need an assistant?" Wilder said.

On the night King Vidor was awarded his special Oscar by the Motion
Picture Academy, Wilder was one of those waiting to congratulate him
at the Dorothy Chandler Pavilion. When Vidor thanked him, Wilder
said that it was *he* who should be thanking *him* for Vidor's *The Crowd*.
He considered *The Crowd* "one of the best films anyone ever made."
Not only had *The Crowd* shaped his vision of cinema when he was
starting out, but it had continued to influence him.

A striking scene in *The Apartment,* the seemingly endless rows of
desks in the office, is reminiscent of the celebrated scene in *The Crowd,*
which establishes the anonymity and depersonalization of the individual in his setting. One day on our way to lunch, I. A. L. Diamond was
telling me about how art director Alexander Trauner had created this
illusion of great depth, a forced perspective, within a relatively small
area, for *The Apartment*'s office set.

"The desks and chairs kept getting smaller and smaller as they went
back, until in the rear, they were so little, Billy had to have small children dressed as grown-ups sitting there."

Later, at lunch, Wilder asked me, "Do you know how we got that
effect? Midgets."

Diamond studied his plate as he cut his food and didn't say a word.
Wilder continued:

"Trauner was unique. He was the master of perspective. We had eight hundred desks, then another two hundred desks, but they were smaller size. Farther back, we had extras who were smaller and, ultimately, tiny desks with dwarf extras. Finally, there were tiny little desks and cutouts. In the back you saw a little traffic, things happening on strings, like puppets. He created that illusion. That's when picture-making becomes real fun, when you do it with mirrors, like a magician. You're pulling rabbits out of hats."

The Apartment is about big white lies and little black truths.

According to Wilder, "This picture is not about how beautiful life is. It is about how life *is*."

American corporate life is shown in 1960, a man's world. Women are absent from the executive suites on the top floors of Consolidated Life, except as secretaries or elevator operators who deliver men to the professional heights. The women at their desks, and in bed, are trying to please men in a pre-pill America. The women are getting older, and the men aren't. The 1950s were a time of great prosperity in the United States and, as in the 1990s, not everyone participated in the affluence.

"I did movies for the moment," Wilder said, not thinking about people in the twenty-first century who would be watching his films. "Come to think of it, I didn't expect to be able to see them, myself, in the twenty-first century."

Wilder originally thought of *The Apartment* as a stage play, not believing that the idea would pass film censors during the mid-1950s. By the time he did *The Apartment,* America was better prepared for a story about casual sexual encounters, and the producers were ready to try it.

Paul Douglas was cast as Jeff Sheldrake. "Absolutely ideal," Wilder said. "He had just done a similar part in *A Letter to Three Wives.*

"I saw him and his wife, Jan Sterling, at a restaurant, and I realized he was perfect, and I asked him right there in the parking lot. About two days before we were to start, he had a heart attack and died.

"Iz and I were shattered. After we got over the shock, we thought about our picture and what we were going to do. Then, simultaneously, like one person, we said, 'Fred MacMurray.'

"I called and said, 'Fred, I'm in trouble.' He said, 'You only call me when you're in trouble.' I said, 'Look, this thing happened,' and I explained. Fred said, 'I can't do it. I cannot play a man who has an illicit love affair in the apartment of one of his employees with an elevator girl. And during the Christmas holidays yet. I'm under contract to Walt Disney. I'm the meshuggah professor with the Volkswagen. They'll never forgive me. I'll be through. I'll be finished.'

"That took about twenty minutes. I let him talk till he ran down. Then I talked him into playing that part just like I talked him into playing a murderer in *Double Indemnity*.

"MacMurray was perfect because if the insurance salesman he played in *Double Indemnity* hadn't taken a wrong turn, he might have ended up running the whole company, like Sheldrake in *The Apartment*.

"After the picture was released, Fred MacMurray called me and said some woman attacked him on the street. She was screaming at him and saying he ruined his TV show for her, and she couldn't enjoy *My Three Sons*. She couldn't look at it because he had made a dirty, filthy movie. And then she hit him with her purse. Today, of course, it would be considered a Disney picture."

Making the film actually began with Jack Lemmon.

"Jack is one of my best friends," Wilder said, "and we kind of get together and talk things over. Then, things just kind of happen. Writing obviously is more comfortable when you know who you're writing for.

"He is full of ideas, so I give him a chance, because I already know that he is a thoughtful actor, and I will want to use some of what he comes up with.

"Mr. Lemmon would arrive at the studio at 8:15 in the morning even if we started shooting at 9:00. There weren't so many who got there early. He comes to my office, and he says, 'Look, I've got a great idea. Why don't we do this?' And he talks for a little while, and I look at him in a funny way, and he says, 'I didn't like it either.' Then he leaves, and I don't have to spend until noon listening to him talk, without getting a shot in the can."

When filming of *The Apartment* began, Shirley MacLaine told Billy Wilder how happy and honored she was to be working with him. He said, "I have to tell you, Miss MacLaine, I'm a very happily married man."

She was never certain whether he was joking or not.

"There wasn't much script when I first saw *The Apartment*," she told me. "There were only twenty-nine, maybe thirty pages, that few. Anyway, we started, and then, literally, Billy and Izzy watched Jack and me together. As they observed, Billy and Iz wrote the screenplay, right as we were shooting.

"I'd always wanted to work with Billy Wilder, but I wasn't so sure about the film. I had to trust my instincts, but when we started, I got sort of worried."

Wilder said, "She took the role because she liked my reputation. She was professional and cooperative, and good, but I knew she wasn't so sure she had made a good decision. One day on the set, she asked my wife, 'Does Billy really think this picture is going to make it?'

The Apartment—*Shirley MacLaine steps out of her character as an elevator operator to laugh at a Wilder joke.* (Museum of Modern Art)

"All she got from Audrey was, 'Let's see.'

"And we saw."

Audrey Wilder loaned Shirley MacLaine her own shaggy coat to play Fran Kubelik. It was perfect for the character. Wilder called it "an Audrey Touch."

Ray Walston described how he "won" his part in *The Apartment:*

"I was told to see Billy Wilder in his office. When I arrived, he was seated at his desk, wearing his little hat. He looked up and said in this really funny German accent:

"'Josh Logan tells me that you are a very good actor. Do you have an overcoat?'

"I said I did.

"He said, 'Good. You have the part.'"

In *The Apartment,* Wilder used his favorite triangle situation, but more boldly. It is all about love. Bud loves Fran. Fran loves Jeff. And Jeff Sheldrake loves Jeff Sheldrake. Sheldrake's love of himself may be the most enduring.

> Insurance statistician C. C. "Bud" Baxter (Jack Lemmon) advances his career by making his Manhattan apartment available to executives in his company for their extramarital affairs. His boss, Jeff D. Sheldrake (Fred MacMurray), finds out and promotes Bud in return for the exclusive use of the apartment for his own affair. When Sheldrake's girlfriend turns out to be Fran Kubelik (Shirley MacLaine), a pretty elevator operator Bud likes, he is heartbroken, but accepts the arrangement.
>
> One night, Bud returns to his apartment and finds Fran unconscious. She has attempted suicide after being told by Sheldrake that he won't get a divorce. Bud nurses her back to health, but she returns to Sheldrake when his wife sues for divorce.
>
> When Sheldrake asks Bud for the key to his apartment to continue the affair, Bud resigns. Fran, learning that Bud has quit, leaves Sheldrake, and rushes back to Bud. She calmly resumes their unfin-

ished gin rummy game, telling him to "shut up and deal" when he tries to say how much he loves her.

"Shut up and deal" is another memorable Wilder closing line. This time, Jack Lemmon has Shirley MacLaine instead of Joe E. Brown. Though one of Wilder's most characteristically unsentimental lines, it is more romantic for Wilder than any of the trite words Fran might have spoken.

"It's important that Fran Kubelik is not full of pity for herself," Wilder said. "Even when she attempts suicide, she must not seem sorry for herself."

Wilder had been advised by doctors that an attempted suicide who had taken sleeping pills would have to be slapped very hard, much harder than Wilder allowed Jack Kruschen, as the doctor, to strike Shirley MacLaine. Wilder also refused to reshoot the scene, saying it wasn't necessary. The hardest slap is heard off-camera.

Shirley MacLaine appreciated the consideration, and she told me that contrary to the opinion of some, "Billy Wilder is a very kind man." Wilder said that if she had been slapped any harder, it would have created the wrong emphasis in the scene, and been offensive and painful for the audience, which sympathized and empathized with her.

Props that advance the plot are characteristic of Wilder films. Fran's cracked compact mirror not only tells us that she and Sheldrake had an argument, but it tells Bud that she is Sheldrake's girl. "I find the compact that was left in my apartment," Lemmon explained, "and I give it back to Fred. Then, when I open it up at the office Christmas party, my face is reflected in the cracked mirror, and at that moment I realize Shirley was the girl who was in my apartment. That's about a dozen pages of dialogue saved." This scene combines two of Wilder's favorite film-making concepts, "the exposure scene" and "the power of omission."

Jeanette's compact mirror in *Mauvaise Graine* also serves more than one purpose, as does the mirror in *The Spirit of St. Louis*.

Diamond explained the appeal of Jack Lemmon's character in the picture:

"There is always a certain amount of schnook-identification, especially when the main character is a schnook who is Jack Lemmon. So, it's important that your schnook isn't a total loser and that you hand him a victory he wasn't expecting."

Wilder concurred. "I like the hero who can't make his moment, but his moment can make him. He isn't a hero because he has nothing to be heroic about. Then, something happens, and when he is tested, he learns who he is. Jack Lemmon was the perfect Mr. Ordinary who only seemed that way.

"J. D. Sheldrake is such an effective liar because he chooses women who *want* to believe him. He's a perfect cad. Well, maybe not perfect. Nobody's perfect."

Mrs. Dreyfuss was modeled after a woman who had lived in Wilder's apartment building at Fleischmarkt 7 in Vienna when he was a boy. "She used to visit my mother. I just had to stop a moment and close my eyes, and I could hear her voice in my head, like it was yesterday. I don't remember her name, but I remember that voice. She was a plump muse, always cooking, and she ate most of what she cooked. She spoke German in the Viennese way, and I tried to put that into English.

"Naomi Stevens did it exactly like I told her to do it, and some critics wrote her character was overdone, not real. She was *under*done. I ask, did *they* know my neighbor?

"The question I am most asked is, 'What happened to the characters?' 'Did it work out for Fran Kubelik and C. C. Baxter?'

"I didn't think it was going to work out for them, because they don't seem made for each other. He is out of work and it looks like soon she might be. Lack of money can be a big irritant between people. Neither one of them seems very good at solving their problems. I hoped for them, but as a betting man, small stakes for Monday Night Football, I wouldn't bet on it. I think the apartment was going to have a 'for rent' sign on it."

Wilder was always open to comic business, especially from Jack Lemmon, even when it was accidental.

"In *The Apartment,* I was so happy about one crazy piece of business I contributed," Lemmon said. "I'm called up to the boss's office, and I have this terrible cold, which, incidentally, I really did have, and I had as a prop a nasal spray. And I thought, 'Wait a minute—you've got this thing in your hand, and when you say, "Oh, no," then involuntarily, you squirt it.'

"So, I didn't tell Billy or Fred MacMurray I was gonna do it. And after I hit him in the face with the spray, MacMurray, God bless him, kept right on going. Wilder, I could hear in the background, trying not to laugh, but it didn't pick up.

"These things you remember because they worked, and of course I remember because it was my idea."

Wilder described how Lemmon caught cold in the same way his character, C. C. Baxter, did:

"I have always liked to shoot in a big city like New York. You never have the control you have on a set, but there is a look which is special—when it works. It is easier in New York because people do not stop to look as much as they do in other places.

"There is an exterior scene in *The Apartment* where Jack Lemmon can't go back to his apartment because one of his superiors at the office is passing the evening there with a woman. This is during the Christmas holidays in New York, so it's supposed to be bitter cold outside, which it really was. Lemmon is acting like he has a bad cough and is shivering as he drags himself to Central Park. He is supposed to be catching a cold.

"So, now we have Lemmon sitting down on a long bench, and in the script, it's supposed to start raining, a cold rain, but not snow. We don't want any snow, because that would mean we would have trouble matching scenes. So, since the weatherman has promised us there won't be any precipitation, we have planned carefully and brought along our own water truck with hoses.

"I tell the assistant director to start the background, and pretty soon Lemmon is sitting there being drenched in our artificial rain, coughing and sneezing the way it says in the script. Meanwhile, the water is actually freezing on the ground and in the streets.

"Traffic was slowing down where the ice was forming, and pretty soon a police patrol car comes to investigate these crazy rain-makers at night in the park. The policemen were very understanding and said we would have to stop using the water hoses, which were causing ice to form.

"So, after they left, we shot the scene as fast as we could, dousing Lemmon with water from the hoses again. Lemmon is doing a terrific job of pretending he is catching a cold. What a cold! Academy Award stuff. We didn't realize he really *was* catching cold!

"When we got back to California, Lemmon still had his cold, so we made an even bigger thing of it than we had originally planned.

"It was Iz who suggested that Bud cook spaghetti for Fran. Iz said women love a man who cooks for them, even if he doesn't know how to cook. It's something about the role reversal, his making the effort for her. It's romantic, it's sexy. I thought he was right, but Bud probably wouldn't have had a strainer."

Diamond finished the story: "Billy tells everyone the idea of using a tennis racket as a spaghetti-strainer when Bud cooks was my idea. It isn't an example of giving credit, but of placing blame. Billy's too much of a gourmet to like that joke. I remember the face he made. But he let it go through, so it must have been okay."

———◦———

"*The Apartment* is about the misuse of the American dream," Jack Lemmon told me. "It's about infidelity as a way of life. I'm in the position of running a hotel for philanderers, which is not the most sympathetic thing, and I'm doing it for self-aggrandizement, to climb the ladder of success sort of thing."

Wilder said it was a matter of "How do you get ahead in corporate life and stay a mensch, keeping your humanity, not just toward others, but toward yourself? We sugarcoated the story with a few laughs here and there. In a serious picture you don't hear them being bored. But in a comedy you can hear them not laughing.

"I wanted stark realism. The apartment was small, so we took all the white out to decrease its size. The office was huge. It was Alexander Trauner's masterpiece."

Billy and Audrey Wilder loaned their own Bentwood double bed to Trauner for *The Apartment*. "I was collecting, a long time ago, Bentwood furniture made by Thonet in Austria," Wilder said, "and I thought it would look good in *The Apartment*. I put Bentwood in Bud's apartment, because it is the way I would have done it if I had lived in an Upper West Side bachelor apartment at that time. We looked at a lot of apartments on Central Park West, and this was sort of a composite mishmash."

As a visitor to the Wilder home, set designer Alexander Trauner knew about the Bentwood bed. Trauner, like Wilder, was always meticulous when it came to detail, and he wanted the bed for Bud's apartment. "Later," Wilder said, "there were more collectors, and the bed got so valuable, it wouldn't have looked right in that apartment. So, we furnished C. C. Baxter's apartment with stuff from resale shops and art posters from the Metropolitan Museum.

Wilder told me that he had never used himself as a character in one of his films, nor had he confused what he thought with what his characters thought. "A writer cannot help but draw sometimes on bits and pieces of the world he knows, without his films being autobiographies. When I was writing, I played some of the parts in my mind. *I* was playing gin rummy in *The Apartment*."

———◇———

Revenues from *The Apartment* more than doubled its $3 million investment, and the film was nominated for ten Oscars, winning five. Billy Wilder received the Oscar as best director. It won for best picture and for best original screenplay, and Daniel Mandell won for best editing. Cinematographer Joseph LaShelle, who had previously won an Oscar for *Laura* and had been recommended to Wilder by Otto Preminger, was nominated. Jack Lemmon and Shirley MacLaine were also nominated, as was supporting player Jack Kruschen, who played Dr. Dreyfuss.

Promises, Promises, a musical comedy based on *The Apartment,* ran on Broadway for 1,281 performances, 1968 through 1972. The book, based on the Wilder-Diamond screenplay, was by Neil Simon, with music by Burt Bacharach, and choreography by Michael Bennett. It starred Jerry Orbach and Jill O'Hara.

While filming an exterior on West 67th Street in New York, Wilder was approached by a man who looked vaguely familiar, who spoke to him in German, saying, "*Ich bin Löwenstein.*" When Wilder looked blankly at him, the man said in English, "Don't you remember me? *Koko* Löwenstein?"

Koko was the class clown at the Realgymnasium Juranek in Vienna. He had escaped the Holocaust and was living in the brownstone next door to where *The Apartment* was filming.

He greeted Wilder shyly, inhibited by the fame of the director and the distance in time since they were young. Wilder was happy to see his boyhood friend. Löwenstein reminded Wilder about the times they had gone to the movies instead of studying Latin.

———◇———

I. A. L. Diamond said Wilder could not stop thinking about his scripts even after they were up on the screen. "About four months after we had finished *The Apartment,* we were sitting at a bar waiting for a table in a restaurant, and Billy said, 'I know how we should have done the picture! We should have given Lemmon some sort of handicap so he would have been a more sympathetic character.'

"By now, of course, the picture's in release, a big success, and Billy's still rewriting it in his head, and probably redirecting it, too."

"Some of the critics said the message of *The Apartment* is 'Be a mensch,'" Wilder said. "I'll go along with that, but I prefer what Fran Kubelik says: 'I should've learned, when you're in love with a married man, you shouldn't wear mascara.'

"But my customary answer to people who ask, 'What is the theme of your picture?' is, 'You can't eat soup with a fork.'"

—One, Two, Three—

One, Two, Three was originally conceived by Billy Wilder as a political farce with characters who represented attitudes rather than real people. "I wanted it to be in the spirit of *Duck Soup,* but the setting was not Fredonia or Sylvania. It was the two Berlins in 1960. Both films are about Marxism, but one involves Karl, and the other Groucho, Chico, Harpo, and Zeppo. Karl proved to be less funny. Like *Duck Soup, One, Two, Three* was supposed to be funny, but something not funny happened on the way to the Brandenburg Gate.

"I had always admired *Duck Soup.* It is a wonderful picture. When we started out to do the Molnár farce, I thought of the Marx Brothers in Berlin, and how they would have approached the Cold War. I wanted to make a picture like *Duck Soup,* but we got *Cola Soup."* It was around this time Wilder had been considering a picture about Groucho, Chico, and Harpo at the U.N.

Wilder didn't correctly judge the basic premise, that the Cold War could be a subject for comedy. The Berlin setting was too realistic, and it quickly became even more grim. The Cold War was *not* the Cola War, and the line "The situation is hopeless, but not serious" was no longer funny.

Horst Buchholz recalled the situation: "When we did *One, Two, Three,* we were going to shoot it, of course, in Berlin, but the damned Wall went up, and we still needed two or three days at the Brandenburg

Gate. So, they built the Brandenburg Gate on the Bavaria grounds outside Munich. They built it out of papier-mâché, but in the original size.
So we shot the rest there."

In 1929, Wilder had seen the German production of the play *Eins,
Zwei, Drei,* in Berlin, starring Max Pallenberg, an actor noted for his
breakneck staccato delivery, which Wilder had admired.

The play's story is very close to that of the film, except that the
leading character, a banker, has become a Coca-Cola executive, and the
young woman staying with his family is the daughter of his boss rather
than the daughter of an important client. In the play, she falls in love
and secretly marries a socialist cab driver. When the daughter becomes
pregnant, the young man has to be transformed into an aristocrat so
the banker won't lose the account.

Wilder saw the play's situation as still valid, with Berlin again the
ideal place to set it. He wanted to bring it up to date by making Coca-
Cola the symbol of capitalism and the rubble of East Berlin, communism. James Cagney seemed the ideal actor to duplicate Pallenberg's
rapid speech.

"I'd seen this incredible guy in Berlin," Wilder recalled. "He was
the fastest talker in the world. You could hardly believe it. It seemed
impossible. Well, maybe it was, and maybe I remembered him talking
faster than he did. Memory plays tricks."

When the movie opened in Berlin, the Cold War was far from a
subject for comedy, if it ever was. "A great miscalculation," Wilder
admitted, "as people were being shot trying to climb the Wall."

West Berlin Coca-Cola head C. R. MacNamara (James Cagney)
hopes to expand their market into Eastern Europe; but while he is
dealing with corrupt commissars (Leon Askin, Peter Capell, Ralf
Wolter), his boss's daughter, Scarlett (Pamela Tiffin), arrives from
Atlanta for a visit. During her stay, she secretly marries an East German communist, Otto Piffl (Horst Buchholz), and learns she is
pregnant just as her parents are about to arrive.

MacNamara saves the day by converting Piffl into a capitalist so
the couple can meet Scarlett's extremely anti-communist parents

(Howard St. John and Lois Bolton), but he doesn't get his anticipated promotion to the London office. Piffl gets that job, and MacNamara is sent back to Atlanta, which is where his wife and children wanted to go.

"I invited Cagney to join our little group for dinner," Wilder recalled, "and Cagney said, 'I'm having dinner with my wife.' I said, 'Well, your wife's invited, too.' He said, 'We're going to have a nice quiet dinner, the two of us.' I guess he was tired of being with all of us all day. He'd had enough of us on the set.

One, Two, Three—*Lilo Pulver does a shish kebab à la Khatchaturian Saber Dance-on-the-Table for East German commissars Peter Capell, Leon Askin, and Rolf Wolter.* (Anthology Film Archives)

"People wrote I was not satisfied with Cagney. They couldn't have been more wrong. He had a phenomenal memory. We'd rehearse, and he'd just do it."

Years later, James Cagney told me that it was the most difficult and exhausting picture he ever did because he was expected to speak so fast and never miss one word.

Horst Buchholz recalled Cagney telling him, "'I don't want to make another film with this man. He makes me speak too fast.'

"I came to the set one morning a bit early, and nobody was there, still the studio lights were on. I heard, *tacka-tacka-tacka-boom, tack-tacka-tack.* It was behind the set somewhere. So I sneaked around, and I saw Cagney hoofing. I said, 'What is that for?'

"He said, 'That's my way of getting the rhythm for this damned dialogue quick enough out of my mouth.' He was doing it through his feet! He was using his feet to get up to speed verbally."

Buchholz told me of his own problems with Wilder's dialogue. "In the middle of a scene, he stopped me from going on, because I'd said, like one sometimes says in real life, 'Oh, well.' And he called the script girl, and said, 'Where is it written, "Oh, well"?' She says, 'There is no "Oh, well."' And he said, 'Horst—no "Oh, well's," please. I've worked with Izzy Diamond for eight months on this script. If we had thought of one "Oh, well," we would have written it down.' I thought, 'This is just normal speech, like in real life,' but I put it out of my mind."

I asked Buchholz about his relationship with Cagney. "Not easy," he said. "He was a strong-minded guy, but a real talent. Cagney told me a funny story. Before he had left for Germany, he had bought a German shepherd to protect his wife and his children, and when he came back, the shepherd wouldn't let him in!"

Buchholz remembered an older man who was always on the set and treated with the greatest respect by Wilder. Even though it was summer, he wore a hat and overcoat. He was Doane Harrison, one of the associate producers of this and many other Wilder films.

Buchholz described Alexander Trauner as "a funny little guy. I liked him very much. Very talented. I don't know whether he's still alive."

Learning that Trauner had died, Buchholz was visibly affected. "That really gets me. When I lose people, most of the time I don't even hear about it. We're comrades in arms, and all of a sudden they're gone."

Just a few days before *One, Two, Three* was to complete shooting in Germany, Buchholz had an almost fatal automobile accident.

"Just outside Munich, I was driving to my house, where my wife was waiting. It was a bloody, stupid accident. Thank God I had a Cadillac at the time. I ran into three trees. The trees did better than I did.

"I was unconscious, in a coma. When I awoke, the doctor said, 'You have a bruise on your head, but you may have internal injuries.'

"Billy waited in the hospital with my wife. The doctor asked her for permission to operate because the steering wheel had been bent, which indicated that I might have internal injuries. My wife didn't think I would like the idea of exploratory surgery. She said no.

"Billy said to my wife, 'If nothing is wrong, he will have a little scar. If something is wrong, they will find it and fix it.' Billy had faith in doctors. My wife had great respect for him. He was always the director. So, she was persuaded. I owe my life to Billy Wilder.

"It was what the doctors call 'the golden hour.' That is the *last* hour. My injuries would have quickly caused my death if Billy Wilder had not made my wife give her consent. You could say I was already dead when Billy saved my life.

"I was away about ten days. Then I had to fly to L.A. and shoot the rest, which was the Tempelhof Air Field scene, the end of the film. They built it in L.A., and we shot the rest there in the studio."

———◦———

One, Two, Three sometimes echoes *Ninotchka*. It has a similar plot situation, with Horst Buchholz instead of Greta Garbo playing the dedicated communist who is won over to capitalism by love, both romantic and materialistic. There are three trade commissars, as in *Ninotchka,* and they frequently go into a huddle to discuss secret matters. At the end, one of them defects, as did all three in *Ninotchka,* to become a capitalist.

There are several other references to earlier Hollywood classics. When the doctor informs the family that Scarlett is pregnant, MacNamara exclaims, "Mother of mercy, is this the end of little Rico?" echoing Edward G. Robinson's last words in *Little Caesar*. Later, Cagney mimics himself in an exchange with MP Red Buttons. In response, Buttons does his own Cagney imitation.

"The film was not a success in the beginning," Buchholz recalled. "It was a flop! In Germany, people thought it was about the Wall, which, of course, it wasn't. It took generations of people who had lived with the Wall to make it, years later, a success. In cinemas, here in Germany, they are still showing *One, Two, Three,* and of course it's on television."

—◁◦▷—

Around the time of *One, Two, Three,* Wilder noticed a change in his status as a director. "I started getting more of the credit and none of the blame for a picture. It was a movement that came from Europe, a sort of *Cahiers du Cinema* thing. The writer-director became not an author, but an *auteur.*

"It was a moment when I couldn't do anything wrong, and I did everything wrong."

—Irma la Douce—

"*Irma la Douce,*" Billy Wilder told me, "is the story of a girl who was born on the wrong side of the tricks.

"My favorite Fellini film was the wonderful *Nights of Cabiria,* with his wife, Giulietta Masina, who was so good. *Irma la Douce* was my treatment of the same subject, that of prostitutes, but *Cabiria* was better."

Irma la Douce was a successful stage musical, running for three years on the stage in Paris and two on Broadway. Wilder liked the story, but felt that Marguerite Monnot's music would serve better as part of the background score rather than sung, as it was in the theater. To do the music for the film, he chose André Previn, who had just scored *One, Two, Three* for him.

Wilder and Diamond rewrote the musical play, changing the Paris locale from Montmartre to Les Halles. "I wanted the action of the market," said Wilder. "Nobody ever mentioned the symbolism of raw meat for sale. Just as well."

After finishing work on *The Apartment,* Wilder turned to casting *Irma;* the first actress he considered was Marilyn Monroe. "Marilyn was like smoking," Wilder said, "I knew she was bad for my health, but I couldn't give her up." When Marilyn wasn't available, Elizabeth Taylor, Brigitte Bardot, and Shirley MacLaine were considered.

"Casting makes a big difference," Wilder said. "If Marilyn Monroe was Irma, it would have been a totally different picture. It might have saved her life. It might have cost me mine. Elizabeth Taylor brought Cleopatra and Elizabeth to the part, too high-powered for Irma, girl of the streets.

"With Bardot, there was the problem of her French accent in English. It wouldn't match the way anyone else was speaking. Lemmon and everybody else would have had to adopt a French accent in English. It wouldn't have worked.

"One actor I was sure of was the great Charles Laughton, the perfect Moustache, the bartender and narrator. He was enthusiastic about the part, had a million ideas for his character. But he was very, very sick, and he died before we started shooting. Poor soul."

Paris policeman Nestor Patou (Jack Lemmon) loses his job because he is too honest. Returning to his old beat, he rescues a prostitute,

Irma la Douce (Shirley MacLaine), from her brutal pimp (Bruce Yarnell). thus becoming "numero uno" himself and Irma's man.

Jealous of her customers, he disguises himself as Lord X, a wealthy Englishman who pays Irma just for her company. To afford this, Nestor takes a backbreaking night job in Les Halles, and he returns home every morning too exhausted to be a satisfactory lover. Displeased by his inattention, Irma seduces Lord X, who had claimed to be impotent.

When Lord X disappears, Nestor is convicted of his murder and sent to prison. He escapes and returns to Irma, who is pregnant and retired from streetwalking. The father is Lord X, in reality Nestor. Nestor marries her after resurrecting the Englishman. Following a church wedding, Irma gives birth, making the baby legitimate, very important to Irma, who wasn't.

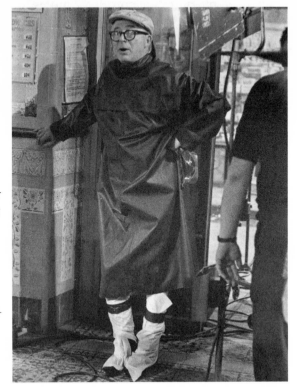

OPPOSITE: Irma la Douce—
*Joseph LaShelle (left) watches
over his camera while Billy Wilder
inspects Alexander Trauner's set
with Les Halles in the background, and Jack Lemmon gets
into, or out of, character.*
(Museum of Modern Art)

RIGHT: Irma la Douce—*Directing can be a hazardous occupation. Wilder anticipates an
inclement interior scene.*
(Anthology Film Archives)

Although Wilder described *Irma la Douce* as "a misfire," it became one of his most financially successful films, earning $20 million. "It was a top grosser for '63," he said, with some pride. "You never know . . .

"You don't know when the Midas Touch is going to become the minus touch. I never set out just to make a lot of money. It's a lot easier to figure out how to make a film that will win a film festival than it is to figure out one that will make money.

"The critics weren't enthusiastic, but the audiences were. The only people who objected to the immorality were men. I guess they had dirtier minds. Women found it amusing.

"We all love success, so I cannot say anything bad about *Irma*. It is not the kind of picture you do an autopsy on.

"Trauner did some great sets. He should have had an Oscar. I told him I was giving him a 'Billy.' "

Shirley MacLaine missed hearing some words of praise "or at least reassurance" from Wilder at the end of the film. "I didn't feel Billy really liked me much, personally or professionally. I couldn't feel he disliked me, because he cast me twice. He was a very important man in my life, but he didn't pay the same attention to me he did to Jack.

"Professionally speaking, Billy was infatuated, big-time, with Jack Lemmon, professionally enamored. Billy didn't want to hear much from me, an idea about a line, a bit. I couldn't quite get his attention, which was unusual and jarring for me. Directors had wanted to hear my ideas, physical bits, even if they didn't use them all. When I spoke with him, his eyes seemed to be somewhere else, and I think maybe his mind was, too. I think he was watching Jack to see what he might come up with.

"Billy was willing to do take after take of Jack to see what he could come up with. I knew if I had a scene with Jack, I had to be good every time because Billy would choose the one he liked best of Jack's. Maybe the picture should have been called *Nestor, the Sweet*. But a lot of people liked it and liked me as Irma, and they're still telling me about it.

"Well, I used to have some negative feeling because I felt I was being ignored, but I don't anymore. *The Apartment* and *Irma la Douce* were wonderful for my career. I loved *The Apartment*. It's wonderful to get an Oscar nomination. You have a better chance to get one if you work with one of the best directors ever. It doesn't hurt not to win, if you didn't expect to win. *Irma la Douce* is one of my favorite pictures.

"Doane Harrison was a wonderful person, very special, and I think Billy Wilder owed a lot to him. He was very kind and patient, and had an intuition that was part intuition and part experience. Billy really thought a lot of him."

Harrison was nominated for three Oscars: *Five Graves to Cairo* in 1943, *The Lost Weekend* in 1945, and *Sunset Boulevard* in 1950. He never won.

Shirley MacLaine was nominated for an Academy Award as best actress. The other nominations for *Irma* were Joseph LaShelle for the best color photography and André Previn for the best musical adaptation. Previn was the only winner. Alexander Trauner's Rue Casanova set cost $350,000 and took three months to build. It was almost a neighborhood, including forty-eight buildings and three converging streets, but Trauner wasn't nominated.

———◦———

Wilder always liked to have an atmosphere on the set in which people felt good. "They do their best when they are happy," he said. "There shouldn't be tension on a set."

Publicist Jerry Pam remembered, "One day, Billy came out, and he danced and sang, 'I'm the Jew who put the Ju in Jujitsu.' Everyone enjoyed it. It really broke the ice. I never forgot it."

Pam couldn't remember the rest of the song, and neither could Wilder. Perhaps that was all there was.

—Kiss Me, Stupid—

Wilder decided early in the filming of *Kiss Me, Stupid* that he might have made a mistake. "It happens sometimes. You write the film, you start to direct it, and it seems flat, so what do you do? No choice.

"You designed the plane; you took off; you thought it was going to soar; now it just kind of stalls, so you try to get to your destination or it's going to crash on you, right? You just try to do the best you can.

"It happens like it does to the best of cooks with the best of recipes, tremendous experience, and the soufflé falls flat. If it happens to a play, and you're trying it out in Pittsburgh, you can rewrite it, and if that does not work you just don't bring it into New York. If you lay an egg with a picture, they're going to open it, anyway. *Kiss Me, Stupid* is a soufflé that dropped.

"We don't bury our dead. It's just going to stink years from now on television. But I think if you bat four out of ten, terrific. It's better than Mickey Mantle. For me, *The Apartment* was one of those hits that soared. I like to think of it as my home run with the bases loaded. *Kiss Me, Stupid* was a strikeout."

The film was based on an Italian stage play, *L'Ora della Fantasia,* by Anna Bonacci. Peter Sellers and Marilyn Monroe were Wilder's original choices for the roles of Orville Spooner and Polly the Pistol. Sellers began the film on location in Nevada, but he had a heart attack. "That's when Iz and I should have quit," Wilder said.

"Nobody caught on to what we were aiming at," I. A. L. Diamond told me, "a *Tom Jones*–style picture in modern dress. They understood this in Europe, and we got some great reviews in Paris and London. If we had done it like the stage version, maybe people would have understood." Anna Bonacci's *L'Ora della Fantasia* was set in Victorian England, and the English-language version, *The Dazzling Hour,* in nineteenth-century France.

At the time Ray Walston was chosen to play Orville Spooner, he was in a successful television series, *My Favorite Martian.* "I was overjoyed to be able to take off those antennae," Walston said.

Diamond said that Billy Wilder thought Dean Martin, also cast in the film, was "the funniest man in Hollywood, and on the set, Martin kept him in stitches." When I asked Diamond for an example, he remembered Martin reaching deep into his pocket and saying, 'Where did I get these plums?'"

Kim Novak spoke with me when she came to New York to attend the Film Society of Lincoln Center showing of the newly restored *Vertigo.*

"I was so thrilled to learn I'd be working with the great Billy Wilder. I know he liked me in *Vertigo.* When we did *Kiss Me, Stupid,* he gave me more direction than Hitch had.

"I didn't call him 'Billy' or 'Mr. Wilder,' but I thought of him as 'Mr. Wilder,' because I never really got to know him personally. I enjoyed my part. My only disappointment about the film was that it wasn't a hit. At the time, a lot of people didn't like it. Now, all these years later, nobody seems to remember it.

"It's wonderful the way they have restored *Vertigo,* and to be here with it. But I don't think I'll ever be asked to appear with *Kiss Me, Stupid.*"

Piano teacher Orville Spooner (Ray Walston) sends his beautiful wife, Zelda (Felicia Farr), away for the night while he tries to sell a song to famous singer Dino (Dean Martin), who is stranded in town. To entertain Dino, Orville's musical collaborator, Barney Millsap (Cliff Osmond), contacts the village tart, Polly (Kim Novak), employing her to pretend to be Orville's wife for a night. She doesn't like Dino, but does love being Orville's surrogate wife. Dino goes to a bar, where he meets Zelda, and they spend the night together while Polly spends it with Orville. Afterward, Orville and Zelda are happily reunited, and Dino sings Orville's and Barney's song on television.

"They have both committed adultery and enjoyed it, and the world didn't come to an end—and they're back together," Wilder explained.

"What was too shocking for some people when our picture opened seems tame stuff now. It is on every soap opera. Now, she would have to do it with a woman, and he with a man, and then they would get back together."

In the film, the songs written by the team of Spooner and Millsap are actually unfamiliar tunes by George and Ira Gershwin. Ira was a friend of Wilder's. André Previn arranged the music and wrote the score. The name Sheldrake appears again in a Wilder film, this time given to Dr. Sheldrake the dentist, played by Mel Blanc, the voice of Bugs Bunny.

Kiss Me, Stupid was the first of a three-picture contract Wilder had signed with the Mirisch Company after the success of *Irma la Douce.*

The film received the Legion of Decency's C rating, which meant that it was deemed inappropriate for Catholic moviegoers, the first film to receive this rating since Tennessee Williams's *Baby Doll,* directed by Elia Kazan. The Production Code approved *Kiss Me, Stupid.* Critical reception of *Kiss Me, Stupid* was poor, so it was relegated by United Artists to a limited run in a few theaters.

"You could do me and yourself a favor by not wasting much time on this one," Wilder said. "Each picture cost at least a year and a half of my life, and I cannot get a refund."

—The—
Fortune Cookie

 "I like working with Lemmon and Matthau," Wilder said, "because they are fine actors. They are fine people. The director has to go into the cage, so it is natural he would want to select friendly animals who are well trained."

The Fortune Cookie was the first time that Walter Matthau and Jack Lemmon worked together. Matthau told me about being approached for his first Billy Wilder film:

"After I did *Odd Couple* on Broadway, Billy and Jack Lemmon dropped by to see me, and they asked me if I would like to do a film with them. Billy was telling me about *The Fortune Cookie,* and I said, 'Where's your script?' not because I needed to see it, but because that's what you think you're supposed to say. And Wilder said, 'There's no script yet.' So I said, 'Okay. Who needs a script? I'll do it.' And that's how it happened.

"While I was making *Fortune Cookie,* I had 'a mild cardiac infarction.' That's a heart attack, in layman's parlance. We had been shooting for two months, and Wilder and Lemmon waited another five months for me to recover. Luckily for me, because I got a supporting Oscar, very important for my acting career."

Jack Lemmon said that the decision to wait for Matthau was made shortly after he went to the hospital: "The only other thing Billy could have done would have been to reshoot all of Walter's scenes with another actor. This would have been understandable under the circumstances, and it's what most directors would have done, but Billy would have none of that. That's Billy. He said, 'We'll wait.' And I think it was very wise. There was only a little more than a week left to shoot, and Walter was so important.

"When Walter came back, he looked about a hundred pounds lighter. Billy threw an overcoat on him and did the scene. The audience never knew."

"I was about thirty-five pounds lighter," Matthau said. "And some people did ask me, 'How did you do that?' You were about two hundred pounds at the bottom of the stairs. You went up, and at the top of the stairs you were 165 pounds. I told them, 'I acted lighter.'

"A couple of days before I got the Oscar, I broke my elbow falling off a bike. What saved me was, before I fell off, I had a very large glass of scotch. I just got right up and kept on riding. I was all busted up, but I wasn't feeling a thing. I made it home, sobered up a little, and went straight to UCLA. They X-rayed me and found sixteen breaks in the elbow. All I remember about the Academy Award was when Shelley Winters gave me the Oscar, and I gave her a kiss, I looked out front, and I don't remember anything after that."

Slightly injured in a sideline collision during a football game, TV cameraman Harry Hinkle (Jack Lemmon) reluctantly follows the advice of his lawyer brother-in-law, Willie Gingrich (Walter Matthau), and feigns paralysis to collect a large insurance settlement. Suspicious, the insurance company sends a private detective, Purkey (Cliff Osmond), to spy on Harry.

Luther "Boom Boom" Jackson (Ron Rich), the black football player who injured Harry, feels such remorse that he devotes himself to helping Harry recover, at the expense of his own career. When Harry's estranged wife, Sandy (Judy West), returns, Boom Boom realizes she is there only for the money. Unhappy for Harry, Boom Boom gets into a barroom brawl, and is suspended from pro football.

Just as Harry is about to collect the insurance money, Purkey makes a racial slur about Boom Boom, and Harry jumps out of his wheelchair and hits him. He then literally kicks his faithless wife out and goes to cheer up the discouraged Boom Boom. Meanwhile "Whiplash" Willie, undeterred, thinks about another insurance scam.

"I got the idea from a real sideline collision I saw on TV," Wilder said. "Nothing happened, but I put the incident into my idea bank, where it didn't collect interest."

The Fortune Cookie alternates between the wide-open spaces of Cleveland Municipal Stadium and the claustrophobic confines of a hospital room and Harry's small apartment. Wilder shot footage during an actual Cleveland Browns game, and then matched it to a staged game with a local college team and a large number of extras in the stands.

This was Doane Harrison's last film. Harrison had worked with Wilder on every one of the films Wilder directed in Hollywood, first as Wilder's editor, and then as a producer. He died in 1967.

The Fortune Cookie—*Walter Matthau makes certain Ned Glass's diagnosis fits in with his plans to collect a huge insurance settlement for Jack Lemmon's feigned injuries.* (Anthology Film Archives)

—The—
Private Life of
Sherlock Holmes

In 1969, while *The Private Life of Sherlock Holmes* was telling a tale of man's exploration of space beneath the seas, an epic exploration was taking place in outer space. French actress Genevieve Page described for me how she felt at that moment, "in between two worlds":

"At the same time we were in Scotland, making *Sherlock,* there was the famous night that men walked on the moon! I remember that little hotel in Inverness where Colin Blakely and I stayed up all night long to watch it on TV. My children, who were in Paris, were two and three, and we woke them up in the middle of the night so they would see this and remember.

"It was all very strange, especially with the moon up above where nobody had ever walked. All of a sudden, in the middle of the night, in the middle of the picture. with all of its illusion and reality, I remember it seemed to me a very, very strange moment."

—◆◇◆—

Billy Wilder had always admired Arthur Conan Doyle's fictional sleuth, but he had never taken any steps toward dramatizing Sherlock Holmes until 1957. During his visit to London to shoot film exteriors for *Witness for the Prosecution,* he contacted the writer's estate and negotiated for the rights to produce a Broadway musical based on Sherlock Holmes for the centennial of Conan Doyle's birth. Wilder approached Moss Hart, and Lerner and Loewe, who were interested, and he expected to work with his *Witness for the Prosecution* collaborator, Harry Kurnitz. Wilder also wanted to work with I. A. L. Diamond, who shared his interest in Sherlock Holmes.

"I would have preferred doing it as a movie," Wilder told me, "but at that time, you couldn't show on the screen the things about Holmes I wanted to show. I wanted a serious study of Holmes in depth. He was a most intriguing character, a dope addict and a misogynist, yet in every movie ever made about him, nobody ever explained why. You couldn't talk about such things on the screen in those days, but you could on the Broadway stage. This was during the time of the great stage musicals, like *Brigadoon* and *My Fair Lady.* I thought Holmes would make a good musical, but nothing happened."

After the success of *Irma la Douce,* Wilder determined that it was the right moment to make the Holmes musical as a film. The lyrics and music were to be by Lerner and Loewe, and Peter O'Toole would be Holmes and Peter Sellers, Watson. O'Toole, however, was unavailable, and after working briefly with Sellers on *Kiss Me, Stupid,* Wilder lost interest in him as Watson. Lerner and Loewe became involved in other projects, and the Sherlock Holmes musical film languished.

In 1968, Wilder revived the idea, but without Diamond, who was working on *Cactus Flower.* He turned to Harry Kurnitz, who worked with him on a script, but Wilder was not happy with what they produced. Kurnitz later characterized Wilder as "Mr. Hyde and Mr. Hyde."

Diamond returned and began working with Wilder on a four-part Holmes film which would be 165 minutes long, with an intermission, and would tour as a road show. The film would be shown only at one of the best theaters in each city, charging higher admissions and offering reserved seats, very much like a touring stage show. Films such as *Lawrence of Arabia* and *West Side Story* had been extremely successful as road shows. Wilder said that he envisioned his film as a "symphony" in four movements, each movement a new Holmes mystery written in the Conan Doyle style. The tentative titles were: "The Curious Case of the Upside-Down Room," "The Singular Affair of the Russian Balle-rina," "The Dreadful Business of the Naked Honeymooners," and "The Adventure of the Dumbfounded Detective."

The Private Life of Sherlock Holmes would be the most ambitious film of Wilder's career, with a budget of $10 million.

———◇———

One of Wilder's favorite LPs was a Heifetz recording of Miklós Rózsa's Violin Concerto. He found it the perfect mood music for writ-ing about Sherlock Holmes, so he played it in the background as he and Diamond worked. It struck Wilder that the music he was playing for personal inspiration would suit a film about Sherlock Holmes. Rózsa was engaged to do the music, and Wilder asked him if he could use the concerto as titles music, as well as for the piece Holmes plays on his violin. Rózsa makes a brief appearance in the film as the conductor of the ballet.

Wilder announced that there would be no stars in *The Private Life of Sherlock Holmes*. "I wanted to avoid the expectations audiences have when they see famous faces," he told me. "I thought the actors should seem like the real characters, and that would have been impossible with someone like Richard Burton or Rex Harrison playing Holmes." Robert Stephens was to be Sherlock, and Colin Blakely, Dr. Watson.

Christopher Lee talked with me about becoming Sherlock's brother, the brilliant Mycroft Holmes:

"'Billy Wilder wants to see you,' I was told. So, after some trepida-tion, I went down to Pinewood, where there was a caravan, what you call in America a trailer, by the set. He was with Iz Diamond.

"'I know quite a lot about you,' he said, and I thought, 'Oh, dear,' after some of the films I'd been in! He said, 'I expect you, like most British people of your generation, have read the stories of Sherlock

Holmes.' I said, 'Yes, of course.' He said, 'Then, you're pretty well acquainted with the character. In fact, you may even have played Sherlock Holmes.' I said, 'As a matter of fact, I did, Mr. Wilder, in Germany, but I'd rather not talk about it.' He thought that was funny.

"He said, 'Do you know "The Affair of the Greek Interpreter"?' I said, 'Yes.' He said, 'Do you know the story of Sherlock and his brother, Mycroft, standing in the window of the Diogenes Club, each trying to top the other as they saw a man moving down the street towards them? Mycroft was the brains of the family according to Sherlock.'

"He told me, 'We have seen Laurence Olivier . . . ' My heart sank. I thought, 'What's he seeing me for?' 'And we've seen George Sanders and James Robertson Justice. I think you might be the right man to play it.' I thought, 'Oh, my God!'

"He wanted several things. He said, 'I know all about you, and I'm not concerned with what you may have done.' I said, 'Thank God!' He said, 'All I'm interested in is, are you the right actor to play Mycroft Holmes in my picture? I want to change your appearance completely, you know, bald cap and all that sort of thing.' I thought, 'This is marvelous. Wonderful.' He said, 'You don't mind changing your appearance?'

" 'Not at all, Mr. Wilder. I have done it before, you know.' He smiled and said, 'Yes, I know, but you won't mind changing it so people won't know who you are right away?'

" 'No, Mr. Wilder. Not at all.' So he said, 'Fine, fine,' and within two days, the deal was done, and I was engaged.

"Oddly enough, I met George Sanders at the London airport a few days after I'd started shooting. He said, 'You're playing my part.' I didn't know quite what to say to that. Laurence Olivier, George Sanders. How lucky can you be? Because that was what really turned my career around."

In Paris, Genevieve Page described for me her first encounter with Billy Wilder.

"I remember I went to London to meet Billy Wilder, and I loved him. He has a way of making a little world around him right away, which makes things easier. He has such a sense of humor, the way he laughs and makes *you* laugh at his funny stories.

"However, our first encounter was a bit surprising for me, because it was a long, long time ago, and people thought differently. He asked me whether I could be photographed naked to the waist. In that time, it was very surprising. Do you remember the scene where she gets up in the middle of the night and has this number on her hand? I suppose he wanted to cover himself for this scene, so we shot two versions.

"That kind of question about being naked to the waist surprised me and probably shocked me, but I thought it was all right. He made everything seem so comfortable around him."

————◦————

Production started at Pinewood Studios, just outside London, in May 1969, with Inverness, Scotland, as a location. The director of photography was Christopher Challis, who had worked as Jack Cardiff's camera operator on *The Red Shoes* and as cinematographer on *The Tales of Hoffmann*.

"When we started," Challis told me, "I think we were all rather in awe of each other, because the relationship which we had then between the crew and directors was rather different here than in Hollywood. We didn't know how to take him, and he didn't know how to take us, I think. But very quickly he formed a very happy relationship with the whole crew, and from that moment on, it was absolutely wonderful. He was just marvelous to work with.

"He had the most wonderful sense of humor. I think the ice broke on about the fourth day of shooting. We were on very, very formal terms. It was always, 'Mr. Wilder, this,' and 'Mr. Challis, that.'

"I had a wonderful cockney camera operator. One day, we had an involved tracking shot, and we lined it all up and rehearsed it a couple of times. Then Freddie Cooper, the operator, said, 'Mr. Wilder, would you like to look through the camera at the rehearsal?' And Billy looks at him and says, 'Oh, Freddie, let's cut out all this crap. I'm not technical. I don't know how the radio works when the window's shut,' and from that moment on, we had a great time."

Wilder's favorite scenic artist, Alexander Trauner, designed the sets. Challis described what it was like working with Trauner:

"He was a very good art director, really. But I don't think he was always quite aware of the problems of lighting some of those sets. A lot of art directors were like Trauner. They were designers, and they weren't aware of the technicalities of lighting and the problems one had with it. I didn't have the closest of relationships with him compared to other art directors I've worked with.

"Baker Street was a huge set out on the lot, with a forced perspective, a fantastically expensive set. Trauner laid real cobblestones, and that sort of thing, which, to my mind, was nonsense. It was all night shooting on it, anyway. I thought it was a terrible waste of money.

"Holmes's apartment, in particular, I mean, it was a real *building!* Nothing was made to float. You had to tear it apart. If you are going to build a set in a studio, you build it in such a way that you can take it apart very easily, because in many cases you have to, to get the sort of shots you want to do. Well, you couldn't do that with his sets. You could have lived in them."

In November of 1969, when British producer Mark Shivas, writing for the *New York Times,* visited Billy Wilder, Baker Street was covered with snow. It was, however, not Baker Street in London, but miles from there, where Wilder's Baker Street was located, in a field at Pinewood Studios. It was, Shivas said, "an enormous cobbled creation of staggering authenticity when viewed from the correct angles. Wander off the eye-lines and you see that most of the houses are just fronts. Number 21B has its own hallway inside, but its other rooms were to be found on a soundstage a quarter of a mile away. Scarcely anything was what it seemed to be."

Wilder told Shivas that he had personally selected many of the small objects that decorated the shelves of Holmes's Baker Street flat as re-created by Trauner. Wilder loved shopping for the flat not only because of his feeling for Holmes, but because he loved shopping for this kind of object, the subtle reflection of the character. He sometimes referred to him as "my Sherlock." This process was, for Wilder, a part of the writing.

Challis described Wilder as being "quite tough on actors, very tough. He gave the French girl a very hard time." Genevieve Page, however, described her relationship with Wilder quite sympathetically, the experience a precious memory:

"I was sometimes a little sad because I didn't know if I really fulfilled what Billy hoped from me. We started, and one of the first things he did, he changed the position of my head for the seduction scene, and that put me a little bit off, because I thought, 'Oh, I'm going to do everything wrong!' From the start, my head was not in the right position. But, in the other way, it's so extraordinary to work with a man like that, because you know he's right, so you don't ask yourself, 'Why does he do that?' You thought, if he asks that, that's the way it should be done. It doesn't happen too often that an actor is certain the director is right, whatever he says. You are afraid you are going to disappoint somebody who's so strong about the idea he has of the character in front of him, someone who is so great.

"I remember when he liked something, he said, 'Good.' That was the word I dreamed to hear. I know he didn't like my accent, and very often he was correcting it. I thought perhaps he found it too Parisian and wanted something more Orient Express, Belgian, with a hint of something strange, the hidden German. It's funny because he has a very strong accent himself. So when he was saying, 'Not like that,' and he would say how he wanted it, at first I thought he was making fun of me.

"He was very pleased with my German at the end. He personally taught me exactly how I should say '*Unter dem Schloss,*' and he was very pleased by my German pronunciation. I didn't know German at all.

"Robert Stephens was a very precise man. I am just the contrary, and I thought that he was so good in all the little things he had to do, just what Billy wanted. I thought it was one thing that Billy didn't like about me. I wasn't very precise about things I had to do, and Robert absolutely was. Robert was doing so well at first, and I wasn't as good as he was. So I was jealous, because I thought that Robert fulfilled much more of what Billy wanted than I could.

"With a French woman there is a sort of a strange suspicion that we are more female than the others. My character seemed to me to have a French mind. The character was a German, speaking French, pretending to be Belgian. It worked better to have her be a Belgian, because that is more mysterious."

Christopher Lee's first day on the Sherlock Holmes set began on a somewhat worrisome note:

"I reported for work. The makeup thing, my head and everything, was all done. My first scene was in the club, which was the interior of the Diogenes Club, built by Trauner. It was the first time you've seen Mycroft, holding on to the reins of the family, very much the power behind the throne. He virtually ran the country from the Diogenes Club. That's the implication, anyway.

"And so I got down there, and there were these rather taut-looking actors, Colin Blakely and Bob Stephens, whom I knew slightly. We talked, and they seemed a bit rigid to me. I thought, these two very distinguished, eminent actors who had done a lot of work in films and theater were sort of frozen. They looked slightly, decidedly on the verge of being alarmed. You can imagine the effect that had on *me,* because I said, 'Is anything wrong?'

"They said, 'No, no, no, not at all! It's the most wonderful experience either of us has ever, ever had. But by God, you'll see! You can't make any mistakes. You've got to get it right.' Well, of course, my heart went into my boots, because this tied in with some of the stories I'd heard. I thought, 'Well, I'm pretty good on lines, thank God.' Then they said, 'Oh, he's the greatest director we ever worked with.' I thought, 'Oh, God. I hope I don't make a mess of things.'

"Billy was charming, very nice. He said, 'I'm very glad to have you in the movie. I'm sure you'll do very well,' and so on. It made me more nervous, of course, because I had to live up to that!

"The crew were all very professional and experienced. They were almost entirely British, and I'd worked with a great many of them before. Of course, I've made a tremendous number of films at Pinewood. So, I didn't feel like a fish out of water. But here was this legendary director behind the camera, almost always wearing a hat, and we rehearsed. And the scene's the first one where I'm in a private room in the Diogenes Club, full of books and everything.

"It so happened that when they came in, I start talking. 'Ah, Sherlock,' or whatever, 'Dr. Watson.' And at the same time, I have this bottle of red wine, which is in a metallic cradle. And in order to pour the wine into three glasses, I had to turn a lever on the side of this cradle, which tilted it, so the bottle of wine came down to a point where it could release the wine, which came out of the bottle. I didn't have to work with the bottle, it was open. I had to turn this little lever on the side, which tilted this metallic frame, which in turn, released the wine from the bottle into the glasses.

"Now, I had to pour out three glasses of wine, one for myself, one for Sherlock, and one for Dr. Watson and talk to a very specific moment. You know you have to time a scene. You can't go on too long. 'No, that's too long. No, that's too quick.' Very precise. 'And don't take so long saying that,' or, 'You're too fast on that one,' or whatever. I thought, 'Oh, heavens, this is going to be murder.' I'm sure the wine is going to slop all over the place, or I'm going to spill it, or it's going to go all over my hands. Or I'll have enough in one glass, and there'll be nothing left for the third one. And I'm going to forget my lines, and Mr. Wilder will be furious. I've heard terrifying stories of the legendary things he's said to people, which I may say, I never saw or experienced. But I'd heard stories that he'd cut people off at the ankles, because he could be devastating. He had a very abrasive wit. He said, 'I think we better shoot this, don't you?' And I thought, 'Well, yes,' because we could go on rehearsing for the next six weeks before I get it right.

"So, in a bit of panic, quite frankly, I sort of mentally worked it out in my mind. I thought, 'I've got all these lines to remember. I've got to talk to Sherlock, I've got to look at him, I've got to talk to Dr. Watson, while at the same time, I'm doing this all the time, turning this wretched thing, this cradle with the bottle. And I've got to pour out, more or less the same amount in three glasses without spilling any.' Not easy.

"Somehow, I don't know how, it was a miracle, I managed it. We only did one take. To say I went on with the scene, inwardly, with relief is an understatement. I managed to fill the glasses, say the dialogue, and do it on time! And I thought, 'Well, I think I did it all right. I don't think I got the words wrong.' They said to me before, you know, there are a lot of words, but you better get everything right. You can't change anything.

"At the end, Billy turned around to Iz, who was always standing there with a script in front of his face for every shot, and Billy said, 'Words?' And Iz said, 'Um-hm. Yeah.' And that was it. One day he said,

'We spent two and a half years writing this so I have every right to expect the people will get all the words right.' And he is right. It's our job—and our privilege.

"So, we got that over, and he said, 'I want to chat with you.' I thought, 'Oh, Lord! That's it. I've had it. I'm going to be fired.'

"He put his arm around me, and he walked me down the long corridor on the set, the corridor in the club. He said, 'I'm very happy with my Mycroft.' And I thought, 'Oh, thank God!' and I gave it the knees.

"He said, 'You might be interested to know we had bets on whether or not you could do that, because we all tried, and none of us could. We bet on how many takes you'd need. But nobody bet that you would do it in one take.'"

Actors frequently characterized Billy Wilder as "the captain of the ship." Genevieve Page saw him just that way:

"The most important symbol of his way of being was when it poured, the way it did in Scotland, he was always the last to go in and take cover, like the captain of a ship. There were clouds, and then the rain. It's the way I always think of him. Billy Wilder was like a captain on a vessel. You know, in Scotland, it sort of rains and is cloudy, and then, all of a sudden, the sun shines. And we have to do that ride on the tandem bicycle, the bicycle built for two.

"We would be all prepared, with the hats, and everything. They would cover the bicycles with a sort of plastic bag with holes in it while it was raining. We would be ready to shoot as soon as the sun would shine, and jump on our bicycles as soon as the sun would show its nose.

"And while we were in all these showers, which were very strong and very rapid, I never saw him going inside, getting under cover while the rain was pouring until everybody else was under cover. He was always the one to stay outside until the last man was under cover. A true captain of the ship!

"When we lost our Loch Ness monster, he wasn't too concerned, even though he was also the producer. He was more concerned about how the man who made it felt when all his work sank to the bottom of the Loch Ness. He went over and comforted him." She was referring to special effects man Wally Veevers's elaborate "monster," which worked beautifully until they gave it a test run in the Loch Ness. After its failure, Wilder decided to shoot it in miniature in the studio.

There were other mishaps and delays on location in Scotland. For Mark Shivas's first interview with him, Wilder had chosen the graveyard. It is there that the four kneeling schoolboys are revealed as middleaged men who, though only the height of children, have achieved their full physical stature. It is what Wilder termed "an exposure scene."

"The sun was beating down on the graveyard," Shivas recalled. "Though it was supposed to be a day of overpowering gloom, the sky is azure blue and any clouds quickly disappeared. So the crew, the midgets, Diamond, and Wilder all had to wait. Wilder actually sat down, an event in itself. Most of the time, he paced back and forth, gazing at the ground. He said:

"'We can't work because the shots we did yesterday would not match this Capri sky. In this business, you make mistakes like that, and they haunt you forever.'

"He stopped for a moment, noticing the dates on an adjacent tombstone.

"'The people around here died so old. They can't have had anything to do with the movie industry.'"

There were other problems in Scotland.

"We had a location in Scotland at Loch Ness, of course," Christopher Challis said. "I never was part of picking that location. Billy picked it, I believe with Izzy Diamond, several months earlier. I don't think they did very much walking. I think they looked at it through a limousine back window on the road. And when we all came out there to shoot it, there were several problems which they hadn't been aware of.

"The visit of Queen Victoria to the place where they were building the submarine took place at night. There was absolutely no way that her carriage could drive to the castle, because it was a steep hillside, and there was no road, so they had to build a road.

"I said to Billy, 'You know, if we shoot it at night with lights, then we see nothing of the background of the mountains, or the loch, or anything like that. Obviously we can't light the countryside. The alternative is to do things 'magic hour,' which is the period at dusk where there's just enough light to see the background, and yet you can light it. You can use lights, and you can light the foreground with the flaming torches and things like that. That period lasts only two or three minutes each day. So, you can be there for fifteen years, you know, shooting the scene. Billy said, 'Well, we'd better go ahead and we'll see what we can do.'

"Well, we shot two or three nights. We didn't see the dailies, because they had to go to London and then come back up. But we went into the town along about the second day to see them, and, of course, it's as I said. You couldn't see anything except the area we were able to light. He said, 'It's not what I want. It's not right. We'll have to build it.' And that's what we did.

"We shot some material up there. We did some magic hour shots and things like that. But the basis, the main thing, was built in the studio, so that we could light it, and we could see the painted backing of the mountains, and the loch, and things like that. We hadn't done very much anyway when he made up his mind that it wasn't what he wanted. So, that was why there was a change of plan.

"But I don't think he's a great location man. He loves to have things under control, really. There were little problems, but by and large, no. Once you were in the studio, you knew exactly what you were doing."

The actors had their problems on location, too, as Christopher Lee remembered:

"When Queen Victoria arrives, we shot that on the bank of Loch Ness, in Scotland. We were on location up there, up in northwest Scotland. And we shot that on the edge of Loch Ness at Urquhart Castle. Very grim. It's a ruin. And you remember—Sherlock arrives, gets out, walks up the red carpet. 'Ah, I'm expected,' or something like that. And I come out of the tent. We have a chat. I'm holding a bottle of champagne, you know. They had to christen the submarine. We're talking, and suddenly a very august personage duly arrives, with her lady-in-waiting. She walks up, and I have to introduce her to all these scientists.

"They all have different names, they all have different initials, and I have to get every—single—one—right in one long take. I couldn't possibly change 'W. W. Prescott,' coinventor of the revolving periscope. I couldn't change it to 'W. J. Prescott,' only that. 'That's not what we wrote. W. W. sounds better. Do you see what I mean?' And it does. So, I got through that somehow.

"We then left and came back to London to the studio, and the decision was then made that it didn't look right because there was no light on Loch Ness. And as Christopher Challis, the cameraman, said, 'Well, Mr. Wilder, I cannot light Loch Ness! I'm afraid we would need several thousand lamps, to put it mildly.' So they reshot the whole thing, from the time he gets out and walks up, it was all rebuilt in the studio. And there was the backing, with some little lights and houses and things, all done in the studio."

If everything didn't work out perfectly in Scotland, at least there was always good food and a lot of it. "I remember that we had catering," Genevieve Page said, "because he didn't want to have pauses, so we had the catering all day long. There was a lot of food, and my corset was getting tighter and tighter."

Each person who worked with Billy Wilder found him different from any other director they had ever worked with. Christopher Lee found one of Wilder's directorial idiosyncrasies to be a bit disconcerting:

"His way of saying 'Action' was actually quite unnerving. I mean, one's used to directors who say softly, 'Action,' and others who yell it, and others who just say it in a normal voice. But Billy used to shout, 'GO!' which if you're playing a quiet, intimate scene is slightly unnerving, to say the least. But that was it: 'GO!' and quite sharply."

Genevieve Page contrasted him with Spanish director Luis Buñuel:

"Working with Billy Wilder was a wonderful and different kind of experience, but to tell you the truth, I never worked twice under the same kind of director. Every one of them was different. It's like if all of a sudden you find yourself married to another man.

"Luis Buñuel created a sort of mystery about himself. When I shot with him, he already didn't hear very well. He was a shy man when he was directing, but he knew exactly what he wanted, and he could surprise you.

"I remember in the scene at the end of *Belle du Jour*, where I kiss Catherine Deneuve on the lips. He came to me and said, 'In this scene, you will kiss her on the lips,' but he didn't tell her. I remember that I was a bit flabbergasted when she didn't know I was going to kiss her on the lips. We got it on the first take, but there was a big laugh afterwards."

Christopher Challis felt that Wilder was more interested in what he was shooting rather than in how he was shooting it:

"He had a different approach. I don't think he was a great visual director. By that, I mean that he knew exactly what he wanted, and he knew how he wanted it to look, but he wasn't sure whether he'd got what he wanted until he saw the dailies.

"He had certain things that he liked. I mean, he liked rather long takes, and I was amazed. He once said to me quite early on, 'You know, I hate this modern method of filmmaking. I don't like all these hundreds of huge close-ups,' and of course now, it's got very much worse. He said, 'The close-up is a jewel. It should just be set in the right place in the overall picture, and it shouldn't be used indiscriminately, or it loses all its impact.' Well, now, that's typical of Billy, and I think he was absolutely right.

"Another thing that I found very interesting with him was that he was primarily a writer. I think the written or the spoken word was all-important to him, and the actors had to do it his way. I mean, he didn't let them have a lot of freedom. He insisted on them playing lines the way he wanted them played. He would play quite important dialogue on people's backs, with them walking away from you, because he knew exactly what the impact would be, whereas most directors would go around the other side and cover it the other way in case it wasn't right. Well, Billy didn't do that. He didn't cover things. It had to be right, the way he did it, and that was it. He was quite unique like that."

Genevieve Page appreciated Wilder's impromptu performances for the cast and crew. "He loved to tell stories, and he was very good. He was always prepared to make people joyful on the set."

Wilder told Mark Shivas, "Holmes has come to seem more real than people who really lived. I wanted to show him as one of the great minds of his time or any time. I think of this picture as my valentine to Sherlock."

> Dr. Watson's safe-deposit box, opened fifty years after his death, contains an unpublished manuscript.
>
> There is a story about a Russian ballerina who requests that Holmes father her child, which he declines, implying that he (Robert Stephens) and Dr. Watson (Colin Blakely) share something more than lodgings.
>
> A more substantial story involves a beautiful Belgian woman, Gabrielle (Genevieve Page), who is really Ilse, a German spy, children who are really midgets, Trappist monks who are really German sailors, a Loch Ness monster which is really the first submarine, and Holmes's brother, Mycroft (Christopher Lee), who is really a secret service agent.
>
> Finally, there is Sherlock's stoic heartbreak when he learns of Ilse's death.

"I should have been more daring," Wilder said. "I have this theory. I wanted to have Holmes homosexual and not admitting it to anyone, including maybe even himself. The burden of keeping it secret was the reason he took dope."

Genevieve Page never suspected this from Wilder's writing or direction. "I don't think Billy thought Holmes was homosexual. Holmes loved his way, something deep and important that he felt for a woman. But that doesn't prove that he was homosexual. It's like people who are so much in love with the theater or movies that they are their main preoccupation. I feel when Sherlock Holmes took the dope, it was only for pleasure, not for any negative reason.

"I think that Holmes was probably falling for Ilse more than she was for him. Her character is supposed to be the one woman he loved in his life. But I was a spy, so I guess he wanted me more because I was unattainable. I felt certain that Holmes was in love with me. Maybe I represented something, a little mystery, that aroused him."

Production lasted from May to November of 1969, and the first rough

The Private Life of Sherlock Holmes—*Wilder directs Robert Stephens in a scene with Colin Blakely and Genevieve Page.* (Museum of Modern Art)

cut of the film ran three hours and twenty minutes, according to Diamond.

The popularity of the road-show-film concept was waning, and United Artists was reluctant to release another such film, especially one with no stars. They decided to release the film in regular distribution, which meant that Billy Wilder, who had the right of final cut and for whom every word was crucial, would have to cut more than an hour. Wilder reluctantly agreed, though he told me that he regretted that decision. "If I had refused, they might have given in." The abbreviated version was released in November 1970.

"When I saw the way they had cut it, I had tears in my eyes," Wilder said. "It seemed longer when they made it shorter."

The original opening, with Watson's grandson (also played by Colin Blakely) receiving the contents of the safe-deposit box, was simplified. The "Upside-Down Room" and the "Naked Honeymooners" were taken out, as was a short episode on a train and a flashback to Holmes as a student at Oxford.

The final release version was two hours and five minutes long. Some of the deleted footage, long assumed lost, has been found. The soundtrack for "The Upside-Down Room" and the film without sound for "The Naked Honeymooners" exist.

Christopher Challis, who viewed the final complete copy, thought that all of the sequences, including those cut, were "good and were all unusual," though he thought the film "as it stood, probably would have been too long."

The flashback to Holmes's student days at Oxford concerns his winning a boat racing pool in which the prize is a night with the town's most beautiful prostitute. Young Holmes wins only to discover that the "prize" is a girl with whom he has been secretly in love.

The short episode on a train involves Holmes proving to Watson that he can solve any case with only the slightest evidence. He does so when a crazed Neapolitan breaks into their compartment and Holmes encourages him to jump off the moving train, which he does. He tells Watson that the man was fleeing a jealous husband, and Holmes simply pretended to be that husband.

"The Upside-Down Room" is a seemingly impossible-to-solve case ending with all of the furniture in a room being on the ceiling. Holmes correctly deduces that it's all a hoax perpetrated by Watson to persuade him that cocaine is affecting the detective's mind, the only possible way to convince him.

The longest deleted sequence is "The Dreadful Business of the Naked Honeymooners," which involved an ocean liner set. "That was quite an elaborate sequence with a big set built in the studio," Challis said.

During a cruise, Watson offers to solve the case of two apparent corpses discovered in a stateroom. His deductions prove erroneous when the corpses turn out to be a naked honeymoon couple lying in bed exhausted.

———◇———

Christopher Challis remembered Billy Wilder as a legend who was not a disappointment in person. "He's someone I've admired all my life as a director, and I've admired all his films. I think with some other people I've worked with, who also had made wonderful films and had great reputations, when I actually came to work with them, it was sometimes rather a disappointment. I, in fact, even wondered how they'd ever made the pictures that they had. Well, that wasn't the case with Billy; he lived up to all our expectations."

"He's not a laughing person," Christopher Lee said. "I don't think I ever saw him laugh. I saw him occasionally smile.

"I remember once, we were waiting between shots, and somebody said Moët wine. And somebody said another champagne, and they reeled off the names of all the great champagnes. And of course, the translation is something else. Veuve Clicquot means 'the widow Clicquot.' And somebody said something else about another champagne, which could be translated into another word, rather like a pun. Suddenly Billy said, 'We shall have absolutely no more champagne jokes at all!' And I said, 'No. Mumm's the word.' He shot 'round, and he looked at me like that. There was the beginning of a twinkle. And he said to Iz, 'Did you hear that?' And Iz smiled slightly. It wasn't that what I said was that funny, but it was fast."

For Genevieve Page, *The Private Life of Sherlock Holmes* coincided with a memorable period in her life:

"I was delighted when I saw the film. But it's very difficult, because so many things are attached to it when you see the picture after you have appeared in it. So many things are remembrance and moments that you lived during the picture. It's very difficult to separate the film and your own experience, to be aware of the whole thing. But it was a very happy period for me.

"London was so extraordinary for us. The hippie touch had not reached France yet, but it was just beginning in London. So, I didn't go to bed very much when we were in London.

"Everything was different. Probably because I was away from my family, alone, away from France, away from dressing according to fashion, I felt a kind of freedom from my own normal identity. I think it helped me to capture Ilse's spirit of adventure.

"I remember I wore boots and a tiny fur coat, things I never thought I would ever do. People were wearing what they found nice, and there was not a sort of a taboo about fashion, or whatever. We were very classic still in Paris, and my godfather was Christian Dior. So, I had a certain way of dressing, and all of a sudden, I find myself in rags, and enjoying it.

"I enjoyed *The Private Life of Sherlock Holmes* treasurably. When we did the scene with me naked, I was feeling a little shy. It was another time, I had never done that before. I was blond, and my nipples were light. Billy said to the makeup woman, 'Make them darker so we can see them.' So, she was brushing them with rouge, and I was so embarrassed. I felt that somehow my nipples had failed.

"I was more than naked to the waist. It was to the bikini line. If the film had shown then, probably I would have been embarrassed. When they said it was to be reissued, I was worried that my nude scene would be in it.

"So there's still a version of me. I hope they will show it sometime. It's a different time now. The truth is, I was beautiful, so if they showed it now, thirty years later, I would be proud."

All of the nude scenes, those of the naked honeymooners and of Genevieve Page, were cut from the final version of the film that was shown.

———◇———

At the end of October 1970, *The Private Life of Sherlock Holmes* opened in one of the great movie palaces of the world, perhaps the greatest, Radio City Music Hall. The theater had more than six thousand seats, and too many of them were empty. Wilder's *Sherlock Holmes* was expected to play through the Thanksgiving holidays, a long and financially big box office weekend, but the film closed before the holiday began.

The entire domestic gross was $1.5 million. It had a limited release everywhere and not only failed financially wherever it played, but was poorly received by the critics. Audiences did not have sufficient time to find it, but when they did, the response generally was, at best, tepid. This was an economic blow to the Mirisches and to United Artists, though the producers had played their part by ordering the extreme cut in the length of the film.

The Private Life of Sherlock Holmes cost more than $10 million to make. A film for which Wilder had such great hopes, it's failure was a blow to his career and to his pride. Usually he avoided indulging in regrets or self-recrimination, but he felt that only he was responsible for *Sherlock's* failure, though even with hindsight, he wasn't certain exactly what he had done wrong. He did regret being timid about going farther into the exploration of Holmes's homosexuality and he wished that he had been able to stay and cut the film himself, but as he told me, "Even hindsight isn't 20/20."

—Avanti!—

 "Nobody cried," Alessandro von Normann, the production manager of *Avanti!* told me. "Billy Wilder never screamed. Everything was so easy, so normal.

"He was like no other movie director. No one else was ever like that. They were usually just directors making a movie. We loved him. Nobody else I worked with ever created that kind of atmosphere on the set. For six months, he was more than a friend with everyone. He had a sense of humor. He was so nice, but professional. Very precise. Very prepared.

"We didn't do a fantastic movie. But we wanted to, every minute. It was a very human experience. For him, every member of the crew was a human being.

"He selected Luigi Kuveiller as cinematographer after he had watched the work of everyone in Italy. He saw a film he liked, I think it was *A Quiet Place in the Country,* directed by Elio Petri. Kuveiller was not so well known as other people, but Billy Wilder always knew what he wanted.

"We finished $100,000 under budget, unheard of in Italy. We were so proud. Everyone tried so hard for him. We wanted to do it for him. Billy Wilder was a gentleman.

"Afterwards, when I went to Los Angeles, I wrote to him, and he showed me his home, with his wonderful paintings, and he took me to a fine restaurant."

Von Normann described how Billy Wilder had the hotel sets designed to accommodate the dialogue, timing how long it would take to speak lines while moving from one spot to another. "Billy Wilder had a light style, but he was at the same time so precise. To ask a production designer about this was unusual. He wanted to be sure the lines covered the movement." The pacing really *was* pacing.

Samuel Taylor's original play of *Avanti!* opened on Broadway in 1968, but ran only twenty-one performances. Agent Charles Feldman purchased the film rights and offered them to Billy Wilder, who believed it would make a good film, but was unable to go forward until after *The Private Life of Sherlock Holmes* was completed. Previously, Feldman had interested Wilder in doing *The Seven Year Itch*. When Wilder started rewriting the play, Diamond was unavailable for collaboration, so Wilder turned first to Julius Epstein and then to Norman Krasna, neither of whom stayed with the project. When Diamond was free, he returned to work with Wilder to finish writing the *Avanti!* screenplay with the help of Luciano Vincenzoni, who had written several successful Italian screenplays, among them *Seduced and Abandoned* and *A Quiet Place in the Country,* as well as Sergio Leone westerns.

"We changed the emphasis," Wilder said, "from a dialogue on American versus Italian values to a bittersweet love story, a little like *Brief Encounter,* which I always admired." *Avanti!* also resembles the theme in Samuel Taylor's *Sabrina Fair,* in which a committed businessman pretends to be attracted to a woman in order to protect his business interests, and then falls in love with her.

While it was being written, Wilder showed his neighbor Jack Lemmon some pages. Lemmon said he would like to play the part of Wendell Armbruster, and Wilder and Diamond, who always liked to write with a specific actor in mind, tailored the script to fit Lemmon.

"Knowing pretty early on Jack was going to be in our film made it more comfortable writing his dialogue," Diamond said.

Wilder had seen Juliet Mills in a TV series which he felt wasted her talents, thought she was a good actress and appealing, so he called her and offered the part of Pamela Piggott.

"I loved Billy Wilder just calling me and asking me to be in his film," Mills told me, "no lawyer or agent, his voice, not asking for an audition or a screen test." He sent her a script but told her that she would have to gain twenty-five pounds. "I told Billy I didn't mind gaining twenty-five pounds, though it was more fun gaining it than losing it. But I'd do it again anytime to work with him. There was also a nude scene, and I agreed to that, too."

"I think nudity hurts laughs," Diamond told me. "I mean if you're watching somebody's boobs, you're not listening to the dialogue." Billy Wilder used female nudity in *Avanti!* and later in *Fedora,* and he had filmed the nude scenes for *The Private Life of Sherlock Holmes,* which weren't used.

Wilder was not trying primarily for laughs in *Avanti!* "I believe whatever you do," he said, "you have to give it both knees, but I do not believe in giving it three knees. Maybe we went a little overboard with some of the comic relief, because *Avanti!* is *not* a comedy. Like Cukor told Mr. Lemmon, 'Sometimes more is less.' If this film had worked the way we wanted it to, it would have had more of the quality of *The Apartment.* I always feel sorry for the disappointment of the actors, and those dear technical people who do so much, when the picture doesn't make it the way they hoped. With *Avanti!* I felt everybody who worked on the film was rooting for it."

Wilder considered *Avanti!* a "European" film. "I directed it in Italy with mostly Italian actors and technicians. Only Lemmon and [Edward] Andrews were American, and Juliet Mills and Clive Revill were British. What makes one film 'European' and another 'American'? [Jean] Renoir said the difference was an American film moves smoothly in a direct way toward its goal while a European film goes indirectly, in a round-about, unpredictable way to get wherever it's going."

The title *Avanti!* comes from the custom of knocking on a door in Italy, asking, "Permisso," and waiting for the word "Avanti" before entering. Avanti means "advance."

The paths of Baltimore industrialist Wendell Armbruster (Jack Lemmon) and London shop girl Pamela Piggott (Juliet Mills) cross when they come to Ischia to pick up the bodies of her mother and his father, who have been killed in an automobile accident after a ten-year summertime affair. Straitlaced Wendell tries to avoid a scandal while plump Pamela is impressed by the romantic setting. After some confusion with the bodies and a blackmail attempt by unscrupulous locals, Wendell and Pamela extend their parents' affair into the next generation.

Avanti! was filmed entirely in Italy, along the Amalfi coast and at the Safa Palatino studios in Rome during the summer of 1972 and released in December of that year. Most of the critical response was negative. "I went much farther with forbidden themes than I had with *Kiss Me, Stupid,* but nobody cared," Wilder said. "Audiences thought it was too long and too bland. I guess they would have liked it better if it turned out the father was having the affair with one of the bellboys at the hotel."

—The Front Page—

"I was getting tired of having to spend 90 percent of my time producing, or trying to produce, and 10 percent on doing a picture, so when Jennings Lang came to me and said, 'How would you like to do a remake of *The Front Page* at Universal?' I said, to quote my partner, Iz, 'Why not?'"

Ben Hecht and Charles MacArthur's 1929 play about the Chicago newspaper world already had been made into two successful films, in 1931 by Lewis Milestone, and in 1940 as *His Girl Friday* by Howard Hawks. The Hawks version changed the Hildy Johnson character into a woman reporter (Rosalind Russell) and her editor, Walter Burns, into her ex-husband (Cary Grant). All three versions, including Wilder's, remained faithful to the plot and characters of the original, while "opening it up" somewhat for the screen.

Some of the expanded scenes in Bartlett Cormack's screenplay for the 1931 film established a kind of cinematic tradition for remakes. When the psychiatrist asks Earl Williams to reenact his crime, the sheriff hands the condemned man the gun with which he makes his escape. This episode, only referred to in the play, becomes important in all three of the films. Wilder liked Dr. Eggelhoffer's character so much that he expanded that part beyond the psychiatric examination. Earl Williams has been changed, too, from wild-eyed George E. Stone in the first *Front Page,* to pathetic John Qualen in *His Girl Friday,* then to Austin Pendleton's anarchist.

Eliminated in Wilder's *Front Page* is Hildy's future mother-in-law and the thug Burns hires to kidnap her. Added is Rudy Keppler, the cub reporter who is replacing Hildy, and Jacobi, a police sergeant played by Cliff Osmond, an actor favored by Wilder.

"Maybe I liked *Front Page* more than I should have because it reminded me of when I was a very young newspaperman," Wilder said.

"A reporter was a glamorous fellow in those days, the way he wore a hat, a raincoat, and a swagger, and had his camaraderie with fellow reporters, with the local police, always hot on the trail of tips from them and from the fringes of the underworld, like stool pigeons.

"The reporter was not likely to be a family man because his work was not dependable enough for anyone with responsibilities. Sometimes you could hardly feed *yourself.* You could be out of a job any time. And you had to be free when the story was happening, because only bank robbers kept bankers' hours."

Added to the problems of a remake were the problems of a period piece. Billy Wilder's *Front Page* was different from all the others, including the stage play, in that it was not contemporary. At the beginning of the film, the date of a newspaper clearly sets it in 1929. Earlier *Front Page* films were set in their own time, but by 1974, this was impossible, since the daily newspaper was no longer the dominant news medium.

Just after reporter Hildy Johnson (Jack Lemmon) quits the *Chicago Examiner* to get married and start a new career, convicted cop killer Earl Williams (Austin Pendleton) escapes from death row, and Hildy can't resist one more scoop. Only he and the condemned man's girlfriend, Mollie Malloy (Carol Burnett), know Williams's whereabouts—in a rolltop desk of the courthouse pressroom. To save him from being discovered, Mollie creates a diversion by jumping out of a third-story window.

When Williams is finally caught, Hildy and his managing editor, Walter Burns (Walter Matthau), are arrested for harboring a fugitive. They are released when it is revealed that the mayor and sheriff were concealing a reprieve from the governor until after the election.

As a going-away present, Burns gives his ex–ace reporter a gold watch, then telegraphs ahead to the next train station to arrest him because it was stolen.

"I had one regret about the film," Jack Lemmon said. "Billy would not let us overlap our lines more. I think that would have made it better. Billy was usually very open to hearing my ideas. Sometimes he liked them, and sometimes he didn't.

"I feel it's a piece in which you *must* overlap. But Billy, the writer, wanted to hear all of the words clearly, and he wanted the audience to hear the words. I would have liked to overlap to the point where you lost some of the dialogue. He would only let us bite the cues, but we couldn't overlap them. I still think we should have."

Real stars of this film were the production designer Henry Bumstead's stylish period sets. "You know, it's funny," Bumstead told me. "Billy never mentions this film. I don't think he's very proud of it. I know I'm proud of it.

"I was just thrilled to work with Billy Wilder, honored to get the chance. I had a very good decorator, Jim Payne.

"I remember they wanted to do it all around Los Angeles. But there was no scale, and I told Billy we're going to have to go to San Francisco. So I went up there, and that's where we did the scale of buildings to match Chicago. We also did the end sequence, the train. Thank goodness there were these train buffs who furnished that nice period train for the final scene.

"The rest of the stuff was all on the lot. I think the city room, the big, big set, was a beautiful set. And the press room, too, upstairs, where the desk was, with the body in it, and the air well and everything outside, it was terrific. That was all set, you know, all on the stage there at Universal. I think really the only things not on the set were the exteriors of what was supposed to be in Chicago, the exteriors of the paper, and then the train sequence. It just worked out beautifully."

At the opening of the train platform sequence, two conductors

The Front Page—*Walter Matthau appreciated Billy Wilder's direct approach to directing, and so did Jack Lemmon. Wilder listened to ideas from both and often used them.* (Museum of Modern Art)

stand in the vapor and steam of the locomotive, beautifully photographed by Jordan Cronenweth. A few years later, he would fill an entire picture with such scenes, *Blade Runner.*

"I had some sketches that we did for *Front Page,*" Bumstead continued, "and I remember taking them over and showing them to Billy. He turned to I. A. L. Diamond and said, 'I don't know what a newspaper office in America looked like in that time,' and he asked him what he thought of my sketch. I remember I. A. L. Diamond said, 'Oh, that's terrific. That's beautiful.' He really kind of relied on me.

"We did have a studio research library. That's kind of a fun part of a film, when you're researching. You design the set to fit the scene, and you use the research as a tool.

"I had just finished *The Great Waldo Pepper,* with George Roy Hill, and Susan Sarandon was in that. She was the one on the wing of the plane. We were getting ready to shoot and Billy was rehearsing on the big set, when she came in. I'll never forget, she saw me and ran up and threw her arms around me and kissed me. Everybody was quite impressed.

"I remember Walter Matthau in the dressing room with Susan, and it was five or six takes of this scene, because he was missing some of the dialogue. Billy said to him, 'Look, I want it exactly like it's in the script.' He finally got it, but it took a while. Most directors aren't that fussy.

"Hitchcock was very demanding, too, word by word, because he worked, just like Billy Wilder, very hard with the writer, even though Hitchcock didn't consider himself a writer and didn't take credit as a writer. With Hitchcock, and Billy Wilder, too, you could almost edit the picture in the camera, because they didn't fool around. They would start a scene, and then say, 'Cut,' and then they'd move in, and that's almost all the film editor had to do. Billy and Hitch both had great taste."

Front Page first assistant director Howard G. Kazanjian shared some of his memories with me of working with Wilder:

"I remember Billy and I. A. L. Diamond being very precise, working very, very hard on the script. They examined and thought about *every* word. 'Should it be an "a" or should it be an "an"?' When we would shoot, I.A.L. was there listening to every word, and those two would not allow an actor—and we had some strong actors there—to say one word that wasn't written. You couldn't change one phrase, you couldn't substitute a word, like actors do all the time. Billy would say, 'Cut,' turn around, look at I.A.L., who would acknowledge that the right words were said. Izzy was not directing. He was just approving the dialogue.

"I was given the script in advance to read so I could talk with some intelligence when I met Billy Wilder. They were still writing up until the very last minute, just making those minor little changes. A lot of the locations were not finalized until just a couple of weeks before shooting, even though I came on a couple of months earlier. You have to change a few words and certain things to accommodate the sets and the locations.

"Without putting any of the directors down that I've worked with, I think the two most brilliant people I've ever worked with were Billy Wilder and Alfred Hitchcock. They came from the old school, where they absolutely learned their trade. They studied film. They knew what they wanted. They meticulously planned.

"Billy was like a kid. He could stand up most of the day, he could move fast, he's full of energy. He's always moving. He's watching the lighting. He moved fast, and he thought fast. You could ask him a question and he could come back with a joke, and you say, 'How could he *think* that fast?'

"Careful planning was one of Billy Wilder's traits. The sets and everything had to be built and ready, and he would continually walk into those sets. Now, he was lucky, because the sets were at Universal, and his offices were at Universal. Oftentimes we're shooting in Indianapolis or somewhere, and the director can't get there, can't see the building taking place, where you can say, 'Stop, let's move that door over two feet because such and such is going to happen.' Or, 'I want the staircase to go two feet higher because I'm going to have a camera here.' A lot of that is done early on, and a lot of filmmakers don't even think of that stuff.

"The one thing Billy did that I've never seen before or since was when he did a pickup. Every other director would say, 'Okay, start at the beginning of the sentence, and go through the whole scene,' or, 'Go through those five or six lines we're picking up,' whether it's a pickup for the master or a close-up, but Billy knew in his mind exactly how he was going to cut this. So, if the sentence was, 'I'm gonna walk out of here, slam the door, and get into my car and go home,' and he only wanted, 'slam the door, and get into my car and go,' that's all he insisted the actor say. Actors need to build up! I mean, they just can't start in the middle of a sentence. He insisted that his actors just say the words he needed. He was worried that Universal would recut his picture. He gave them no choice. This was the movie!

"He turned that picture over in four days, from the time he fin-

ished shooting, and he had a wonderful Academy Award–winning editor on it [Ralph E. Winters], and he really had a top-notch crew. And
then you bring in the sound effects crew, the music, and all that.

"We had an upright piano on the set, and Jack Lemmon, as I understand he did on most of his pictures, he'd go down and sit there, and
he'd play the piano while the rest of us were getting the next shot
ready. It was a very quiet set, a very, very quiet set. Everybody worked
extremely quiet. I didn't like people shouting and bells ringing. Nor did
Hitchcock, Billy Wilder, and Robert Wise. They were all very quiet souls.

"Jack Lemmon would shave twice a day. He'd shave in the morning, get his makeup on, and then he'd shave at two o'clock or so.

"When we were shooting *Front Page,* Billy got a telephone call in
the afternoon, and somebody said, 'The Samuel Goldwyn Studio is
afire.' And he calmly said, 'What stages?'

"With me, I'd drop everything and run. But he was very calm, he
didn't say too much, and he said to me, 'Call and see if you can find out
anything else. I have a great deal stored there.'

"And then, at the end of the day, we heard that everything burnt
down. Somebody said to him, 'What do you have there?' He said, 'I
have my art. I have my Oscars and scripts. Those are replaceable, the art
isn't.' I don't think I've ever heard a value on that art, but it must have
been millions. His secretary had all of the Oscars duplicated, and she
got copies of all his scripts, and bound them in leather, but they were
all new. They weren't his original stuff. He went through that traumatic
experience while we were shooting *The Front Page,* but he didn't miss
any time or let it show to the rest of us how he felt.

"I remember one time I went to his office, and he had this painting
on the floor, leaning up against the wall. He said, 'What do you think of
that?' I said, 'I don't quite know what to say, Billy, and I don't know
what it's worth, but it's probably something I wouldn't hang in my
house.'

"He said, 'Well, let me describe that picture to you. That has presence. Whether you like it or not.' And he was absolutely right. It was
something I learned. It wasn't, do I like the painting or what not, but it
sure did catch your eye, and you looked at it."

For the film, Wilder wanted to cast old-time actor Frank McHugh, who had appeared in the first *Front Page,* but Universal vetoed him. He was able to have Allen Jenkins, who was the garbageman in *Ball of Fire,* who appears as the telegraph operator near the end of the film.

The Front Page was the first Wilder film to show a profit since *Irma la Douce.* The picture cost $4 million and grossed $15 million.

He still felt, however, that his longtime instinct about remakes was correct. He said a few years after making *Front Page,* "I'm against remakes in general, because if a picture is good, you shouldn't remake it, and if it's lousy, *why* remake it? People remember and sometimes they think they remember something that never was there. We were younger, we were more impressionable, and it was fresher. For fifty years, people have been ripping off *Front Page.*

"It was not one of my pictures I am particularly proud of. But I never think about my old pictures. Good, bad, indifferent, whether it's a hit or flop, that's all kind of out of my mind. It's 'What are we doing now? The games we lost, forget it! There's a game on tonight. Let's win it, because we've got a chance to win the pennant and go into the World Series.'"

PART IV

A Legend in Somebody Else's Time

—Fedora—

Fedora was intended by Billy Wilder to be his "memorial tribute to a vanished Hollywood," the Hollywood in which he had thrived. It is a story of lost hopes revived momentarily, lost youth relived vicariously.

"Youth had been a habit of Fedora's for so long that she could not part with it," was how Wilder saw it. "She was sort of like *Dorian Gray*, except it was herself she kept in the closet instead of a portrait. Maybe we should have called our film *The Picture of Fedora Gray*, by Oscar Wilder. Fedora was a strong woman who wanted to write her own third act.

"What attracted me to *Fedora* in the first place was what I finally could not resolve: Could I find someone who seemed to be twenty and at the same time eighty, decrepit in a wheelchair but still young-looking, without revealing my secret? Would the audience notice if I used a double, photographed from the back? Or would it be like trying to shoot Katharine Hepburn as Audrey Hepburn? It's one thing to fool the audience, and another to fool yourself.

"I needed a Bette Davis in her prime. I wanted her to be an 'imported' star, someone like Dietrich or Garbo. After I cast Marthe Keller and Hildegard Knef, I had the idea of working entirely with Knef's voice, so that afterwards the bad operation would explain the difference between the two faces.

"Originally, I wanted Marlene Dietrich to play both the mother and the daughter. Iz and I had written it with her in mind, and I thought she could still do it. I sent her the script and it came back by return mail, special delivery. She must have had the postman wait. She had written in large block letters just five words: HOW COULD YOU POSSIBLY THINK! It wasn't a question. Smart girl. No matter what you write, casting is important.

"I wanted Bill Holden. My only problem was, I knew Bill was going to bring the ghosts of *Sunset Boulevard* along with him. But I couldn't make *Fedora* without him. You couldn't get somebody *like* Bill Holden because nobody was like him. He had a seriousness, a presence, a maturity, an inner strength which made him absolutely indispensable. He made it look easy.

"When he made *Fedora,* Bill was just about the only actor of his age who had not had any cosmetic surgery. That in itself is remarkable in a town where the leftover scraps of flesh from the face-lifts of just one star could be sewn together to make half a dozen stars."

Fedora was based on a story from *Crowned Heads,* by Tom Tryon, about a legendary actress who returns to the screen after a seventeen-

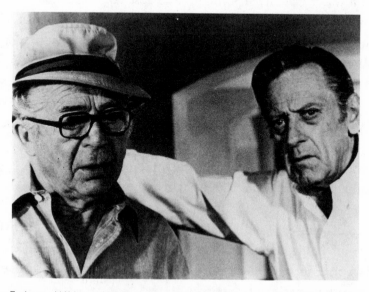

Fedora—*Wilder and Holden contemplating serious cinematic problems while shooting in Greece.* (Museum of Modern Art)

year absence, miraculously unchanged. Wilder and Diamond expanded Tryon's story, adding characters and plot complications.

Universal rejected the Wilder-Diamond *Fedora* script in 1976, putting it into "turnaround." Wilder tried unsuccessfully to sell the property elsewhere. "No wonder the young directors have all got beards," Wilder said. "They don't have time to shave! They have to spend all their time pitching—and not baseballs."

Wilder originally wanted to shoot *Fedora* in Hollywood, but when Marlene Dietrich said no, and Universal rejected his script, he turned to his old friend, agent Paul Kohner. Willy Egger, the production coordinator on *Fedora*, described the meeting:

"Mr. Kohner asked him, 'What's happened, Billy? You want to make this picture or not?'

"He said, 'Yes, but Universal doesn't want to do it.'

"'Okay, then we can do it in Germany, with German money.'

"So Kohner called Bavaria in Munich and asked them, 'You want to make a Billy Wilder picture?' and everybody said, 'Yes!'"

Wilder referred to the European backing as "a German production, tax-shelter-wise." The budget was $6.7 million. Wilder bought out Universal's interest in *Fedora,* including distribution rights. The film was scheduled to begin shooting in June of 1977 somewhere in the Mediterranean, then to go to Paris and to finish at the Bavaria Studios in Munich, where much of *One, Two, Three* had been shot. Madouri island in the Ionian Sea off the west coast of Greece and the village of Nydri were chosen as the Mediterranean locations.

Hollywood producer Barry "Dutch" Detweiler (William Holden) attempts to put together a picture by luring the legendary Fedora out of her second retirement. He finds her in Greece, as beautiful as ever, but living with an old woman in a wheelchair who won't allow her to return to the screen. Two weeks later, Fedora commits suicide.

At her ostentatious funeral near Paris, Dutch learns that the young woman in the coffin is not Fedora, but her secret illegitimate daughter, Antonia (Marthe Keller). The real Fedora is the old woman (Hildegard Knef). Antonia took her mother's place when a cosmetic surgeon, Dr. Vando (José Ferrer) disfigured Fedora's face, but the burden of playing her mother drove her to return to drugs and finally to suicide. As Dutch leaves, Fedora lets him know that she remembers their brief romantic rendezvous years earlier.

For "old times' sake," Dutch keeps her secret, and the real Fedora dies, unnoticed, six months later.

This is a film about people who are searching for something they have lost. Fedora wants to find a way back to the days of her beauty, youth, and screen stardom. Antonia wants the love of the mother who rejected her. Dr. Vando wants to regain the respect, even envy, of the medical world. Dutch Detweiler wants to make his comeback as the producer of a Fedora film.

For Michael York, being in *Fedora* was an especially memorable experience. "Billy said the role he wanted me to play was an extremely difficult one. 'Very difficult for anyone, but you.' Billy wanted me to play an actor and the actor would be Michael York. Intriguing. It was a unique offer I certainly couldn't refuse, especially when he said he would pay me in part with a piece of art! I think that was a joke, but I didn't care. I wanted to be in a Billy Wilder film, as any actor would. It was also an opportunity to be one of the few actors who could tell Billy and his collaborator, Iz Diamond, something about the charac-ter—me. When I made the film, I never said anything, because who could write a character better than Billy Wilder could?

"*Fedora* took me to Paris and Munich, one of my favorite cities. I could hardly wait to get to Dalmayer's, the Munich Fortnum & Mason, with all of its delightful foods. The story was about a faded movie star of olden times who, it seemed, had fallen in love with, of all people, Michael York. It was all very flattering, but I must say, I did feel a bit awkward about it. By a really odd coincidence, Tom Tryon, who wrote the original story, was the previous owner of our home in California, which my wife, Pat, and I love. Real life has its strange turns, too.

"I was in just a few scenes: the ballroom, the funeral. But I must say it's one of my great fantasies, one of my most cherished possessions, that memory. And, in fact, I've got it on a demo reel, that moment when William Holden pulls down the sheet to reveal the shrine—to actor Michael York, whom I am playing! He says, 'Michael York? Yes, I've seen him in the movies.' It was definitely an odd sensation.

"There was an echo of *Sunset Boulevard*. As in *Sunset Boulevard,* there was a great star who couldn't face that last act of life. Old age is such a taboo in Hollywood. The casting of William Holden was a further tie with *Sunset Boulevard*. When I was in Paris, I rode out with William Holden to the scene of Fedora's funeral. It was a great thrill.

"I think of Billy wearing one of his signature hats he always had. When there was some talk about the possibility of going over budget, he told us, 'Nobody ever says, "Boy, I've gotta see that film—I hear it came in under budget.""

"We were in Paris at the tomb. And Billy was doing his own art direction. He was arranging roses on the tomb, and he murmured wickedly, 'Ah, this is living!'"

In the scene with the mourners, Michael York places a red rose on Antonia's chest. Wilder had never forgotten the story of actress Katharina Schratt, Francis Joseph's mistress, placing white roses on the chest of the emperor at his funeral.

————◦————

Wilder had seen a rough cut of Sydney Pollack's *Bobby Deerfield*. He was impressed by the young Swiss actress, Marthe Keller, and he signed her to star in his new film, envisioning her as both the young and the old Fedora.

"When we were almost ready," Wilder said, "we put on a kind of mask to make her old. It's not so difficult to make someone age. Making someone young, that is not so easy. I would like one of those masks myself.

"All of a sudden, I saw the mask was crying. We got it off quickly. It turned out that our star couldn't wear the mask. She had been in an automobile accident, and the mask was painful for her.

"We had to quickly find another actress to play the old Fedora. We had to make the two Fedoras match. Not so easy."

The part of the old Fedora went to Hildegard Knef. A problem in having two actresses play the same part, even though they are far apart in age, was the difference in their voices. It was easier to make them look alike than to sound alike. Keller's voice did not sound like Knef's, so Wilder brought in a German actress, Inga Bunsch, to "loop" both voices. When this didn't prove entirely satisfactory, Keller and Knef were given back their voices except in scenes where both voices had to match. As a further compromise, Keller's voice was used for both actresses in the French version, and Knef's in the German version.

"It was my idea to ask Knef," Marthe Keller told me during lunch at the Russian Tea Room in New York. "Being in a Billy Wilder film was a dream come true, a dream I wouldn't have expected to come true, and then it happened: *He* asked me.

"I expected to learn a lot. I felt he would inspire me to draw out from inside me something that even I didn't know was there.

"I had such respect for him. I wanted him to help me to be good, my best. And then, I wanted him to tell me I *was* good. He paid more attention to the crew, the makeup people, to anyone but me.

"Everyone thought he was very funny. He didn't seem funny to me. But everyone laughed at his jokes, and he was always full of jokes. I was never certain if they were all laughing because he was so funny or because he was our director.

"I don't have a good memory for jokes, but I remember one he was telling while I was trying to get into my character for a difficult scene. Actually, I found it all difficult, especially since I wasn't getting help, only criticism. I'm not the kind of person who can work well without encouragement. I need approval. I found myself losing my confidence. I was very tense. And then I heard him saying:

"'Miriam found Moses in the bulrushes and showed him to the pharaoh, and the pharaoh said, "What a homely baby," and Miriam said, "He looked good in the rushes."'

"At the time, it didn't seem funny to me. It still doesn't. It seemed to me then that he was talking about me, that I was the joke. Looking back, I still don't know if it was just a joke, if I was meant to hear it . . . I wish I hadn't.

"The person who *did* try to help me was Bill—Bill Holden. He was wonderful. But what could *he* do? It was Bill *Wilder* I needed.

"He was a genius. I'm not a genius, so I don't like to say anything critical of him. But he came looking for me. I didn't go to him. It was not a natural part for me. I am not a diva. I am more introspective.

"I was thrilled, and I had such high hopes. I have no regrets, but it was a difficult experience. It didn't turn out the way I had hoped, but I am not sorry I did it. He wanted me, and then he didn't.

"I like harmony on a set for the best work. We didn't have that. It wasn't just for me.

"Sometimes when we were alone, he would go into German. He never did it if there were other people around who didn't speak German. It was especially when we were in a German-speaking place. He spoke eloquent, educated German, though the humor was the same. I think after all those years, Billy Wilder was still thinking in German and translating into English.

"I'd worked with wonderful people. I'd just been directed by Sydney Pollack. It was a perfect experience, professionally. He is a fine human being. It was he who recommended me for *Fedora*.

"But Billy Wilder liked everyone else better than me. I don't know why he cast me if he didn't like me. Sydney Pollack's recommending me wouldn't have been enough. Wilder was a person who would decide for himself. He must have liked what he saw when he watched my work. I suppose I disappointed him in my performance. I think having two actresses play the same part, one young, one old, spoiled it for him. We didn't rehearse. I was accustomed to rehearsing."

"Keller had just done *Bobby Deerfield*," Wilder remembered, "and she came on the set with her nose high in the air and said, 'With Sydney Pollack, we rehearsed, and rehearsed, and rehearsed.' And I said, 'Okay, then we won't have to rehearse anymore. Let's do the scene.'"

———◦———

Vienna-born Willy Egger, who had been working in European films since 1945 when he was fifteen, was overwhelmed when he was chosen by Billy Wilder to be his production coordinator on *Fedora*.

"When we were first on location, we always spoke English. Then, after the first week, I asked him what's the problem with shooting this picture. Are we shooting in three months, in five months? He said,

'Maybe in three months, maybe four, I don't know now.'

"So, I go to my room, and I think, 'We *must* have a schedule.' So, for two nights, I work with cups of coffee—coffee, coffee, coffee. And then, on the third day I come, and I say, 'Mr. Wilder, I have a schedule.'

"He said, 'When have you done this?'

"I say, 'In the last two nights.'

"'Ah, great!' and this was the first moment he speaks German. Once he had spoken German with me, I felt he had accepted me. He recognized I was a professional." On Wilder's next picture, *Buddy Buddy,* Egger was his personal assistant.

———◇———

"When I was asked about doing *Fedora,*" Henry Fonda told me, "I was pretty pleased to be in a Billy Wilder picture. I'd always wanted to work with him, but he took a long time in getting around to asking me. The trouble was, I wasn't sure I could do the part. I would like to have worked with him when I was younger. And I also would have liked a more interesting part. He wanted me to play Henry Fonda!

"I'm not really a very interesting person myself. I haven't ever done anything except be other people. I'm best at being other people. I ain't really Henry Fonda!

"When I'm doing a part, it's more real than the real world for me. I'm more comfortable in my part than I am in real life. I never know what to say if I don't have lines somebody else wrote for me.

"I'm never nervous when I'm performing. Some actors have said they hate me for that. They were only joking, of course, but there's always a little truth in a good joke. I guess sometimes they don't like it.

"I like being the guy the writer conceived, whatever. It's the old make-believe, let's pretend. There's no reason to be nervous, 'cause it's not me.

"I thought about how much fun I was gonna have. Then, I found out it was only half as much fun when Billy said to me, 'I don't have to tell you how to play Henry Fonda. Just be yourself.'

"Those were the most fearsome words anyone could tell me. Be myself. What is that? How do I do that? I don't know that character.

"Billy and Iz Diamond wrote lines for me, but the lines seemed to be written for Henry Fonda rather than for a character. Anyway, I had trouble finding a character I could disappear into.

"I tried to switch the focus off myself. I thought about all the presidents of the Academy and some public-figure executives, and tried to figure how they would do it.

"I'm afraid I was only semisuccessful. I would've liked it a whole lot better being the president of the Academy with any name in the world except Henry Fonda."

"I know Billy was disappointed in *Fedora*," William Holden told me, "both in the reception of it, and in the picture itself. The criticism hurt Billy even though he never showed it. You would think you'd get more thick-skinned with time, but you only get more thin-skinned. He never blames anyone but himself. But a lot of things went wrong. For instance, me.

"Just having me in the film invited comparison to *Sunset Boulevard*. It was a picture about Hollywood, with an old film star dreaming of bygone days, and *Fedora* had a better chance of being judged on its own if someone else had played my part. *Fedora* couldn't stand up to *Sunset Boulevard*. What could? It was daring of Billy to make another picture about Hollywood.

"Of course, I said yes without even looking at the script, hearing the story, knowing what my part was. I trusted Billy totally."

From time to time, an actor plays a part from which he takes away something that influences him not only in future performances, but in real life as well. William Holden said he was not certain how much he brought of himself to Joe Gillis, or how much of Joe Gillis he took away with him into his future life, but he did feel that people expected him to live up to *Sunset Boulevard,* on the screen and in real life. He believed that the comparison was made and that in real life, he failed the test; and he believed that in *Fedora* he had "let Billy down."

"It's not easy being fabulous," Holden said. "You really should be talking with Billy Wilder. He says all those clever, cynical things I'm supposed to say."

Holden preferred talking about Africa where he said it was refreshing to be with dumb animals who hadn't seen *Sunset Boulevard* and didn't expect him to be that character. "I try not to let people down, but I see the disappointed looks on their faces."

Holden said that whenever he returned to Hollywood, he understood how wild animals feel when they are put in a cage with people staring at them. It made him feel restless and anxious. He wanted to get back to Africa where he felt free. "But I'll never be able to or want to say no to Billy."

———◦———

Fedora was completed on August 31, 1977. The world premiere took place at the Cannes Film Festival on May 30, 1978, with Billy Wilder in attendance. Though the film was well received at Cannes, reviews in the United States were mixed and distribution was limited.

"I felt rushed in strange locations where I had so little control," Wilder said. "And there are so many things I would do differently.

"It's terrible when you believe in a picture, you think you are doing something good, and then, only after you have begun, you realize it's a mistake. But it's already too late to go back, so you have only one direction to go in. When you are climbing a mountain, there is a point where mountain climbers say it is easier to try to make it to the top than to go back down. The trip is only half over, but you have to finish it.

"Iz and I wondered if we were giving away too much too soon. We decided *Fedora* was not a mystery, like *Sunset Boulevard* was not a mystery. It is the characters that make it or break it.

"We decided it wasn't a problem to know about Fedora that much before the end of the film. To judge from what critics said and audiences thought, maybe it was. Maybe the story was too tricky. Maybe it wasn't tricky enough.

"Maybe one day, when I am concealed under another name in a rest home, I will find an unfortunate young man who resembles me a little. I will acquaint him with my movies. After making him suffer through a plastic surgery operation, so he'll seem a little bit older, he will have the strength to continue to make pictures under my name, the ideas I did not have time to carry out. People will say, 'Billy Wilder looks so young for his age, which is a hundred.'"

—Buddy Buddy—

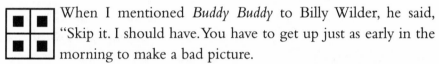When I mentioned *Buddy Buddy* to Billy Wilder, he said, "Skip it. I should have. You have to get up just as early in the morning to make a bad picture.

"It was brought to me. I didn't have to pitch it. I didn't have to audition. No screen test. No birth certificate. I didn't have to pass through Checkpoint Charlie.

"I hadn't been working enough, and I was anxious to get back on the horse and do what I do—write, direct. This wasn't a picture I would have chosen. It chose me. At that point, maybe I was a little lazy about hitting my head against the wall, or maybe a little dented."

Buddy Buddy was based on *L'Emmerdeur*, a 1973 French film starring Lino Ventura and Jacques Brel. It was written by Francis Veber, an author of *La Cage aux Folles*. *L'Emmerdeur* was released in U.S. art houses as *A Pain in the A—*. MGM decided that an American version might do well, and Wilder was offered the property to rewrite and direct.

Jack Lemmon and Walter Matthau agreed to be in the film, even before the script was written. "I couldn't say no to Billy," Matthau told me, "and I didn't want to say no to being in a Billy Wilder picture. But this wasn't a Billy Wilder picture."

"We took a wrong turn," Wilder said. "If we'd been doing this the way we'd always worked, I would've been back to the drawing board and started again when we saw we were going wrong. But we didn't have time.

"Sometimes scenes that play beautifully in the typewriter don't work on film," Wilder noted. "That's where the director takes over from the writer. Personally, I prefer to do most of my directing on paper.

"I watch when something isn't clear with the eyes of a writer because I am mostly a writer. The writer in me screams at the director to get it right. The writer is always stronger in me. Sometimes there is a conflict between the writer in me and the director in me, and the two parts of me don't speak to each other for days.

"Wilder the writer let Wilder the director down. We had to write too fast. This script was done in three months. We always took much longer, but the wheels were rolling, and we had to go forward. If I'd backed out, they would have said it was because I was too old.

"If I met all my old pictures in a crowd, personified, there are some that would make me happy and proud, and I would embrace them. There are others I would say a casual 'Hello' to, polite, nothing more, and walk on. I might nod to *Fedora,* but *Buddy Buddy* I'd try to ignore."

Hit man Trabucco (Walter Matthau) has trouble completing a contract because a suicidal man, Victor Clooney (Jack Lemmon), won't leave him alone. Trabucco tries everything to get rid of him, but Victor is convinced he has found a new friend. Complicating matters for Trabucco is Dr. Zuckerbrot (Klaus Kinski), a sex clinic guru for whom Victor's wife (Paula Prentiss) has left home. Zuckerbrot fears her husband's suicide will ruin the reputation of his clinic. After assorted plot exposures and payoffs, Victor successfully carries out Trabucco's contract, then follows his new friend to a tropical island as Victor's wife runs off with a female employee (Joan Shawlee) from Zuckerbrot's sex clinic.

"After two weeks of shooting," Wilder said, "I realized I'd made a mistake in casting. It didn't work to have two comics together. I needed someone serious like Clint Eastwood as the hit man instead of a comedian like Matthau."

Jack Lemmon noticed a difference in the way Wilder directed on the set of *Buddy Buddy:*

"Billy seemed more tense. He seemed to be pushing harder, forcing it. I'm capable of overacting. Billy never overdirected. It was something I couldn't put my finger on exactly. He had always been open to suggestions I had for my part, a way to say something, a way to play it, business, but this time, I didn't feel as welcome with my ideas, so I didn't say anything. Who am I to tell Billy Wilder what he should do?" as Lemmon frequently said when speaking about his favorite director.

I had the opportunity to ask Klaus Kinski about his part in *Buddy Buddy.* He said, "I wasn't in the picture." I tried to go on, having *seen* him in the film, but he only repeated, "I wasn't in the picture."

When I mentioned to Billy Wilder what Kinski had told me, he said, "He's right." Then he added, "But European irony doesn't travel well."

Filming began on February 4, 1981, and ended on April 23. It was shot in Riverside, California, Hawaii, and at MGM in Culver City, and released at the end of that year.

Critical reaction was almost entirely negative. Among major critics, only Vincent Canby of the *New York Times* liked the film, though with reservations. It was a box office failure and lost money for MGM.

"The best thing for me about *Buddy Buddy* was that not very many people saw it," Wilder said, "but that wasn't good for MGM and the producers. It was dead on the vine, Hollywood and Vine.

"I said to myself, 'You committed the game-losing error, but it wasn't the World Series. It was just another game, and there would be more at bats. Only there weren't.

"It hurts to strike out on your last picture. It *was* my last picture— only I didn't know it."

Producer David Brown remembered talking with Billy Wilder in the days after the director found himself retired, far sooner than he wanted to be.

"I met Billy, and we were talking about an honor he was receiving, and he was complaining. He said, 'I get offered all these prizes and they say how great my pictures are, but they don't offer me any to do.'

"So, I offered him one. It was a comedy. Billy read it, and he came back to me and said, 'This is either going to be the biggest success ever, or the biggest failure ever, and that range is too great.'"

———◦———

One day, shortly after *Buddy Buddy* had opened, I was sitting in Billy Wilder's office, and the phone rang.

As soon as he heard the voice at the other end of the line, he began speaking in German. It was a very long call. I had spoken on the phone many times with Wilder, and I knew that he didn't enjoy long calls. Always very correct, he considered it rude to have a long phone call while someone was sitting there with him. I could understand enough German to know that he was discussing a movie deal.

After the call, he explained, "I'm trying to get work."

———◦———

Austrian friend Fred Zinnemann, who had known Wilder since their youth in Europe, wondered why his old friend spoke with him in English, even when no one else was there. "English was no problem for me after all those years in California and England, and my wife is English, but it seemed odd. Billy wanted so much to be an American."

Wilder told me about Fred Zinnemann, when he was past seventy, going to one of the Hollywood studios.

"He had a project to submit for a picture, and he had an interview with a twenty-five-year-old producer. The producer began by saying to Freddy, 'Tell me something about yourself,' and Freddy just looked at him, and he said, 'You go first.'

"Emeric Pressburger, who worked with Michael Powell in England on those wonderful Archers pictures, said to me, 'You have to bring your twenty-year-old grandson with you and say he's your collaborator.'

"I said, 'Youth has to protect itself, because it doesn't have very long.'"

———◦———

After *Buddy Buddy,* Wilder and Diamond returned to the office on Brighton Way to create their next film. Anxious to do a movie that pleased the world, and them, too, more than had *Buddy Buddy,* they worked harder than ever.

"Iz and I, when we collaborated, we'd get to the office at nine o'clock in the morning, like employees of a bank. And we'd sit there, and we'd try to find something. Sometimes nothing." Diamond told me that the highest accolade an idea of his could receive from Billy Wilder was, "Write it down."

Billy had begun what he was later to call "the rest of the time."

"I was retired, but I didn't know it, because I was too busy and working too hard. If someone had told me I wasn't going to get another picture through, I would've said they were crazy.

"The awards kept arriving. I didn't have room in the office, and the phone kept ringing with offers to accept all kinds of honors, but not offers to make a picture. I was a burnt child. I'd lost my confidence. I'd done my best. I'd tried my hardest, and what I did wasn't liked, so you lose confidence in your judgment.

"Iz and I had so many ideas, we'd work on one for four weeks, and then we'd start another. We'd been burned; we chose wrong with *Buddy Buddy,* and we didn't want to make another mistake. We'd had some failures, so our confidence wasn't as good.

"But when two people work together as collaborators, it's more than just one plus one equals two. It equals eleven. You prop each other up. The important thing is not to go down in spirits at the same time. If you can alternate being discouraged, you have the other guy saying, 'The new thing we're working on is great. I think we've got something.'

"Then, when *he* loses hope, the other guy comes in and picks him up, *if* you can get this coordinated. Iz and I did."

One day Wilder received a call from Diamond. "Iz had not been feeling well. He told me he wouldn't be in. I said, 'Well, maybe tomorrow or next week. Get better, Iz. We'll work when you feel better.'

"He said, 'I won't be coming in at all. I won't be getting better. I'm dying.'"

Wilder rushed over to his house. "He looked terrible. I didn't know what to say. He didn't know what to say, either. He looked at me, and he said, 'Oh, shit.'"

Four weeks later, on April 21, 1988, I. A. L. Diamond died.

"He had met with me every day, and he never said anything about being sick. Not a word. We worked together every day. He was as funny as always. He worked on our future stories, but he knew he wouldn't be there to see them. Then, only four weeks before he died he called me and said he couldn't meet me."

Years later, Wilder wondered, "Why didn't Iz tell me?"

I believed that I understood why. Sharing such terrible news would have interfered with or stopped their creativity and the ability of both of them to concentrate on a new film, especially on a comedy.

If Diamond had told Wilder, each day would have been filled with doom and gloom instead of hopes and dreams. Working with Wilder was constructive, something for Diamond to do when there was nothing to be done about his illness, multiple myeloma, a form of cancer. Wilder agreed.

"It's true. He knew if *I* knew, I wouldn't have been able to do it. How can you be funny? So, he kept his secret—for maybe four years!" Wilder paused. "But he should have told me.

"We had a good time, Iz and me. Even though we weren't going to sell anything, we didn't know it, so it gave us both something to get up for in the morning."

It might have surprised Diamond to know exactly how much he meant professionally and personally to Wilder. Even Wilder may have been surprised by the depth of the emotion he felt at the loss of Iz.

"That was years ago, and there hasn't been a day that has gone by that I have not missed him. Iz and I went to lunch, and we stayed together for more than thirty years.

"I loved Iz."

—Lights!—
Camera!
Auction!

In 1989, a year after Diamond's death, Billy Wilder parted with most of his art collection.

"I thought, these pictures are leaving their parents' house where they have been loved and well treated, some of them for fifty years, and now they are going out into the world to stand, *hang* on their own," Billy Wilder told me.

"I said good-bye to each one that was leaving home, and that was that.

"Pictures don't talk back."

Wilder discussed his decision to sell his art, a collection he had put together during more than half a century in America, the acquisition of which had been one of the great rewards of his Hollywood writing-directing career.

"I am not an art collector; I am a squirrel. I definitely do not consider myself a collector. To be a collector, the madness needs a method. I had no plan, only the craziness. I consider myself an accumulator. I've accumulated things like a pack rat. I cannot help myself. It is like a sickness, a sickness that brings me pleasure.

"This pleasure of accumulating was a part of my work, because the acquisition of a new work of art was a shot of adrenaline, and that adrenaline went right into my work. It was *La Ronde.* The films fed the collection, and the collection fed the films. When I finished a movie and felt good about it, my conscience didn't complain when I went out and bought a few things to hang on my walls.

"I had to buy, acquire, even though I had too much stuff. There was always room for something more. I had it hidden under the beds, in all the closets, except the ones with Audrey's clothes, and I've had to use warehouses. I just could not stop buying, buying.

"When they came to me about selling the pictures, my first thought was, no. Maybe, I felt, as long as I am accumulating, I am alive. I rethought it. As long as I am *breathing,* I am alive.

"After a while, there were so many paintings in our apartment, they were stacked against the walls, in the bathroom, everywhere. The hallway got so narrow, I had to put one foot in front of the other because there was only space for one shoe, and what if that went? I nearly broke my toe more than once.

"Audrey never complained. She understood. I know men who had to hide what they bought from their wives or lie about the price they paid. I would never lie to Audrey. And I do not say much about what she spends on clothes, only about how good they look on her.

"It was always pictures that attracted me, even when I was a boy. I cut out pictures I liked from magazines. I was fascinated by Klimt, Kokoschka, and Schiele. As a teenager cutting out pictures of Schiele's work from magazines, I felt I was one of the first to spot him, and to understand him.

"I was affected by the Wiener Werkstætte, which existed from 1903 to about 1932. That kind of design had a great influence on me when I lived in Vienna. If I had any talent for it, I would like to have drawn and painted.

"We had to leave behind my grandmother's Thonet rocker, which I liked very much, when our family ran to Vienna. When Hitler came to power, I knew people who collected Dresden, and Dresden is not a good thing to try to take away with you. Some people made the mistake of staying in Austria and Germany with their Dresden, but people are as fragile as Dresden. I had a friend who collected wonderful Austrian glass, but if you have pictures, you can always roll up a few and put them under your arm. I don't expect to have to run for it in Los Angeles, I'm happy to say, because I don't run very fast these days. And Audrey couldn't help because she would have her hands full with her jewelry."

For Wilder, the worst part of selling his collection was making the decision. "Indecision is the most wearing. Once you have made the decision, not just yes or no, but feeling right with it, you let go inside yourself. When you do, *that* is the moment of decision.

"I made the big decision to sell, and then I made the little decisions, about each one that was going; that's when it was over for me, not the night of the auction. By that night, I had already parted with my old friends. When I agreed to the auction, that was when I said my good-byes to the pictures. By the night they were sold, I didn't feel they belonged to me anymore."

Wilder said the sale didn't mean he would not be buying anymore, but he didn't feel he would ever be driven as he had been when he began buying art before he was twenty years old.

His taste had been shaped by his Vienna childhood, his Berlin years, and even his brief stay in Paris on the way to Hollywood. Though his stop in Paris was short, less than a year, he looked as much as he could, and promised himself he would return someday with the money to buy. The memory of what he had seen in Paris stayed with him.

Wilder had begun serious art collecting in Berlin, readily giving up meals to purchase a drawing. There was nothing in his background to account for the strength of his passion for art. No one else in his family had shown any such interest. Wilder had no education in art except for his casual viewing of the beauty of Vienna shortly after the turn of the century; however, in his childhood, he had experienced the city of Vienna at a time when personal standing in the society was not just based on money, but on one's appreciation of beauty.

---◦---

At 7:00 P. M., on the evening of Monday, November 13, 1989, the auction of Billy Wilder's paintings and objects took place. Christie's had advised Wilder that he would receive more by selling the art as a collection. Christie's would send it on tour, accompanied by parties and extensive promotion, so many potential buyers could see it. Buyers were expected to pay more because the collection had belonged to Billy Wilder.

"Why would people pay more for the pictures because I owned them?" Wilder asked. "Are they afraid to trust their own taste? It was like I was putting my autograph on it, along with the artist. The price people are willing to pay would be influenced by how much people thought my taste was worth.

"I knew there were people who were going to think I was needy. They would be saying, 'Oh, poor Billy Wilder,' and I knew that the 'poor' would be referring to my financial state. They would say, 'He's run out of money, so he *has* to sell his pictures.' It wasn't like that at all. I just wanted to write my own third act.

"I admired Preston Sturges. He was a writer who became a direc- tor, and he had respect for words. His work was his life. He would have worked free, and when he couldn't get the money to make pictures, he put up his own money.

"The last time I saw him was in Paris. He was sitting at an outdoor café. Old friends would stop and have something with him, and they'd pick up the check. It seemed he was hard up. He'd had a great life, but it didn't end up great. He didn't know how to write a third act for his own life.

"I heard someone say, 'Poor Sturges!' I never wanted pity. I did not sell everything. I sold the most valuable, because that made the whole collection valuable. I miss a few of those. I was able to hang on to some of my favorites, which were *not* the most valuable.

"When Christie's called me, first I said I'd think about it. Selling the pictures one at a time would have been more painful, and bad busi- ness. Christie's offer to tour the collection was like a road show movie. It was what I'd wanted for *The Private Life of Sherlock Holmes.* It was like my art collection was a Billy Wilder production. Well, it was.

"So, I said yes to Christie's. They said it was important for me to be at the auction. I told them they couldn't keep me away. I wanted the *fun* of being there. And I saw it that way, once I decided to do it, as fun. Andy Warhol missed seeing his cookie jar go for $10,000."

Christie's had a private preview and reception for the Wilder collection at the Beverly Hills Hotel. In the ballroom was Picasso's *Head of a Woman,* which had an estimate of $5 to $7 million.

"I never wanted a yacht or horses or junk bonds," Wilder said. "I put everything I got into art. I had so much fun, and I never collected a picture because it was a bargain, or as an investment or a hedge against inflation. A hedge is what you have in your yard.

"Everything I bought was something I could live with, something that made me feel better. It was going to live with me in my home. It's like the movies I made. My taste. If the movies I did or the pictures I bought were worth something, it was because my taste was somebody else's taste, too. What pleased me, pleased some other people. It is a kind of confirmation of your taste. When the price increases a lot over what you paid, it is even more confirmation. I sold at the high. I enjoyed that. There was a satisfaction, not just for the money, which was nice, too."

He remembered the occasion on which he had bought each picture and object, but rarely its price.

———◇———

The largest part of Wilder's collecting was done in the late '40s, the '50s, and the early '60s, his prime years as a film writer and then as a writer-director, the period of his Oscars, and of films beloved by audiences, such as *Double Indemnity, The Lost Weekend, Sunset Boulevard, Some Like It Hot,* and *The Apartment.*

By the 1950s, art collecting on a grand scale had become important in Southern California among film people and among those making new fortunes. According to Wilder, "The advantage of collecting art in Los Angeles is that American burglars are unsophisticated and uneducated. In Europe, a burglar would grab a Picasso off the wall faster than you could say Picasso, even if it was a fake. In Los Angeles, a Picasso is safer than anything in the house signed 'Sony.'"

Wilder, spending less than most noted collectors, was able to build a collection of fine quality. "I bought from my heart for my happy obsession.

"It is difficult to say why you buy one drawing instead of another, why one painting calls out, why there is a watercolor you feel you can't live without. I did not ask a lot of opinions. I listened to my heart, and heard it go, 'Boom, boom, boom.' "

The collection did not entirely represent his first choices, as Wilder had never been in a financial position to buy many of those. He had limited time to travel to his favorite buying haunts in New York and Paris. His selections were based on what was there when he went looking, on what caught his fancy, and on what he could afford.

"Life is choices. I didn't get to buy everything I wanted. I had to shop according to my pocketbook. There are pictures I could have afforded, and they would've gone up a lot in value, but I couldn't imagine living with a Francis Bacon. I can look at Mr. Bacon in the museum, but I would find it depressing to live with his pictures."

Wilder frequented the galleries with the best reputations—for quality and variety, those best known for judging authenticity. He was ready to pay high but fair prices. He developed personal relationships with the dealers, so that they came to understand his taste and preferences. They could call him when they had something of interest which he could afford, or could *almost* afford.

"I enjoyed talking with some of the dealers who really knew a lot. It was an education. I could have bought some more expensive pictures if I had been willing to skip a few of the smaller things, a drawing here, a watercolor there, but I wasn't ever willing to save up. I wanted instant gratification, the pleasure of the moment. When I went out to buy, I wanted to go back to the hotel with a package I was carrying, or a receipt for something that was being shipped, if it was too big for me to carry.

"I was never one to dwell on 'the ones that got away.' They got away when I couldn't afford their price. No complaints. I've had my share of art. I've had my share of everything.

"They said it was because I had a good eye. I had two of them. I was influenced by Eddie [Edward G.] Robinson and Joe [Joseph von] Sternberg. His 'von' was as real as von Stroheim's.

"Sometimes what seems like an unlucky break can be lucky. I was walking around a gallery exhibition in Paris, talking with Anatole Litvak. I was deep in what I was saying, not really looking where I was going, when

I stepped back, and there was a loud crash. I had backed into a glass case.

"The gallery owner came rushing over, terribly upset. I tried to make a little joke. 'I stand behind the damage, but not far enough behind.' He did not laugh. It wasn't a good joke.

"He had a terrible, *terrible* expression on his face. I looked to see how much damage I had done. It wasn't just the money. It would have made me sick to have destroyed a work of art. Fortunately, I hadn't broken anything but the glass case.

"While I was trying to reassure the owner of the gallery that I would be responsible for the damage, I caught a glimpse of a bronze figure. I liked it. I was also feeling guilty. So I asked him how much it was even before I found out *what* it was. He said it was a Giacometti. When he said a thousand dollars, I said I'd take it. It seemed a little high, but I didn't bargain. The owner didn't charge me for the broken glass case. Maybe it was built into the price of the figure."

The twenty-one-inch-high bronze figure was that of a woman sculpted by Alberto Giacometti in 1953. In November of 1989, the figure sold for $1 million at the Christie's auction. "If I had been more careful and looked where I was going, I wouldn't have had the pleasure of knowing the little lady, and I would be one million dollars poorer."

Some at Christie's auction assumed that Wilder was selling because of his age, rational for a man in his eighties. They didn't know Billy Wilder. Before he had left New York, before he had deposited his almost $30 million check, the amount his art brought from the auction minus commissions, he was thinking about new works of art. After the auction, back in Los Angeles, I was in his office as he took calls from dealers about Benin sculpture, another interest. On his desk was an auction catalogue for paintings by Latin American artists.

"I don't give advice," he told me, "but what I might say to anyone buying art is, don't collect. It's like being a writer. You have to write to please yourself.

"Buy what you like. Enjoy it. Hold on to it."

Wilder had invited me to Christie's. As I watched the auction, I was reminded of how Wilder had sympathized with Otto Preminger when we had talked about Preminger's being forced to sell his art collection to raise cash to finish a film. Like Wilder, Preminger had loved art and was a passionate collector, but when it came to working as a director or parting with some of his treasures, he cared more about making a film than keeping his possessions. Preminger was prepared to part with everything except the Henry Moore figure of a lady in the garden of his New York City house.

Preminger, like Wilder, had come to America from Vienna, just ahead of the Nazis. Unlike Wilder, Preminger's family was wealthy and very much interested in the arts. Preminger's father had been the equivalent of attorney general at the end of Emperor Francis Joseph's reign.

"Poor Otto Preminger," Wilder had said, "selling his paintings to pay for his movies. Especially for that Graham Greene thing [*The Human Factor*]. Hard enough to do anyway, but for a bad picture! Perhaps he didn't know yet that the picture didn't work. Or perhaps he did. That would *really* be terrible. Calling back from a hotel in France to his dealer to sell the tall Giacometti, so he could pay the hotel bill for everyone when they went over budget.

"But you can't hold on too tightly to possessions. They are yours only on loan, and my library card isn't good for much longer."

The auction was not the first time Wilder had parted with his possessions. When he left Vienna, he left behind the little he had. With his success in Berlin, he had more to lose when the Nazis arrived on the scene and forced him to sell his treasures in "a kind of garage sale" in order to finance his trip to Paris. By the time he left Paris, he had nothing left to leave behind.

After the fire on the Goldwyn lot had destroyed some of his art, Wilder said, "It was like losing a piece of myself.

"I've learned that when such things happen to me what I have to do is think of a bigger tragedy. It works for me. For example, I think, Hitler might have won World War II."

As I stood next to him at Christie's, Audrey Wilder passed us on her way to chat with playwright Garson Kanin and actress Marian Seldes. Wilder watched her, then turned to me and said softly the two words which for me summed up the reason he had sold his art:

"For her."

The true extent of his caring for Audrey was expressed in this sale of the larger, most valuable part of his art collection. He could not predict the future, and he wanted to be certain his younger wife would have everything she needed. He did not want her to be burdened with the responsibility of selling the art.

As a writer, Wilder, the public and professional person, always wanted control of his words in his films. The private person wanted control of his future days. Of course, at the time, Wilder had no idea that there were so many days left ahead for him.

———◇———

The auction was a glittery event, by invitation only. Those who wished to attend needed to apply to Christie's. There was no room for all who wanted to be there. Bidders in cocktail attire, with their paddles poised, were ready in the sales room. Claudette Colbert, who had starred in *Bluebeard's Eighth Wife, Midnight,* and *Arise, My Love,* early in Wilder's Hollywood career, starred at the auction, though not as a bidder. The biggest star in the sales room was Wilder himself. The sale was attended by art collectors and leading art dealers from around the world.

Hellmuth Karasek, *Der Spiegel's* noted film critic, had journeyed from Hamburg to write about Wilder and the auction. Wilder, looking around the room at the collection, told Karasek with pride, "I only had $11 when I came to this great country."

Wilder was "tickled" by the high prices. "That was very interesting to me. It's like a scorecard."

He had wanted to see some of the happy new owners. The auction reassured him that the pictures would be getting good homes. He expected that the new owners would be much younger than he, "not too many in their eighties," and that they would have years ahead in which to enjoy what they acquired.

The catalogue with a Balthus on the cover, a painting of the artist's nineteen-year-old niece, was much sought after, and twenty years later, some of those catalogues were being sold at auctions.

There were works of Klee and Miró, Calder and Henry Moore, as well as drawings by Grosz and Renoir. When Wilder was writing scripts in Berlin, he had been attracted by the works of Grosz, when many were finding them unattractive and objecting to their strong, painful comments on the times in Germany.

Picasso's *Tête de Femme* brought the top price in the auction, $4.8 million. Wilder was disappointed because he had expected this 1921 pastel portrait of Olga Koklova, Picasso's first wife, to bring more.

The Balthus pictured on the catalogue cover, *La Toilette,* was sold for $2 million, and Ernst Ludwig Kirchner's painting *Two Nudes on a Blue Sofa* went for $1.5 million. A Joseph Cornell box brought $495,000. Georg Tappert's *Schwarze Strümphe (Black Stockings),* from 1910, was sold to Barbra Streisand for $580,000.

The collection included many pictures of women, often nude. "It was a grand farewell to my harem," Wilder said.

When the 1989 evening auction at Christie's had ended, and the final bids were totaled, the Billy Wilder collection had brought in $32.6 million, less commissions, more than Wilder had earned from his work on all of his films. "And it was less nerve-wracking than a film preview," Wilder commented. The auction exceeded Christie's most optimistic estimate by more than $1 million. Billy Wilder had, as he put it, "cashed out" at the top of the market. He told me, "Life is strange. I didn't get rich making pictures, I got rich collecting pictures." He didn't become a really wealthy man until he was in his middle eighties. "I was lucky I liked pictures that moved, and pictures that don't, too."

Shortly afterward, the art market dropped.

———◁◦▷———

Not long after the Christie's sale, there was a fire in the luxury apartment building where the Wilders had lived for many years. Though the fire did not touch their apartment, there was extensive smoke damage. Everything they owned, their clothes and their remaining art, had to be deep-cleaned. Because of the smoke damage, the Wilders had to move out for several months.

There was sufficient insurance to cover the cleanup of all their possessions, but according to Wilder, had he not sold the bulk of his art collection, the insurance would not have been adequate to cover all that would have been there, and the fire would have been even more devastating. As it turned out, Billy Wilder's most valuable pictures had fled only just ahead of the conflagration, very much as Wilder himself had left Berlin just in time.

Wilder's comment after the fire was, "Getting the stuff out of the apartment and listing it for the insurance company was the first time in years I knew how many sweaters I had. I'll have to live to be two hundred instead of one hundred to wear them all." Wilder typically covered more deeply felt emotions with an attempt at humor.

"If you have a lot of clothes and you like to keep your clothes that are still in good condition and you live to be ninety-four, you have more of everything than you ever intended to own. They say cashmere sweaters wear out, but they don't. I'm wearing out faster than the sweaters."

—Nefertete—

Late in life, in his eighties, Billy Wilder tried his hand at sculpt-ing. He had been thinking about doing so for about sixty years. "Living a long life gives you a chance to try a lot of things you never thought you had time to do," he told me.

He had a strong desire to see the three-dimensional representation of his imagination, as he had seen his words on paper and then on the screen. Then it struck him that as he enjoyed collaboration in writing a film, why not try it in creating objects?

"I would have tried sooner to paint or draw or sculpt, but I knew I didn't have the talent for it," he said. I suggested that he might have been setting his standard too high, that his artistic appreciation was so developed that perhaps he didn't believe his hand could achieve what his eye admired.

He agreed. "No one stops you like you stop yourself."

After his arrival in Hollywood, Wilder felt insecure in English, so he was more than happy to find a collaborator, Charles Brackett, who had full command of the language. Applying the same principle to sculpting, he found a collaborator who had command of the language of sculpting, the technique to give life to the images in Wilder's mind.

There was one area, however, in which Wilder believed there was no possibility for collaboration, because one had to have the authority to speak totally for what would go up on the screen—directing.

In 1993, he took me to see the art show of his work at the Louis

Stern Gallery, near his office in Beverly Hills. Stern was Wilder's friend, an art dealer with whom he liked to chat at length about art. We walked from Wilder's office, and he left me at the door of the gallery so I could "look in peace." He told me not to miss "the Nefertete-Groucho."

"I am not trying to out-Warhol Andy," he said. "I am just trying to be Wilder than Billy."

There were works for sale, created by Wilder in collaboration with artists Bruce Houston and Richard Saar, as well as some art collected by Wilder. The exhibition, called *Billy Wilder's Marché aux Puces*—Billy Wilder's Flea Market—had been Stern's idea.

The pièce de résistance was a group of fourteen plaster busts of Nefertete, as interpreted by Wilder and executed by Bruce Houston, called *Variations on the Theme of Queen Nefertete I*. Each bust was a humorous homage to a famous twentieth-century artist or personality. Matisse was represented by a ring of dancers painted on the queen's headband. Picasso's Nefertete had two faces and a straw hat. Frank Stella's queen wore a pin-striped neckline. For Jackson Pollock, Nefertete's painted clothing appeared as if the paint was dripping. The Nefertete that Wilder had specifically reminded me to see, a bust of Nefertete, had a Groucho mustache.

"I got the idea that the head of Nefertete could be reinterpreted in the styles of other artists by them, but they were all too busy," Wilder said. Then he met Houston, a special kind of artist Wilder described as "an assemblagist." They began their Nefertete series with an Andy Warhol version using a can of Campbell's soup as Nefertete's headdress. They followed with a Modigliani-style Nefertete with a long neck, a Salvador Dali, and others. The busts were cast from molds, but each one required hand adjusting and, of course, hand painting.

With his first sculpting collaborations, Wilder enjoyed the experience of seeing objects come to life that he had imagined, and the experience had lived up to the anticipation of the pleasure he had expected to derive from it. But once was enough.

When Wilder was a young man in Germany, he saw the famed painted limestone bust of Nefertete at the Berlin State Museum, and Nefertete made a lasting impression on him. He told me, "I always liked brunettes."

—"Alone from—
My Time"

"I'm an old ship captain," Billy Wilder told me. "I've known the storms. I know all of the dangers, all of the bad things that can happen. Only the ones who have not experienced the storms can sail out into oblivion. Those starting out, they don't have the fear because they don't know any better. If you know the dangers, it's harder to start, but easier to finish."

For almost a decade after Diamond's death, Wilder did not give up hope. He continued to work regularly, alone, believing he would write and direct another picture. "In my line of work, you don't know you have retired until years after it happens. You wonder why you're not working, then, all of a sudden, you know. I'm very proud of my six Oscars, but that's the past." In 1988, he also received the Acadamy's Thalberg Award.

In his eighties and nineties, he found himself with time to do all the things he always had intended doing someday. "I read a lot. I read books I didn't have time to read when I was working. Now I'm read- ing Proust and Kafka. After all these years talking about them, I have time to read them. I'm learning a lot, but learning is more rewarding when you have something to apply it to.

"Old age is when your dreams have become memories."

———<o>———

In December of 1995, as I arrived at the coffee shop where we were meeting for breakfast, I saw Billy Wilder getting out of his car. He was leaving, not from the driver's side, but from the passenger's side. Someone I didn't know drove the car away.

Wilder joined me, saying, "I am not able to drive anymore. I have begun old age."

Old age, for Wilder, was linked to not being able to drive a car. Not only is the ability to drive essential in Southern California, but Wilder had always loved it, and wanted to be the one doing the driving. In his early nineties, there was a clear line of demarcation. Vertigo had forced him to give up driving. "Without Kim Novak, vertigo is very undesirable," he said.

When he believed he could never drive again, he no longer felt middle-aged, still in control of life. For him, there was a correlation between driving and directing.

As we ate breakfast, he said, "I'll never direct another picture, but maybe someone else can direct one of my scripts, like having someone drive for me.

"I thought of myself as middle-aged until I was ninety. Then it came to me. How many people do I know who are 180?"

One of the more memorable events of Wilder's Viennese childhood was the funeral of the Emperor Francis Joseph. "When he died at eighty-six, it seemed to me that Francis Joseph must have been the oldest man in the world. It was hard to imagine anyone being that old. And here I am, almost a decade older than he was when he died, and, you know, it doesn't seem so old, after all.

"Sometimes I am reminded of something, a memory seventy or eighty years old. I see a painting, or a Sacher torte. I have a vague remembrance of Salzburger Nockerl past. For a minute I think I am that boy who is there, deep inside me, very deep. Then, I try to get up, and my legs remind me I am not.

"When you get older, your world gets smaller. No more Europe. No more New York."

"Do you know the Spanish saying, *El mundo es un pañuelo,* 'The world is a handkerchief'?" I asked.

"Kleenex," he said.

———<o>———

In 1998, we were having coffee and croissants at the Brighton Way coffee shop next to his Beverly Hills office when a teenage messenger approached.

"I have a letter for you, Mr. Wilder. I was at your office, but you weren't there."

"No, I wasn't there because I am here, and I never learned how to be in two places at once." The messenger looked puzzled.

Wilder said, "Give me the thing to sign."

The messenger handed him a sheet of blank paper. Wilder said, "What's this? What am I signing?"

"I need your signature for the letter, but I'd like to keep this one—with your autograph."

"Give me the other one."

The crestfallen messenger handed it to him, and Wilder signed for the letter. Then he tore off a corner of the blank paper, signed it, and handed it to the messenger, who left pleased. Wilder never signed a whole sheet of blank paper, on which, as he pointed out, anything at all could later be typed.

"These days I understand you can get one Spielberg autograph for three of mine," Wilder told me, "unless I'm slipping. I may be. It's like a *New York Times* obituary. If you outlive your fame, you lose paragraphs."

———<o>———

In December 1999, when I visited him in his office, he greeted me with, "Do you know how old I am now? Ninety-three and a half. After you get to be ninety, it is like when you were very young and you are a year and a half, two and a half, three and a half. When you reach a certain age, each half year counts again.

"No, ninety-three is not the same as ninety-two. I am still fighting, but one thing I have given up on: I no longer believe some day I am going to lose my accent.

"I don't have enough time left to find new friends. Having a friend takes a long time. When you are very young, you make friends easily. Youth is most easily shared with youth. You grow up, you get older together. When you're old, your address book is closed because *you* are closed.

"I no longer need to keep an address book. I can remember the numbers of my friends. It's not that my memory got better. It's because I have so few left. My closest friends are alive in the past. I am alone from my time.

"If I were starting out now to be a writer or a director, I don't know how I'd do it. Those big budgets change everything, the responsibility for all that money, and you don't need dialogue because you can't hear it with the explosions. Maybe I would go into special effects or stunts. They will always need bigger and better special effects and they will always need a stuntman because somebody's got to break his ass.

"You have to be flexible. When Cinemascope came in, I thought about making the love story of two dachshunds.

"Trust your own instincts. Your mistakes might as well be your own instead of somebody else's. Everyone has the right to be wrong about his own life, but not about another person's. In Berlin, I remember being asked my advice by someone who wanted to leave his wonderful job, where he made a lot of money and knew all the beautiful women, so he could write a novel. I laughed. I advised him to stay where he was well off, that the gamble was too big, and how did he know he could do it? So he quit, and Erich Maria Remarque wrote *All Quiet on the Western Front*.

"I've taken chances, and I've been lucky. The hardest thing now for me to talk about is my own life. I'm too involved. It leads to wanting to change some things in the past, which is a very great waste of energy. Also, if you change one thing, maybe you change everything.

"God writes with a pencil that has no eraser.

"I don't like to look back. It's no use saying, 'What if . . . ?' You could drown in what-ifs, especially if you make it past ninety, which I have. If you're going to say, 'What if?' you might as well save it for something like, 'What if Hitler had been a girl?'

"At ninety-four, there aren't many goals to work for except longevity. The ninety-fifth birthday. The ninety-sixth. Maybe trying to make it to a hundred as long as my mind is good, and I look forward to each day, and am happy with the third act of my life."

Billy Wilder had all of his mental powers, and his mind still dashed about, but some of his physical powers had let him down. The massages he had enjoyed as a luxury, he referred to as physical therapy. "A massage is not a luxury when there's no choice. Choice is a luxury. This is what happens to you when you get old."

"You could say your 'trainer' is coming," I suggested.

"I could never imagine myself being old. An old man was someone who was forty, then fifty, then sixty. When I was a young man in Vienna, if someone had offered me a deal to guarantee I'd make seventy, I'd have grabbed it. Seventy would have sounded pretty good to me. You never know what life holds. If somebody had asked me, did I want to live to be ninety, I might have said, 'No, that's too old. What can you do at ninety?' Now, I know the answer. Quite a lot, if you are lucky.

"The difference between being ninety-four and twenty-four is when I was twenty-four, I thought in terms of years, what would I be doing ten years later, twenty years from then, in thirty years. I thought I'd always feel the same. Now, I don't make an appointment for tomorrow.

"At ninety-four, it's not long enough. It seems short. Too bad. But it has to end sometime."

Before his ninety-fifth birthday, when I called him from New York to say I would be in California, he said, "I have to use a wheelchair now. Do you remember what I said about David Lean at the AFI, that no one would ever see me in a wheelchair? Well, I've changed my mind."

———◇———

Billy Wilder had chosen not to revisit his own films, but he was pleased others did. "I've wanted only to continue entertaining audiences with stories that are close to my heart. To see them gripping their seats with fear or bent over with laughter is all I ever wanted. That was the reaction to *Some Like It Hot,* and that gave me a real thrill. I heard people saying, 'I spent two wonderful hours in the theater, and I am going to see that film again.' That was better than any award or medal, though I found those enjoyable, too.

"They just chose *Hot* at the AFI as the best American comedy, number one. Well, I'm happy for it, but it's not true. It's not the best because there is no best. It's *one* of the best. It's a good picture, and I'm proud of it. I'm happy people still like it so much." Wilder had received the American Film Institute's Lifetime Achievement Award in 1987.

At the turn of the century, I called to wish Billy Wilder a happy New Year. He said, "I'm old enough to remember when people thought it would always be the twentieth century. Now that I've made it to the twenty-first, I'm going for a hundred. I never liked celebrating birthdays, but I'll have a party for that one. I'll invite you."

Shortly after I met him, Wilder told me, "You have to have a dream so you can get up in the morning. But that dream can't stay the same all your life. If I'd been a boy in America, I would have dreamed of being a batboy. Of course, that dream couldn't have sustained me all my life."

———◁◦▷———

He asked me how I was going to end my book about him, what the final chapter would be called.

"I don't know. How about 'Loose Ends'?"

"It sounds like a bad beauty salon."

"I like what you said, 'Alone from My Time.'"

"To borrow Iz's words, 'Why not?' Maybe you'll get something better. But write it down. I always wrote everything down. You never know."

I asked if there was anything in his life that had been written about him that he would like to have the opportunity to correct.

"Plenty.

"Somebody wrote I quit the university and left Vienna because I fell in love with a young, pretty prostitute I didn't know was a prostitute, and had a broken heart. Some guy wrote this years ago, and others copied it. I left Vienna to go with Paul Whiteman and his band to Berlin, which was where I wanted to go. I didn't fall in love with a prostitute. I wasn't running away from anything. I was running *to* something.

"Another story that made the rounds was I was a gigolo. In Berlin, I was what they call an *Eintänzer,* a tea dancer. It was a respectable job at the leading hotel in Berlin. I wanted to write an article about my experience, which I did. That was all that happened.

"People say I am cynical. I am not. I deal with the rat race and the human condition, the people who aren't rats who are caught up in it.

"I am not a mean and bitter person. I don't go around belittling people. I have never been a jealous person. I live in a place where too many people are happy when they hear bad news about someone. They seem happier about the failure of someone else's movie than they do about their own success. A lot of time when people hate other people, it's really themselves they hate.

"In Hollywood, they think not having success could be a contagious disease. You are cut from the team. If *you* could strike out *they* could strike out. For everyone in the business I know and like, I only wish them very well. The others, I don't think about.

"And you can say I wasn't punching all the time to make jokes. Sometimes they make me seem like that.

"A favorite question they are always asking me is, what would I like to have written on my tombstone? It's *their* favorite question, not mine.

"I'll tell you what it is: 'Here lies a writer.' It is what I am. I only became a director so they wouldn't get my script wrong. I had to protect my script. I don't write camera angles and dialogue. I write character and dialogue. It doesn't matter what is happening to your characters unless people care about them.

"Interviewers would ask me, 'How do you see yourself?'

"I'm the lion tamer who has lasted and not been eaten by the lions."

I asked him what he would change about himself if he were living his life again and knew how it was going to turn out. "I'd be less anxious," he answered. "I'd enjoy more and worry less."

I asked him if there was something else he would like to say for the summing up.

He answered that he would like to thank all of the wonderful helping hands throughout his life, first those who helped him up, and then, along the way, those who played their parts in his films, not just the stars, but the bit parts, the technical people, those on every crew, everyone who did his best to help him do the only thing he wanted to do—make movies.

"One other thing. People still ask me about *The Apartment*. They ask, 'Did Fran and Bud live happily ever after?' I always used to say the cards were stacked against it. I've changed my mind. Maybe my marriage to Audrey made me more of a romantic. Now I think it worked out for them. The marriage lasted, and they got a better apartment."

"Is there anything more you want to say?"

"God bless you. God bless you all!"

————◄○►————

At ninety-four, Billy Wilder said to me, "I have been alive so long, there is only one explanation: God forgot me."

I remember some years before, he had told me, "When you are older, the time is going by much faster. Since I came to the United States, I have lived in Los Angeles. When you are young in a place without seasons, time goes slower. When you are past ninety, it goes faster. It was just New Year's Eve, and now it's March.

"The snowball tumbles into oblivion with increasing speed . . ."

—Filmography—

Der Teufelsreporter: Im Nebel der Grossstadt *(The Devil's Reporter: In the Fog of the Big City)* (1929). Deutsche Universalfilm Verleih. Black and white, silent. Director: Ernst Laemmle. Screenplay: Billie Wilder. Cinematographer: Charles Stumar. Sets: Gustav A. Knauer, Willy Schiller. Cast: Eddie Polo (Eddie, the reporter); Maria Forescu (Madame Lourdier); Robert Garrison (Jonas); Fred Grosser (Maxe); Gritta Ley (Bessie). 65 minutes.

Menschen am Sonntag *(People on Sunday)* (1929). Filmstudio Germania. Black and white, silent. Director: Robert Siodmak. Producer: Moritz Seeler. Assistant director: Edgar G. Ulmer. Screenplay: Billie Wilder and Kurt Siodmak. Cinematographer: Eugen Schüfftan. Assistant cameraman: Fred Zinnemann. Cast: Brigitte Borchert (record salesgirl); Christl Ehlers (aspiring actress); Annie Schreyer (model); Erwin Splettstösser (taxi driver); Wolfgang von Waltershausen (wine salesman); with Kurt Gerron, Valeska Gert, and Ernst Verebes. 74 minutes extant.

Der Mann, der seinen Mörder sucht *(The Man Who Sought His Own Murderer)* (1931). UFA. Black and white. Director: Robert Siodmak. Producer: Erich Pommer. Screenplay: Billie Wilder, Kurt Siodmak, and Ludwig Hirschfeld, based on the play *Jim, der Mann mit der Narbe,* by Ernst Neubach, and the novella *The Tribulations of a Chinaman in China,* by Jules Verne. Cinematographers: Otto Baecker and Konstantin Irmen-Tschet. Music: Friedrich Holländer. Musical director: Franz Wachsmann. Sound: Fritz Thiery. Cast: Heinz Rühmann (Hans Herfort); Lien Deyers (Kitty); Raymund Janitschek (Otto Kuttlapp); Hermann Speelmans (Jim); Gerhard Bienert (Schupo), Friedrich Holländer (conductor); Hans Leiberlt (Adamowski). 98 minutes.

Ihre Hoheit befiehlt *(Her Highness Commands)* (1931). UFA. Black and white. Director: Hanns Schwarz. Assistant Director: Carl Winston. Production manager: Max Pfeiffer. Screenplay: Paul Frank, Robert Liebmann, Billie Wilder. Cinematographers: Konstantin lrmen-Tschet and Günther Rittau. Music: Werner

Richard Heymann. Lyrics: Ernst Neubach, Robert Gilbert. Sound: Hermann Fritzschling. Cast: Willy Fritsch (Lt. von Conradi); Käthe von Nagy (Princess Marie-Christine); Paul Hörbiger (Pipac); Reinhold Schünzel (Minister of State); Paul Heidemann (Prince von Leuchtenstein); Michael von Newlinski (conductor); Eugen Tiller (major); Erich Kestin (young man with Conradi); Erik Schütz (singer); the Comedian Harmonists; with Attila Hörbiger, Ferdinand Martini, Edgar Pauly, Fritz Spira, Wolfgang von Schwind. 96 minutes. Remade by Fox as *Adorable* (1933), directed by William Dieterle, and starring Janet Gaynor. Wilder received a screenwriting credit.

Seitensprünge (*Stepping Out*) (1931). UFA. Black and white. Director: Stefan Székely. Screenplay: Ludwig Biro, Bobby E. Lüthge, and Karl Noti, from a story idea by Billie Wilder. Cinematographer: Walter Robert Lach. Music: Karl M. May, Fritz German. Lyrics: Karl Brüll. Cast: Oskar Sima (Robert Burkhardt); Gerda Maurus (Annemarie, his wife); Paul Vincenti (Carlo); Jarmila Marton (Lupita); Otto Wallburg (Uncle Emil); Paul Kemp (Anton Schiller); Adele Sandrock (Hanne); Lieselotte Schaak (Frieda). 81 minutes.

Der falsche Ehemann (*The Counterfeit Husband*) (1931). UFA. Black and white. Director: Johannes Guter. Screenplay: Paul Frank and Billie Wilder. Cinematographer: Carl Hoffmann. Music: Norbert Glanzberg. Editor: Constantin Mick. Sound: Erich Leistner. Cast: Johannes Riemann (Peter and Paul Hannemann, twins); Maria Paudler (Ruth Hannemann); Tibor Halmay (Maxim Tartakoff); Fritz Strehlen (Maharaja); Jessie Vihrog (Ines); Gustav Waldau (H. H. Hardegg); Martha Ziegler (Fraülein Schulze); with Klaus Pohl. 85 minutes.

Emil und die Detektive (*Emil and the Detectives*) (1931). UFA. Black and white. Director: Gerhard Lamprecht. Producer: Günther Stapenhorst. Screenplay: Billie Wilder, based on Erich Kästner's novel. Cinematographer: Werner Brandes. Music: Allan Gray. Cast: Rolf Wenkhaus (Emil); Käte Haack (Emil's mother); Fritz Rasp (Grundeis); Rudolf Biebrach (policeman); Olga Engl (Emil's grandmother); Inge Landgut (Pony Hütchen); Hans Joachim Schaufuss (Gustav); Hubert Schmitz (professor); with Hans Richter, Hans Loehr, Ernst-Eberhard Reling, and Waldemar Kupczyk. 75 minutes. Remade by British Gaumont (1935), directed by Milton Rosmer. Wilder received original screenplay credit.

Es war einmal ein Walzer (*Once Upon a Time There Was a Waltz*) (1932). Aafa-Film AG. Black and white. Director: Victor Janson. Screenplay: Billie Wilder. Cinematographer: Heinrich Gärtner. Music: Franz Lehar. Editor: Ladislas Vajda, Jr. Cast: Marta Eggerth (Steffi Pirzinger); Rolf von Goth (Rudi Möbius); Hermann Blass (Sauerwein); Fritz Greiner (coachman); Paul Hörbiger (Franz Pirzinger);

Lizzi Natzler (Lucie Weidling); Albert Paulig (Pfennig); Ernst Verebes (Gustl Linzer); Lina Woiwode (Frau Zacherl); Ida Wüst (Frau Weidling). 79 minutes.

Ein blonder Traum (A Blonde Dream) (1932). UFA. Black and white. Director: Paul Martin. Producer: Erich Pommer. Screenplay: Walter Reisch and Billie Wilder. Cinematographers: Otto Baecker, Konstantin Irmen-Tschet, and Günther Rittau. Music: Werner R. Heymann and Gérard Jacobson. Cast: Willy Fritsch (Willy 1); Willi Forst (Willy 2); Lilian Harvey (Jou-Jou); Paul Hörbiger (Scarecrow); C. Hooper Trask (Mr. Merryman); Hans Deppe (secretary); Trude Hesterberg (Ilse). 84 minutes.

Scampolo, ein Kind der Strasse (Scampolo, a Child of the Street) (1932). Bayerische Filmgesellschaft. Black and white. Director: Hans Steinhoff. Screenplay: Max Kolpe and Billie Wilder, based on the play by Dario Niccodemi. Cinematographers: Hans Androschin and Curt Courant. Music: Franz Wachsmann and Artur Guttmann. Editor: Ella Ensink. Cast: Dolly Haas (Scampolo); Karl Ludwig Diehl (Maximilian); Paul Hörbiger (Gabriel); Hedwig Bleibtreu (Frau Schmidt); Oskar Sima (Phillips, the banker). 87 minutes.

Das Blaue vom Himmel (The Blue of the Sky) (1932). Aafa-Film AG. Black and white. Director: Victor Janson. Screenplay: Max Kolpe and Billie Wilder. Cinematographer: Heinrich Gärtner. Music: Paul Abraham. Editor: Else Baum. Cast: Marta Eggerth (Anni Mueller); Hermann Thimig (Hans Meier); Jakob Tiedtke (U-Papa); Ernst Verebes (Hugo); Fritz Kampers (Tobias); Hans Richter (Tommy); Margarete Schlegel ("Zigaretten-Cilly"); Walter Steinbeck (Piper). 82 minutes.

Madame wünscht keine Kinder (Madam Wishes No Children) (1933). Lothar-Stark-Film. Director: Hans Steinhoff. Producer: Lothar Stark. Screenplay: Max Kolpe and Billie Wilder, based on Clément Vautel's book. Cinematographers: Willy Goldberger and Hans Androschin. Editor: Ella Ensink. Music: Bronislau Kaper. Lyrics: Walter Jurmann, Fritz Rotter, and Max Kolpe. Cast: Georg Alexander (Dr. Felix Rainer); Erika Glässner (Frau Wengert); Liane Haid (Madelaine Wengert); Lucie Mannheim (Luise); Hans Moser (sleeping car conductor); Willi Stettner (Adolf); Otto Wallburg (Herr Balsam). 86 minutes.

Was Frauen träumen (What Women Dream) (1933). Bayerische Filmgesellschaft. Black and white. Director: Géza von Bolváry. Screenplay: Franz Schulz and Billie Wilder. Cinematographer: Willy Goldberger. Music: Robert Stolz. Cast: Nora Gregor (Rina Korff); Gustav Fröhlich (Walter König); Peter Lorre (Füssli); Kurt Horwitz (Levassor, alias John Constantinescu); with Kurt Lilien, Hilde Maroff, Erik Ode, Walter Steinbeck, and Otto Wallburg. 86 minutes. Remade by Universal as *One Exciting Adventure* (1934), directed by Ernst Frank, and starring Binnie Barnes. Wilder received story credit.

Mauvaise Graine *(Bad Seed)* (1934). Compagnia Nouvelle Cinématographic M. Corniglion-Molinier. Black and white. Director: Billie Wilder, with Alexander Esway. Producers: Edouard Corniglion-Molinier and Georges Bernier. Screenplay: Billie Wilder, Max Kolpe, Hans G. Lustig, Alexander Esway, and Claude-André Puget. Cinematographers: Paul Cotteret and Maurice Delattre. Music: Allan Gray and Franz Waxmann. Cast: Danielle Darrieux (Jeanette); Pierre Mingand (Henri Pasquier); Raymond Galle (Jean-la-Cravate); Paul Escoffier (Dr. Pasquier); Michel Duran (the Boss); Jean Wall (Zebra); Marcel Maupi (man in Panama hat); Paul Velsa (man with peanuts); Georges Malkine (secretary); Georges Cahuzac (Sir); Gaby Héritier (Gaby). 77 minutes.

Music in the Air (1934). Fox Film Corporation. Black and white. Director: Joe May. Producer: Erich Pommer. Screenplay: Robert Liebmann, Billie Wilder, and Howard Irving Young, based on the musical by Oscar Hammerstein II and Jerome Kern. Lyrics and libretto: Hammerstein. Music: Kern. Musical adaptation: Franz Waxman. Cinematographer: Ernest Palmer. Cast: Gloria Swanson (Frieda); John Boles (Bruno Mahler); Douglass Montgomery (Karl); June Lang (Sieglinde); Al Shean (Dr. Lessing); Reginald Owen (Weber); Joseph Cawthorn (Uppman); Hobart Bosworth (Cornelius); Sara Haden (Martha); Marjorie Main (Anna); Roger Imhof (burgomaster); Jed Prouty (Kirschner); Christian Rub (Zipfelhuber); Fuzzy Knight (Nick). 85 minutes.

Under Pressure (1935). Fox Film Corporation. Black and white. Director: Raoul Walsh. Producer: Robert T. Kane. Screenplay: Borden Chase, Noel Pierce, and Lester Cole, with revisions and additional dialogue by Billie Wilder, based on the novel *East River* by Borden Chase and Edward Doherty. Cinematographers: Hal Mohr and L. W. O'Connell. Art direction: Jack Otterson. Costumes: William Lambert. Cast: Edmund Lowe (Shocker); Victor McLaglen (Jumbo); Florence Rice (Pat); Charles Bickford (Nipper); Ward Bond (fighter); Sig Ruman (doctor). 70 minutes.

The Lottery Lover (1935). Fox Film Corporation. Black and white. Director: Wilhelm Thiele. Screenplay: Franz Schulz, Billie Wilder, and Hanns Schwartz, based on a story by Siegfried Herzig and Maurice Hanline. Cinematographer: Bert Glennon. Art direction: William Darling. Costumes: Rene Hubert. Music and lyrics: Jay Gorney and Don Hartman. Editor: Dorothy Spencer. Cast: Lew Ayres (Frank Harrington); Pat Paterson (Patty); Peggy Fears (Gaby); Reginald Denny (Capt. Payne); Sterling Holloway (Harold Stump). 82 minutes.

Champagne Waltz (1937). Paramount Pictures. Black and white. Director: A. Edward Sutherland. Producer: Harlan Thompson. Screenplay: Frank Butler and Don Hartman, from a story by Billy Wilder and H. S. Kraft. Cinematographer: William C. Mellor. Editor: Paul Weatherwax. Costumes: Travis Banton. Music: Johann Strauss II. Cast: Gladys Swarthout (Elsa Strauss); Fred MacMurray (Buzzy Bellew); Herman Bing (Max Snellinek); Jack Oakie (Happy Gallagher); Fritz Leiber (Franz Strauss); Rudolph Anders (Franz Joseph); Stanley Price (Johann Strauss). 85 minutes.

Bluebeard's Eighth Wife (1938). Paramount Pictures. Black and white. Director: Ernst Lubitsch. Producer: Ernst Lubitsch. Screenplay: Charles Brackett and Billy Wilder, based on the play by Alfred Savoir. Cinematographer: Leo Tover. Music: Werner R. Heymann and Frederick Hollander. Costumes: Travis Banton. Editor: William Shea. Art directors: Hans Dreier and Robert Usher. Cast: Claudette Colbert (Nicole de Loiselle); Gary Cooper (Michael Brandon); Edward Everett Horton (Marquis de Loiselle); David Niven (Albert de Regnier); Elizabeth Patterson (Aunt Hedwige); Herman Bing (M. Pepinard); Warren Hymer (Kid Mulligan); Franklin Pangborn (hotel manager); Rolfe Sedan (floorwalker); Lawrence Grant (Prof. Urganzeff); Lionel Pape (M. Potin); Tyler Brooke (Clerk); with Armand Cortés. 80 minutes.

That Certain Age (1938). Universal Pictures. Black and white. Director: Edward Ludwig. Producer: Joe Pasternak. Screenplay: Bruce Manning, from a story by F. Hugh Herbert, with uncredited contributions by Charles Brackett and Billy Wilder. Cinematographer: Joseph A. Valentine. Music: Harold Adamson and Jimmy McHugh. Musical director: Charles Previn. Costumes: Vera West. Editor: Bernard W. Burton. Art director: Jack Otterson. Cast: Deanna Durbin (Alice Fullerton); Melvyn Douglas (Vincent Bullitt); Jackie Cooper (Ken); Irene Rich (Mrs. Fullerton); Nancy Carroll (Grace Bristow); John Halliday (Fullerton); Jack Searl (Tony); Juanita Quigley (the pest); Peggy Stewart (Mary Lee); Charles Coleman (Stevens); Grant Mitchell (jeweler). 95 minutes.

Midnight (1939). Paramount Pictures. Black and white. Director: Mitchell Leisen. Producer: Arthur Hornblow, Jr. Screenplay: Charles Brackett and Billy Wilder, from a story by Edwin Justus Mayer and Franz Schulz. Cinematographer: Charles Lang. Music: Frederick Hollander. Art directors: Hans Dreier and Robert Usher. Editor: Doane Harrison. Special effects: Farciot Edouart. Cast: Claudette Colbert (Eve Peabody); Don Ameche (Tibor Czerny); John Barrymore (Georges Flammarion); Francis Lederer (Jacques Picot); Mary Astor (Helene Flammarion); Elaine Barrie (Simone); Hedda Hopper (Stephanie); Rex O'Malley (Marcel); Monty Woolley (judge); Armand Kaliz (Lebon); Eddie Conrad (Prince Potopienko); Billy Daniels (Roger). 94 minutes.

What a Life (1939). Paramount Pictures. Black and white. Director: Jay Theodore Reed. Producer: Jay Theodore Reed. Screenplay: Charles Brackett and Billy Wilder, based on the play by Clifford Goldsmith. Cinematographer: Victor Milner. Editor: William Shea. Art directors: Hans Dreier and Earl Hedrick. Cast: Jackie Cooper (Henry Aldrich); Betty Field (Barbara Pearson); John Howard (Mr. Nelson); Janice Logan (Miss Shea); Lionel Stander (Ferguson); Hedda Hopper (Mrs. Aldrich); Vaughan Glasser (Mr. Bradley); James Corner (George Bigelow); Dorothy Stickney (Miss Wheeler); Kathleen Lockhart (Miss Pike); Andrew Tombes (Prof. Abernathy); Lucien Littlefield (Mr. Patterson); Sidney Miller (Pinkie Peters); George Guhl (janitor); Arthur Aylsworth (MacGowan); Wilda Bennett (Miss Doolittle); Kay Stewart (Marjorie, the drum majorette); Leonard Sues (Harold); Eddie Brian (Don Bray); Janet Waldo (Gwen); Betty McLaughlin (Jessie); Douglas Fahy (Tony Milligan); Roberta Smith (Gertie); Nora Cecil (Miss Eggleston). 75 minutes.

Ninotchka (1939). MGM. Black and white. Director: Ernst Lubitsch. Producer: Ernst Lubitsch. Screenplay: Charles Brackett, Billy Wilder, and Walter Reisch, from a story by Melchior Lengyel. Cinematographer: William H. Daniels. Music: Werner R. Heymann. Art director: Cedric Gibbons. Costumes: Adrian. Editor: Gene Ruggiero. Cast: Greta Garbo (Ninotchka); Melvyn Douglas (Count Leon d'Algout); Ina Claire (Grand Duchess Swana); Sig Ruman (Iranoff); Felix Bressart (Buljanoff); Alexander Granach (Kopalski); Gregory Gaye (Rakonin); Tamara Shayne (Anna); Bela Lugosi (Commissar Razinin); George Tobias (Russian visa officer); Rolfe Sedan (hotel manager); Edwin Maxwell (Mercier); Richard Carle (Gaston); Mary Forbes (Lady Lavenham); Peggy Moran (French maid). 110 minutes.

Rhythm on the River (1940). Paramount Pictures. Black and white. Director: Victor Schertzinger. Producer: William LeBaron. Screenplay: Dwight Taylor, from a story by Jacques Théry and Billy Wilder. Cinematographer: Ted Tetzlaff. Music and lyrics: Johnny Burke, James V. Monaco, and Victor Schertzinger. Musical director: Victor Young. Costumes: Edith Head. Editor: Hugh Bennett. Art directors: Hans Dreier and Ernst Fegré. Cast: Bing Crosby (Bob Sommers); Mary Martin (Cherry Lane); Basil Rathbone (Oliver Courtney); Oscar Levant (Billy Starbuck); Oscar Shaw (Charlie Goodrich); Charley Grapewin (Uncle Caleb); Lillian Cornell (Millie Starling); William Frawley (Mr. Westlake); Jeanne Cagney (country cousin); Helen Bertram (Aunt Delia); John Scott Trotter (himself); Ken Carpenter (announcer); Charles Lane (Bernard Schwartz); Harry Barris (bass player). 92 minutes.

Arise, My Love (1940). Paramount Pictures. Black and white. Director: Mitchell Leisen. Producer: Arthur Hornblow, Jr. Screenplay: Charles Brackett and Billy Wilder, from a story by Benjamin Glazer and John S. Toldy, with additional contributions by Jacques Théry. Cinematographer: Charles Lang. Music: Victor Young. Art directors: Hans Dreier and Robert Usher. Costumes: Irene. Editor: Doane Harrison. Cast: Claudette Colbert (Augusta Nash); Ray Milland (Tom Martin); Dennis O'Keefe (Shep); Walter Abel (Mr. Phillips); Dick Purcell ("Pinky" O'Connor); George Zucco (prison governor); Frank Puglia (Father Jacinto); Esther Dale (secretary); Paul Leyssac (Bresson); Ann Codee (Mme. Bresson); Stanley Logan (Col. Tubbs Brown); Lionel Pape (Lord Kettlebrook); Aubrey Mather (Achille); Cliff Nazarro (Botzelberg). 110 minutes.

Hold Back the Dawn (1941). Paramount Pictures. Black and white. Director: Mitchell Leisen. Producer: Arthur Hornblow, Jr. Screenplay: Charles Brackett and Billy Wilder, based on a treatment and novel by Ketti Frings. Cinematographer: Leo Tover. Music: Victor Young. Art directors: Hans Dreier and Robert Usher. Costumes: Edith Head. Editor: Doane Harrison. Cast: Charles Boyer (Georges Iscovescu); Olivia de Havilland (Emmy Brown); Paulette Goddard (Anita); Victor Francen (Van Den Luecken); Walter Abel (Inspector Hammock); Curt Bois (Bonbois); Rosemary De Camp (Berta Kurz); Eric Feldary (Josef Kurz); Nestor Paiva (Flores); Eva Puig (Lupita); Micheline Cheirel (Christine); Madeleine Lebeau (Annie); Billy Lee (Tony); Mikhail Rasumny (mechanic); Charles Arnt (Mr. MacAdams); Arthur Loft (Mr. Eivestad); Harry Shannon (soldier); Mitchell Leisen (Mr. Saxon); Brian Donlevy (movie actor); Veronica Lake (movie actress). 115 minutes.

Ball of Fire (1941). Samuel Goldwyn. Black and white. Director: Howard Hawks. Producer: Samuel Goldwyn. Screenplay: Charles Brackett and Billy Wilder, based on a story by Billy Wilder and Thomas Monroe. Cinematographer: Gregg Toland. Music: Alfred Newman. Costumes: Edith Head. Editor: Daniel Mandell. Art director: Perry Ferguson. Cast: Gary Cooper (Prof. Bertram Potts); Barbara Stanwyck (Sugarpuss O'Shea); Oskar Homolka (Prof. Gurkakoff); Henry Travers (Prof. Jerome); S. Z. Sakall (Prof. Magenbruch); Tully Marshall (Prof. Robinson); Leonid Kinskey (Prof. Quintana); Richard Haydn (Prof. Oddly); Aubrey Mather (Prof. Peagram); Allen Jenkins (garbage man); Dana Andrews (Joe Lilac); Dan Duryea (Pastrami); Ralph Peters (Asthma); Kathleen Howard (Miss Bragg); Mary Field (Miss Totten); Alan Rhein (Horseface); Eddie Foster (Pinstripe); Aldrich Bowker (justice of the peace); Addison Richards (district attorney); Pat West (bum); Kenneth Howell (college boy); Tommy Ryan (newsboy); Tim Ryan (cop); William A. Lee (Benny the Creep); Geraldine Fissette (hula dancer); Gene Krupa (himself). 111 minutes.

The Major and the Minor (1941). Paramount Pictures. Black and white. Director: Billy Wilder. Producer: Arthur Hornblow, Jr. Screenplay: Charles Brackett and Billy Wilder, based on the story "Sunny Goes Home" by Fanny Kilbourne and the play *Connie Goes Home* by Edward Childs Carpenter. Cinematographer: Leo Tover. Music: Robert Emmett Dolan. Art directors: Roland Anderson and Hans Dreier. Costumes: Edith Head. Editor: Doane Harrison. Assistant director: Charles C. Coleman, Jr. Makeup: Wally Westmore. Cast: Ginger Rogers (Susan Applegate); Ray Milland (Major Philip Kirby); Rita Johnson (Pamela Hill); Robert Benchley (Mr. Osborne); Diana Lynn (Lucy Hill); Edward Fielding (Colonel Hill); Frankie Thomas (Cadet Osborne); Raymond Roe (Cadet Wigton); Charles Smith (Cadet Kornet); Larry Nunn (Cadet Babcock); Billy Dawson (Cadet Miller); Lela Rogers (Mrs. Applegate); Aldrich Bowker (Reverend Doyle); Boyd Irwin (Major Griscom); Byron Shores (Captain Durand); Richard Fiske (Will Duffy); Norma Varden (Mrs. Osborne); Gretl Sherk (Miss Shackleford); Edward Peil, Sr. (ticket clerk); Will Duffy (doorman); Ken Mundy (elevator operator); Stanley Desmond (conductor); with Billy Ray, Marie Blake, Mary Field. 100 minutes.

Five Graves to Cairo (1943). Paramount Pictures. Black and white. Director: Billy Wilder. Producer: Charles Brackett. Screenplay: Charles Brackett and Billy Wilder, based on the play *Hotel Imperial* by Lajos Biró. Cinematographer: John F. Seitz. Music: Miklós Rózsa. Costumes: Edith Head. Editor: Doane Harrison. Art directors: Hans Dreier and Ernst Fegré. Makeup: Wally Westmore. Cast: Franchot Tone (John J. Bramble); Anne Baxter (Mouche); Erich von Stroheim (Field Marshal Erwin Rommel); Akim Tamiroff (Farid); Fortunio Bonanova (General Sebastiano); Peter Van Eyck (Lieutenant Schwegler); Konstantin Shayne (Major von Bülow); Fred Nurney (Major Lamprecht); Miles Mander (Colonel Fitzhume); Ian Keith (Captain St. Bride). 96 minutes.

Double Indemnity (1944). Paramount Pictures. Black and white. Director: Billy Wilder. Producer: Joseph Sistrom. Screenplay: Raymond Chandler and Billy Wilder, based on the short story by James M. Cain. Cinematographer: John F. Seitz. Music: Miklós Rózsa. Costumes: Edith Head. Editor: Doane Harrison. Art directors: Hans Dreier and Hal Pereira. Makeup: Wally Westmore. Cast: Fred MacMurray (Walter Neff); Barbara Stanwyck (Phyllis Dietrichson); Edward G. Robinson (Barton Keyes); Porter Hall (Mr. Jackson); Jean Heather (Lola Dietrichson); Tom Powers (Mr. Dietrichson); Byron Barr (Nino Zachette); Richard Gaines (Mr. Norton); Fortunio Bonanova (Sam Gorlopis); John Philliber (Joe Pete); Bess Flowers (Norton's secretary); Kernan Cripps (conductor); Edmund Cobb (brakeman); Harold Garrison (redcap); Oscar Smith (Pullman porter); Betty Farrington (maid); Sam McDaniel (Charlie). 107 minutes.

The Lost Weekend (1945). Paramount Pictures. Black and white. Director: Billy Wilder. Producer: Charles Brackett. Screenplay: Charles Brackett and Billy

Wilder, based on the novel by Charles R. Jackson. Cinematographer: John F. Seitz. Music: Miklós Rózsa, with the prelude and Libiamo chorus of *La Traviata* by Giuseppe Verdi, sung by John Garris and Theadora Lynch. Operatic sequence supervised by Armando Agnini. Musical director: Victor Young. Costumes: Edith Head. Editor: Doane Harrison. Sound: Stanley Cooley and Joel Moss. Art directors: Hans Dreier and A. Earl Hedrick. Set decorator: Bertram Granger. Special effects: Farciot Edouart and Gordon Jennings. Makeup: Wally Westmore. Medical advisor: Dr. George N. Thompson. Cast: Ray Milland (Don Birnam); Jane Wyman (Helen St. James); Phillip Terry (Wick Birnam); Howard Da Silva (Nat); Doris Dowling (Gloria); Frank Faylen (Bim); Mary Young (Mrs. Deveridge); Anita Sharp-Bolster (Mrs. Foley); Lillian Fontaine (Mrs. St. James); Lewis R. Russell (Charles St. James); Helen Dickson (Mrs. Frink); David Clyde (Dave); Eddie Laughton (Mr. Brophy); Frank Orth (coatroom attendant); William Newell (liquor store proprietor); with Clarence Muse. 100 minutes.

The Emperor Waltz (1948). Paramount Pictures. Technicolor. Director: Billy Wilder. Producer: Charles Brackett. Screenplay: Charles Brackett and Billy Wilder. Cinematographer: George Barnes. Music: Johnny Burke, Richard Heuberger, Fritz Rotter, Johann Strauss, Jr., and Arthur Pryor. Musical director: Victor Young. Costumes: Edith Head and Gile Steele. Editor: Doane Harrison. Art directors: Hans Dreier and Franz Bachelin. Assistant director: Charles C. Coleman, Jr. Set decorators: Sam Comer and Paul Huldschinsky. Sound: Stanley Cooley and John Cope. Choreography: Billy Daniels. Process photography: Farciot Edouart. Special photographic effects: Gordon Jennings. Makeup: Wally Westmore. Cast: Bing Crosby (Virgil Smith); Joan Fontaine (Johanna Augusta Franziska von Stoltzenberg-Stoltzenberg); Roland Culver (Baron Holenia); Lucile Watson (Princess Bitotska); Richard Haydn (Emperor Francis Joseph); Harold Vermilyea (chamberlain); Sig Ruman (Dr. Zwieback); Julia Dean (Archduchess Stephanie); Bert Prival (chauffeur); Alma Macrorie (inn proprietor); Roberta Jonay (chambermaid); John Goldsworthy (officer); Gerald Mohr (Marquis Alonson); Paul de Corday (Prince Istvan); Doris Dowling (Tyrolean maid). 106 minutes.

A Foreign Affair (1948). Paramount Pictures. Black and white. Director: Billy Wilder. Producer: Charles Brackett. Screenplay: Charles Brackett, Billy Wilder, and Richard L. Breen, based on a story by David Shaw and Robert Harari. Cinematographer: Charles Lang. Music: Frederick Hollander. Art directors: Hans Dreier and Walter H. Tyler. Costumes: Edith Head. Editor: Doane Harrison. Assistant director: Charles C. Coleman, Jr. Set decorators: Sam Comer and Ross Dowd. Process photography: Farciot Edouart and Dewey Wrigley. Sound: Hugo Grenzbach and Walter Oberst. Special effects: Gordon Jennings. Makeup: Wally Westmore. Cast: Jean Arthur (Phoebe Frost); Marlene Dietrich (Erika von Schlütow); John Lund (Capt. John Pringle); Millard Mitchell (Col. Rufus Plummer); Stanley Prager (Mike); Peter von Zerneck (Hans Otto Birgel); Raymond Bond (Pennecott); Boyd Davis (Griffin); Robert Malcolm (Kramer); Charles Meredith (Yarndell); Michael Raffetto (Salvatore); Damian O'Flynn (lieutenant colonel); William Neff (Lt. Lee Thompson); Frank Fenton (Major Mathews); James Larmore (Lieut. Hornby); Harland Tucker (Gen. MacAndrew); George M. Carleton (Gen. Finney); Gordon Jones (M.P.); Freddie Steele (M.P.). 116 minutes.

Sunset Boulevard (1950). Paramount Pictures. Black and white. Director: Billy Wilder. Producer: Charles Brackett. Screenplay: Charles Brackett, Billy Wilder, and D. M. Marshman, Jr. Cinematographer: John F. Seitz. Music: Franz Waxman. Costumes: Edith Head. Editors: Doane Harrison and Arthur P. Schmidt. Assistant director: Charles C. Coleman, Jr. Set decorators: Sam Comer, Ray Moyer, and John Meehan. Sound: John Cope and Harry Lindgren. Art director: Hans Dreier. Process photography: Farciot Edouart. Special effects: Gordon Jennings. Makeup: Wally Westmore and Karl Silvera. Cast: William Holden (Joe Gillis); Gloria Swanson (Norma Desmond); Erich von Stroheim (Max von Mayerling); Nancy Olson (Betty Schaefer); Fred Clark (Sheldrake); Lloyd Gough (Morino); Jack Webb (Artie Green); Michael Brandon (clothing salesman); Franklyn Farnum (mortician); Larry J. Blake (finance man); Charles Dayton (finance man); Cecil B. DeMille (himself); Hedda Hopper (herself); Buster Keaton (himself); Anna Q. Nilsson (herself); H. B. Warner (himself); Ray Evans (himself); Jay Livingston (himself): with E. Mason Hopper, Virginia Randolph, Gertrude Astor, Eva Novak, Creighton Hale, Ralph Montgomery. 110 minutes.

Ace in the Hole (1951). Paramount Pictures. Black and white. Director: Billy Wilder. Producer: Billy Wilder. Screenplay: Billy Wilder, Walter Newman, and Lesser Samuels. Cinematographer: Charles Lang. Music: Hugo Friedhofer. Costumes: Edith Head. Editors: Doane Harrison and Arthur P. Schmidt. Set decorators: Sam Comer and Ray Moyer. Process photography: Farciot Edouart. Sound: Gene Garvin and Harold C. Lewis. Art directors: Hal Pereira and A. Earl Hedrick. Makeup: Wally Westmore. Cast: Kirk Douglas (Chuck Tatum); Jan Sterling (Lorraine); Robert Arthur (Herbie Cook); Porter Hall (Jacob Q. Boot); Frank Cady (Mr. Federber); Richard Benedict (Leo Minosa); Ray Teal (sheriff); Lewis Martin (McCardle); Frances Domingues (Mama Minosa); Gene Evans (deputy sheriff); John Berkes (Papa Minosa); Harry Harvey (Dr. Hilton); Frank Jaquet (Smollett); Bob Bumpas (radio announcer); Geraldine Hall (Mrs. Federber); Richard Gaines (Nagel); Paul D. Merrill (Federber boy); Stewart Kirk Clawson (Federber boy); John Stuart Fulton (boy); Robert Kortmann (digger); Edith Evanson (Miss Deverich); Ralph Moody (miner); Claire Du Brey (spinster); William Fawcett (sadfaced man); Basil Chester (Indian). 111 minutes. First released as *The Big Carnival*.

Stalag 17 (1953). Paramount Pictures. Black and white. Director: Billy Wilder. Producer: Billy Wilder. Screenplay: Billy Wilder and Edwin Blum, based on the play by Donald Bevan and Edmund Trzcinski. Cinematographer: Ernest Laszlo. Editorial advisor: Doane Harrison. Music: Franz Waxman. Editor: George Tomasini. Associate producer: William Schorr. Art directors: Franz Bachelin and Hal Pereira. Set decorators: Sam Comer and Ray Moyer. Sound: Gene Garvin and Harold C. Lewis. Special effects: Gordon Jennings. Makeup: Wally Westmore. Cast: William Holden (Sefton); Don Taylor (Lieut. Dunbar); Otto Preminger (von Scherbach); Robert Strauss (Stosh "Animal" Krusawa); Harvey Lembeck (Harry Shapiro); Richard Erdman (Hoffy); Peter Graves (Price); Neville Brand (Duke); Sig Ruman (Schulz); Michael Moore (Manfredi); Peter Baldwin (Johnson); Robinson Stone (Joey); Robert Shawley (Blondie); William Pearson (Marko); Gil Stratton, Jr. (Cookie); Jay Lawrence (Bagradian); Erwin Kalser (Geneva man); Edmund Trzcinski (Triz); Tommy Cook (prisoner); with Herbert Street, Rodric Beckham, Jerry Gerber, William Mulcany, Russell Grower, Donald Cameron, James Dabney, Jr., Ralph Gaston. 121 minutes.

Sabrina (1954). Paramount Pictures. Black and white. Director: Billy Wilder. Producer: Billy Wilder. Screenplay: Billy Wilder, Samuel A. Taylor, Ernest Lehman, based on the play *Sabrina Fair* by Taylor. Cinematographer: Charles Lang. Music: Frederick Hollander. Costumes: Edith Head. Editor: Arthur P. Schmidt. Assistant director: C. C. Coleman, Jr. Editorial advisor: Doane Harrison. Art directors: Hal Pereira and Walter H. Tyler. Set decorators: Sam Comer and Ray Moyer. Sound: John Cope and Harold Lewis. Special effects: John P. Fulton. Process photography: Farciot Edouart. Makeup: Wally Westmore. Cast: Humphrey Bogart (Linus Larrabee); Audrey Hepburn (Sabrina Fairchild); William Holden (David Larrabee); Walter Hampden (Oliver Larrabee); John Williams (Thomas Fairchild); Martha Hyer (Elizabeth Tyson); Joan Vohs (Gretchen Van Horn); Marcel Dalio (Baron St. Fontanel); Marcel Hillaire (professor); Nella Walker (Maude Larrabee); Francis X. Bushman (Mr. Tyson); Ellen Corby (Miss McCardle); Nancy Kulp (maid). 114 minutes.

The Seven Year Itch (1955). 20th Century-Fox. Color by DeLuxe. Director: Billy Wilder. Producers: Charles K. Feldman and Billy Wilder. Screenplay: Billy Wilder and George Axelrod, based on the play by Axelrod. Cinematographer: Milton Krasner. Music: Alfred Newman. Costumes: Travilla. Editor: Hugh S. Fowler. Associate producer: Doane Harrison. Title design: Saul Bass. Art directors: George W. Davis and Lyle R. Wheeler. Special effects: Ray Kellogg. Sound: Harry M. Leonard and E. Clayton Ward. Makeup: Ben Nye and Whitey Snyder. Set decorators: Stuart A. Reiss and Walter M. Scott. Assistant director: Joseph E. Rickards. Cast: Marilyn Monroe (The Girl); Tom Ewell (Richard Sherman); Evelyn Keyes

(Helen Sherman); Sonny Tufts (Tom MacKenzie); Robert Strauss (Mr. Kruhulik); Oskar Homolka (Dr. Brubaker); Marguerite Chapman (Miss Morris); Victor Moore (plumber); Roxanne (Elaine); Donald MacBride (Mr. Brady); Carolyn Jones (Miss Finch); Butch Bernard (Ricky Sherman); Doro Merande (waitress); Dorothy Ford (Indian girl). 105 minutes.

The Spirit of St. Louis (1957). Warner Bros. Warnercolor. CinemaScope. Director: Billy Wilder. Producer: Leland Hayward. Screenplay: Billy Wilder, Wendell Mayes, and Charles Lederer, based on the book by Charles A. Lindbergh. Cinematographers: Robert Burks and J. Peverell Marley. Music: Franz Waxman. Editor: Arthur P. Schmidt. Assistant director: Charles C. Coleman, Jr. Associate producer: Doane Harrison. Art director: Art Loel. Makeup: Gordon Bau. Technical advisors: Harlan A. Gurney and Maj. Gen. Victor Bertrandias. Special effects: Hans F. Koenekamp, and Louis Lichtenfield. Set decorator: William L. Kuehl. Aerial supervisor: Paul Mantz. Sound: M. A. Merrick. Aerial photographer: Tom Tutwiler. Cast: James Stewart (Charles Lindbergh); Murray Hamilton (Bud Gurney); Patricia Smith (mirror girl); Bartlett Robinson (B. F. Mahoney); Marc Connelly (Father Hussman); Arthur Space (Donald Hall); Charles Watts (O. W. Schultz). 135 minutes.

Love in the Afternoon (1957). Allied Artists. Black and white. Director: Billy Wilder. Producer: Billy Wilder. Screenplay: Billy Wilder and I. A. L. Diamond, based on the novel *Ariane* by Claude Anet. Cinematographer: William C. Mellor. Music: Franz Waxman. Art director: Alexander Trauner. Editor: Leonide Azar. Associate producers: Doane Harrison and William Schorr. Songs: Henri Betti, Matty Malneck, F. D. Marchetti, André Hornez, and Maurice De Feaurdy. Sound: Jean De Bretagne. Assistant director: Paul Feyder. Second-unit director: Noel Howard. Cast: Gary Cooper (Frank Flannagan); Audrey Hepburn (Ariane Chavasse); Maurice Chevalier (Claude Chavasse); Van Doude (Michel); John McGiver (Monsieur X); Lise Bourdin (Madame X); Bonifas (commissioner of police); Claude Ariel (existentialist); Olivia Chevalier (child in garden); Alexander Trauner (artist); Audrey Wilder (brunette); Gyila Kokas, Michel Kokas, George Cocos, and Victor Gazzoli (Gypsy orchestra), Olga Valery (lady with dog). 130 minutes.

Witness for the Prosecution (1957). United Artists. Black and white. Director: Billy Wilder. Producers: Arthur Hornblow, Jr., and Edward Small. Screenplay: Billy Wilder and Harry Kurnitz with Larry Marcus, based on the play by Agatha Christie. Cinematographer: Russell Harlan. Art director: Alexander Trauner. Music: Matty Malneck and Ernest Gold. Costumes: Edith Head and Joe King. Editor: Daniel Mandell. Set decorator: Howard Bristol. Assistant director: Emmett

Emerson. Associate producer: Doane Harrison. Sound: Fred Lau. Makeup: Gustaf Norin, Harry Ray, and Ray Sebastian. Cast: Tyrone Power (Leonard Vole); Marlene Dietrich (Christine Vole); Charles Laughton (Sir Wilfrid Robarts); Elsa Lanchester (Miss Plimsoll); John Williams (Brogan-Moore); Henry Daniell (Mayhew); Ian Wolfe (Carter); Torin Thatcher (Mr. Myers); Norma Varden (Mrs. French); Una O'Connor (Janet McKenzie); Francis Compton (judge); Philip Tonge (Inspector Hearne); Ruta Lee (Diana). 116 minutes.

Some Like It Hot (1959). United Artists/Mirisch Company/Ashton Productions. Black and white. Director: Billy Wilder. Producer: Billy Wilder. Screenplay: Billy Wilder and I. A. L. Diamond, based on the film *Fanfaren der Liebe,* written by Michael Logan and Robert Thoeren. Cinematographer: Charles Lang. Music: Adolph Deutsch. Art director: Ted Haworth. Costumes: Orry-Kelly. Editor: Arthur P. Schmidt. Associate producers: I. A. L. Diamond and Doane Harrison. Set decorator: Edward G. Boyle. Makeup: Emile LaVigne. Sound: Fred Lau. Song supervisor: Matty Malneck. Assistant director: Sam Nelson. Special effects: Milt Rice. Cast: Marilyn Monroe (Sugar Kane); Tony Curtis (Joe); Jack Lemmon (Jerry); George Raft (Spats); Pat O'Brien (Mulligan); Joe E. Brown (Osgood Fielding); Nehemiah Persoff (Little Bonaparte); Joan Shawlee (Sweet Sue); Billy Gray (Sid Poliakoff); Al Breneman (bellhop); George E. Stone (Toothpick Charlie); Dave Barry (Beinstock); Mike Mazurki (henchman); Harry Wilson (henchman); Tito Vuola (Mozarella); Beverly Wills (Dolores); Barbara Drew (Nellie); Edward G. Robinson, Jr. (Paradise); Marion Collier (Olga); Helen Parry (Rosella); Laurie Mitchell (Mary Lou); Sandy Warner (Emily); Tommy Hart (second official); Tom Kennedy (bouncer); John Indrisano (waiter); Fred Sherman (drunk); Paul Frees (female voice). 116 minutes.

The Apartment (1960). United Artists/Mirisch Company. Black and white. Panavision. Director: Billy Wilder. Producer: Billy Wilder. Screenplay: Billy Wilder and I. A. L. Diamond. Cinematographer: Joseph LaShelle. Art director: Alexander Trauner. Music: Adolph Deutsch. Editor: Daniel Mandell. Associate producers: I. A. L. Diamond and Doane Harrison. Set decorator: Edward G. Boyle. Sound: Gordon Sawyer and Fred Lau. Assistant director: Hal W. Polaire. Makeup: Harry Ray. Special effects: Milt Rice. Script supervisor: May Wale. Cast: Jack Lemmon (C. C. "Bud" Baxter); Shirley MacLaine (Fran Kubelik); Fred MacMurray (J. D. Sheldrake); Jack Kruschen (Dr. Dreyfuss); Ray Walston (Joe Dobisch); Frances Weintraub Lax (Mrs. Lieberman); Hope Holiday (Margie MacDougall); Johnny Seven (Karl Matuschka); Naomi Stevens (Mrs. Dreyfuss); Willard Waterman (Mr. Vanderhof); Joan Shawlee (Sylvia); Edie Adams (Miss Olsen); David Lewis (Mr. Kirkeby); David White (Mr. Eichelberger); Hal Smith (Santa Claus); Joyce Jameson (the blonde); Benny Burt (bartender). 125 minutes.

One, Two, Three (1961). United Artists/Mirisch Company/Pyramid Productions. Black and white. Panavision. Director: Billy Wilder. Producer: Billy Wilder. Screenplay: Billy Wilder and I. A. L. Diamond, based on the play by Ferenc Molnár. Cinematographer: Daniel L. Fapp. Art director: Alexander Trauner. Associate producers: I. A. L. Diamond and Doane Harrison. Music: André Previn. Editor: Daniel Mandell. Sound: Basil Fenton-Smith. Assistant director: Tom Pevsner. Special effects: Milt Rice. Cast: James Cagney (MacNamara); Horst Buchholz (Otto Ludwig Piffl); Pamela Tiffin (Scarlett Hazeltine); Arlene Francis (Phyllis MacNamara); Howard St. John (Mr. Hazeltine); Hanns Lothar (Schlemmer); Leon Askin (Peripetchikoff); Ralf Wolter (Borodenko); Peter Capell (Mishkin); Karl Lieffen (Fritz); Hubert von Meyerinck (Count von Droste-Schattenburg); Lois Bolton (Mrs. Hazeltine); Tile Kiwe (reporter); Henning Schlüter (Dr. Bauer); Lilo Pulver (Ingeborg); Christine Allen (Cindy MacNamara); John Allen (Tommy MacNamara); Ivan Arnold (M.P.); Klaus Becker (policeman); Max Buchsbaum (tailor); Werner Buttler (policeman); Red Buttons (M.P.); Paul Bos (Krause); Jacques Chevalier (Pierre); Ingrid DeToro (stewardess); Otto Friebel (interrogator); Werner Hessenland (shoe salesman); Jaspar von Oertzen (haberdasher); Abi von Hasse (jeweler); Frederick Hollander (bartender). 115 minutes.

Irma la Douce (1963). United Artists. Technicolor. Panavision. Director: Billy Wilder. Producer: Billy Wilder. Screenplay: Billy Wilder and I. A. L. Diamond, based on the musical by Alexandre Breffort and Marguerite Monnot. Cinematographer: Joseph LaShelle. Art director: Alexander Trauner. Music: André Previn. Costumes: Orry-Kelly. Editor: Daniel Mandell. Associate producers: I. A. L. Diamond and Doane Harrison. Assistant director: Hal W. Polaire. Special effects: Milton Rice. Cast: Jack Lemmon (Nestor Patou); Shirley MacLaine (Irma); Lou Jacobi (Moustache); Bruce Yarnell (Hippolyte); Herschel Bernardi (Inspector Lefevre); Hope Holiday (Lolita); Joan Shawlee (Amazon Annie); Grace Lee Whitney (Kiki the Cossack); Paul Dubov (André); Howard McNear (concierge); Cliff Osmond (policeman); Diki Lerner (Joio); Herb Jones (Casablanca Charlie); Ruth Earl (zebra twin); Jane Earl (zebra twin); Tura Satana (Suzette Wong); Lou Krugman (first customer); James Brown (Texan); Bill Bixby (tattooed sailor); Harriette Young (Mimi the MauMau); Sheryl Deauville (Carmen); James Caan (uncredited extra). 147 minutes.

Kiss Me, Stupid (1964). Mirisch Company/Lopert Pictures. Black and white. Panavision. Director: Billy Wilder. Producer: Billy Wilder. Screenplay: Billy Wilder and I. A. L. Diamond, based on the play *L'Ora della Fantasia* by Anna Bonacci. Cinematographer: Joseph LaShelle. Music: André Previn. Songs and lyrics: George Gershwin and Ira Gershwin. Art director: Alexander Trauner. Costumes: Wesley Jeffries. Editor: Daniel Mandell. Associate producers: I. A. L. Diamond and Doane

Harrison. Set decorator: Edward G. Boyle. Assistant director: Charles C. Coleman, Jr. Makeup: Loren Cosand and Emile LaVigne. Art director: Robert Luthardt. Sound: Clem Portman. Special effects: Milton Rice. Cast: Dean Martin (Dino); Kim Novak (Polly the Pistol); Ray Walston (Orville J. Spooner); Felicia Farr (Zelda Spooner); Cliff Osmond (Barney Millsap); Barbara Pepper (Big Bertha); James Ward (milkman); Doro Merande (Mrs. Pettibone); Howard McNear (Mr. Pettibone); Bobo Lewis (waitress); Tommy Nolan (Johnnie Mulligan); Alice Pearce (Mrs. Mulligan); John Fiedler (Rev. Carruthers); Arlen Stuart (Rosalie Schultz); Cliff Norton (Mack Gray); Mel Blanc (Dr. Sheldrake); Eileen O'Neal (showgirl); Susan Wedell (showgirl); Bernd Hoffmann (bartender); Henry Gibson (Smith); Alan Dexter (Wesson); Henry Beckman (truck driver). 124 minutes.

The Fortune Cookie (1966). United Artists/Mirisch Company/Phalanx/Jalem. Black and white. Panavision. Director: Billy Wilder. Producer: Billy Wilder. Screenplay: Billy Wilder and I. A. L. Diamond. Cinematographer: Joseph LaShelle. Music: André Previn. Costumes: Chuck Arrico and Paula Giokaris. Editor: Daniel Mandell. Associate producers: I. A. L. Diamond and Doane Harrison. Special effects: Sass Bedig. Set decorator: Edward G. Boyle. Makeup: Lauren Cosand. Art director: Robert Luthardt. Sound: Robert Martin. Assistant director: Jack N. Reddish. Makeup: Robert J. Schiffer. Cast: Jack Lemmon (Harry Hinkle); Walter Matthau (Willie Gingrich); Ron Rich (Luther "Boom Boom" Jackson); Judi West (Sandy); Cliff Osmond (Purkey); Lurene Tuttle (Mother Hinkle); Harry Holcombe (O'Brien); Les Tremayne (Thompson); Lauren Gilbert (Kincaid); Marge Redmond (Charlotte Gingrich); Noam Pitlik (Max); Harry Davis (Dr. Krugman); Ann Shoemaker (Sister Veronica); Maryesther Denver (nurse); Ned Glass (Doc Schindler); Sig Ruman (Prof. Winterhalter); Archie Moore (Mr. Jackson); Howard McNear (Mr. Cimoli); William Christopher (intern); Don Reed (newscaster). 115 minutes.

The Private Life of Sherlock Holmes (1970). United Artists/Mirisch Company. Color by DeLuxe. Panavision. Director: Billy Wilder. Producer: Billy Wilder. Screenplay: Billy Wilder and I. A. L. Diamond, based on characters created by Arthur Conan Doyle. Cinematographer: Christopher Challis. Music: Miklós Rózsa. Art director: Alexander Trauner. Costumes: Julie Harris. Editor: Ernest Walter. Cast: Robert Stephens (Sherlock Holmes); Colin Blakely (Dr. John Watson); Genevieve Page (Gabrielle Valladon); Christopher Lee (Mycroft Holmes); Tamara Toumanova (Patrova); Clive Revill (Rogozhin); Irene Handl (Mrs. Hudson); Stanley Holloway (gravedigger); Catherine Lacey (woman in wheelchair); Mollie Maureen (Queen Victoria); Peter Madden (Von Tirpitz); Michael Balfour (cabbie); James Copeland (guide); George Benson (Inspector Lestrade); Michael Elwyn (Cassidy); John Garrie (first carter); Godfrey James (second carter); Robert

Cowdron (hotel manager); Alex McCrindle (baggageman); Frank Thornton (porter); Paul Hansard (monk); Miklós Rózsa (ballet conductor). 125 minutes.

Avanti! (1972). Mirisch Corporation/Phalanx/Jalem. Color by DeLuxe. Director: Billy Wilder. Producer: Billy Wilder. Screenplay: Billy Wilder and I. A. L. Diamond, with contributions by Luciano Vincenzoni, based on the play by Samuel A. Taylor. Cinematographer: Luigi Kuveiller. Music: Carlo Rustichelli. Art director: Ferdinando Scarfiotti. Costumes: Lino Coletta. Editor: Ralph E. Winters. Cast: Jack Lemmon (Wendell Armbruster); Juliet Mills (Pamela Piggott); Clive Revill (Carlo Carlucci); Edward Andrews (J. J. Blodgett); Gianfranco Barra (Bruno); Francesco Angrisano (Arnoldo Trotta); Pippo Franco (Mattarazzo); Franco Acampora (Armando Trotta); Giselda Castrini (Anna); Raffaele Mottola (passport officer); Lino Coletta (Cipriani); Harry Ray (Dr. Fleischmann); Guidarino Guidi (maître d'); Giacomo Rizzo (bartender); Antonino Di Bruno (concierge); Yanti Sommer (nurse); Janet Agren (nurse). 144 minutes.

The Front Page (1974). Universal International. Technicolor. Panavision. Director: Billy Wilder. Producers: Jennings Lang and Paul Monash. Screenplay: Billy Wilder and I. A. L. Diamond, based on the play by Ben Hecht and Charles MacArthur. Cinematographer: Jordan Cronenweth. Music: Billy May. Costumes: Burton Miller. Editor: Ralph E. Winters. Production designer: Henry Bumstead. Illustrator: Bill Major. Assistant director: Howard G. Kazanjian. Cast: Walter Matthau (Walter Burns); Jack Lemmon (Hildy Johnson); Susan Sarandon (Peggy Grant); David Wayne (Bensinger); Carol Burnett (Mollie Malloy); Austin Pendleton (Earl Williams); Vincent Gardenia (sheriff); Allen Garfield (Kruger); Herb Edelman (Schwartz); Charles Durning (Murphy); Martin Gabel (Dr. Eggelhofer); Harold Gould (mayor); Jon Korkes (Rudy Keppler); Dick O'Neill (McHugh); Cliff Osmond (Jacobi); Lou Frizzell (Endicott); Paul Benedict (Plunkett); Doro Merande (Jennie); Noam Pitlik (Wilson); Joshua Shelley (cabdriver); Allen Jenkins (telegrapher); John Furlong (Duffy); Biff Elliot (police dispatcher); Barbara Davis (Myrtle); Leonard Bremen (Butch). 105 minutes.

Fedora (1978). Geria-Bavaria. Color. Panavision. Director: Billy Wilder. Producer: Billy Wilder. Screenplay: Billy Wilder and I. A. L. Diamond, based on a story by Tom Tryon. Cinematographer: Gerry Fisher. Music: Miklós Rózsa. Production designer: Alexander Trauner. Art director: Robert André. Costumes: Charlotte Flemming. Editors: Stefan Arnsten and Fredric Steinkamp. Associate producer: I. A. L. Diamond. Assistant director: Jean-Patrick Constantini. Production supervisor: Willy Egger. Production coordinator: Harold Nebenzal. Makeup: Tom Smith. Cast: William Holden (Barry "Dutch" Detweiler); Marthe Keller (Antonia/Fedora); Hildegard Knef (Fedora/Countess Sobryanski); José Ferrer

(Dr. Vando); Frances Sternhagen (Miss Balfour); Mario Adorf (hotel manager); Stephen Collins (young Barry); Henry Fonda (president of the Academy); Michael York (himself); Hans Jaray (Count Sobryanski); Gottfried John (Kritos); Arlene Francis (newscaster); Jacques Maury (usher); Christine Mueller (young Antonia); Ellen Schwiers (nurse); Bob Cunningham (assistant director); Christoph Künzler (clerk); Mary Kelly (Gladys); Elma Karlowa (maid); Panos Papadopoulos (bartender); Rex McGee (photographer). 113 minutes.

Buddy Buddy (1981). MGM. Metrocolor. Panavision. Director: Billy Wilder. Producer: Jay Weston. Screenplay: Billy Wilder and I. A. L. Diamond, based on the film *L'Emmerdeur,* screenplay by Francis Veber. Cinematographer: Harry Stradling, Jr. Music: Lalo Schifrin. Art director: Daniel A. Lomino. Editor: Argyle Nelson. Makeup: Stephen Abrums and Ron Snyder. Costumes: John A. Anderson and Agnes G. Henry. Executive producer: Alain Bernheim. Associate producer: Charles Matthau. Set decorator: Cloudia. Assistant director: Gary Daigler. Set design: William J. Durrell. Special effects: Milt Rice. Sound: Don Sharpless. Cast: Jack Lemmon (Victor Clooney); Walter Matthau (Trabucco); Paula Prentiss (Celia Clooney); Klaus Kinski (Dr. Zuckerbrot); Dana Elcar (Hubris); Miles Chapin (Eddie, the bellhop); Michael Ensign (assistant manager); Joan Shawlee (receptionist); Fil Formicola (Rudy "Disco" Gambola); C. J. Hunt (Kowalski); Bette Raya (maid); Ronnie Sperling (husband); Suzie Galler (wife); John Schubeck (newscaster); Ed Begley, Jr. (policeman); Frank Farmer (policeman); Tom Kindle (patrolman); Biff Manard (patrolman); Charlotte Stewart (nurse). 96 minutes.

INDEX